DATE DUE

31 DEC '69 CIT
3/27
30 JUL '70 CIT
19 JUL '71 CIT

A Radical Future

A Radical Future

EDITED BY
BEN WHITAKER

JONATHAN CAPE
THIRTY BEDFORD SQUARE LONDON

THIS COMPILATION FIRST PUBLISHED 1967
BY JONATHAN CAPE LTD
30 BEDFORD SQUARE, LONDON, WC1
© 1967 BY BEN WHITAKER

PRINTED IN GREAT BRITAIN
BY EBENEZER BAYLIS AND SON, LIMITED
THE TRINITY PRESS, WORCESTER, AND LONDON,
ON PAPER MADE BY JOHN DICKINSON AND CO. LTD.
BOUND BY A. W. BAIN AND CO. LTD, LONDON

Contents

INTRODUCTION: THE NEED FOR REFORM
Ben Whitaker
M.P. for Hampstead — 9

EUROPE
David Marquand
M.P. for Ashfield — 21

THE REFORM OF PARLIAMENT
John P. Mackintosh
M.P. for Berwick and East Lothian — 36

APPROACHES TO INDUSTRIAL DEMOCRACY
Eric Moonman
M.P. for Billericay — 56

OVERSEAS AID AND DEVELOPMENT
Frank Judd
M.P. for Portsmouth West — 77

PUBLIC OWNERSHIP
James Dickens
M.P. for Lewisham West — 99

FOREIGN POLICY
Evan Luard
M.P. for Oxford — 116

THE WELFARE STATE: REFORM AND DEVELOPMENT
Christopher Price
M.P. for Birmingham (Perry Barr) — 137

CONTENTS

PLANNING FOR THE POPULATION OF THE FUTURE
Gerry Fowler
M.P. for The Wrekin — 155

A SOCIALIST POLICY FOR THE PRESS
John Ryan
M.P. for Uxbridge — 179

MODERNIZING THE LABOUR PARTY
Alan Lee Williams
M.P. for Hornchurch — 188

SOCIALIST LAW REFORM
John Lee
M.P. for Reading — 202

A Radical Future

Introduction:
The Need for Reform

BEN WHITAKER

'What went wrong with [the Attlee] Labour Government? Why didn't we come back for a second five years with an increased majority? Why did we falter, fall out of office and nearly split? I believe that no one who remembers that time has any doubt of the answer. As early as 1949, four years after we had won power, the Government was beginning to lose impetus, and the reason was quite simple. We were running out of intellectual ammunition. We had nearly finished the job we had been sent to do in those first five years. As a result our sense of direction began to go, and a radical reforming Labour Government without a clear sense of direction is sunk. I say to you this must not be allowed to happen again.'

The words are Richard Crossman's, addressing the Labour Party on the eve of the 1966 Conference. Labour cannot afford to forget the relevance of what he said between now and the next election. However deeply its inheritance was mortgaged to defence commitments, however emaciated the social services to which it was heir, the Labour Government can no longer rely on exposing the faults of the Tories' thirteen years. A governing party, and particularly a reforming one, must continually replenish its ideas if it is to have any right to ask the country to renew its mandate. Otherwise, not only will the electorate turn to the Opposition for the sake of variety, but—for a reforming party—this would be to allow creeping conservatism. While change may have no virtue in itself, so often the radicalism of yesterday becomes the Maginot Line of today. Political thought must aim to keep pace with, or preferably ahead of, the ever-accelerating evolution of a world where our children are being taught computer techniques that we will never learn. Today, when length of experience is bought at the price of an increasingly obsolescent education, the ability to be receptive to and to assimilate new ideas is as vital for the Labour Party as it is for Britain.

Hence the reason for this book: these essays by some of the new Labour M.P.s are offered as contributions to a debate whose continuation is essential. To some people it may seem irreverently presumptuous that it is new backbench M.P.s who are giving their views; but Ministers, immersed in the detail of day-to-day government and conditioned by cautious departmental tradition, for reasons of fatigue and preoccupation alone are rarely able to stand aside and look far ahead. There is also an interesting phenomenon of human nature, to which some of the policy of Gladstone is the only exception that comes readily to mind, that politicians' conservatism increases with their age. This tendency cannot be wholly explained by the realization of the practical limitations of power; many people in political life would be less than human if they also did not try to rationalize their own failure to change society by contending that alteration is neither possible nor desirable. Perhaps this may underlie the resentment which the idealism of students and young people often arouses in their elders. It would be a tragedy if, because of the need for solidarity or the weight of office, any other party or organization were able to pre-empt the Labour Party's tradition of radical idealism. At each successive election Labour must raise its sights further and, despite the self-criticism that this involves for a governing party, arouse the electorate to new and higher aims. If the Labour Party modernized its organization it could—despite the Tories' advantages in money and public relations—become the normal majority party in Britain; but it must continually earn its right to be so, and never fall into the Tories' arrogant assumption of a natural right to govern. No Labour Government is elected to fossilize the present imperfections. If ever Labour through having been in power becomes content to rest on its record or to defend the status quo, it will lose its *raison d'être* and will rightly be driven from office.

The views of this book—like those of any twelve people—have inevitable limitations and variation of horizon. Each contributor speaks for himself alone. Others of our colleagues could make contributions of at least equal value; we hope they will. It would be stimulating to read, for example, Willie Hamilton on the reform of many British institutions, or Leo Abse as a one-man social law commission, or Lena Jeger on any subject calling for compassionate fire. Reasons of space alone have also resulted in the omission of vital subjects of which each reader will have his own list. A collection of writers who by coincidence are all male can be criticized as well for not having attacked what is perhaps the most widespread of all injustices remaining in our society: that relic of medievalism, discrimination against women.[1] The scarcely questioned continuance in our national life of such a primitive prejudice as the selection of people on grounds of biology rather than their ability is a remarkable testimony to the effect of conditioning. Less than one British woman in five is being paid the same rate as a man would receive for her work. The cost to the country of the restriction of female opportunities in higher education is difficult to calculate; but prejudice in the medical profession, for example, has the indefensible consequence of our draining less developed countries of doctors they cannot afford to lose. The involuntary levy paid by the women of this country who are not getting equal pay for equal work has received each year since 1885 lip-service condemnation paralleled by almost total inactivity. The full eventual cost is no excuse for not making a start on reform, even if it may be a reason for phasing it; nine years ago the Treaty of Rome fixed the date for the full implementation of equal pay in the European Economic Community to take place by stages but not later than the end of 1964.

If one theme in general permeates the following pages, it is perhaps a realization of how many aspects of British society are still urgently in need of reform. Conservatism, as John Mackintosh and Alan Lee Williams show in their contributions, does not stop outside a Labour-controlled Parliament or the organization of the Labour Party itself. It would be an error if the Party, because it has won two elections, failed to improve the structure or pay of its organization. But it will be a tragedy if either the electorate or the Government of this country felt that after a few years of reforming legislation it was time for the pendulum to swing us back to digestive torpor. The 1964–70 Parliaments, saddled with the sterling, defence and Rhodesian problems they inherited, are likely to make

[1] There are symptoms of this in the Palace of Westminster: in A.D. 1966 the Deputy Prime Minister of Italy, who wished to hear a debate but did not understand English, was deprived of the interpreter provided for him by the Foreign Office, because she was a woman—and women are not allowed in the Distinguished Strangers' Gallery.

little more than a modest start on the backlog of overdue law reform or the reconstruction of social security. Redoubts of reaction in Britain such as the public school system and a partly hereditary legislature[1] — discarded by virtually every other country in the world — seem all too likely to survive this Parliament. Nobody can accuse of precipitousness a Government whose innovations include a restricted form of the Ombudsman which Sweden has had for 160 years, or capital gains and corporation taxes similar to those which have been operating for some time in the United States. And as long as we cling to trying to maintain sterling as a world currency, all our hopes and plans for social reconstruction will be at the mercy of the pressures which it entails. At present, like the finance companies which have recently been in difficulties, we have to borrow short and lend long, and are forced to deflate as soon as we achieve any tangible rate of growth in our economy.

But if our society is to progress, it is not enough merely to resist government from the grave or even to make good the omissions of the past. Our reshaping must organically improve the basis for the future. A breakthrough is effected not by Labour taking office, but by what it achieves; a Labour Government, whose National Plan or whose prices-and-incomes policy succeeds only in preserving the present injustices, will have failed ignominiously. Instead of blaming our recurrent economic malaise for restricting the room for reform, we should recognize that it necessitates drastic remedial action. In order to release our full national potential as well as for reasons of moral justice, we must survey and eliminate every form of inequality of opportunity. How can exhortation or any number of productivity committees outweigh the fact that the gap between those who earn the money in this country, and those who own it, is widening? While weekly wage rates between 1956 and 1965 rose by 64 per cent, ordinary dividends increased by 159 per cent and in addition share values rose by 106 per cent. The United Kingdom's increase in unearned income between 1960 and 1964 was not only the highest in Europe but approximately four times the rise in our productivity in that period. Yet surely it would be more logical to

---

[1] If Britain were a colony we could justifiably be told we were not yet ready for independence because we have not yet developed a fully democratic form of government. It is also time we attained 'one man, one vote' in this country by ending the plural votes which 150,000 local electors have in Britain, even excluding the extraordinary franchise in Ulster.

reverse this bias: to increase incentive by reducing taxation on earnings—while providing equal opportunity for people to earn—and to pay for this by taxing unearned and inherited wealth more? A tax on private capital would also benefit growth by encouraging the owners to put their money to the most productive use. This would promote production at the same time as social justice—the twin mandate that Labour was given.

The illusion that the Attlee Government achieved a classless society has been dispelled by the research of Professor Titmuss and others who have shown that, for example, tax-paying for those who are wealthy enough to have expert advice is often little more than a voluntary levy. (In the absence of a gifts tax, any person whose estate pays duty to the State will probably either have been malicious to his heirs or have had a claim for negligence against his advisers.) The scale of the continuing inequality in Britain is revealed by the fact that four-fifths of all the share capital of private corporate business is held by 1 per cent of the adult population. The imbalance actually *increased* between 1959 and 1964. The Conservatives put the whole direction of redistribution sharply into reverse: the share of wealth belonging to the richest 5 per cent of the population, which had come down from 79 per cent in 1938 to 71 per cent in 1954, had risen to 75 per cent again by 1960. The relative inequality of the distribution of personal taxed income also widened under the Conservatives:[1]

	Group of Income Recipients	1957	1963
PERCENTAGE	Top 1%	5.0%	5.2%
DISTRIBUTION	2%– 5%	9.9	10.5
OF INCOMES	6%–10%	9.1	9.5
AFTER TAX:	11%–40%	38.5	39.5
	41%–70%	24.0	23.5
	Bottom 30%	13.4	11.8

[1] This was so even without taking account of the greater opportunities for capital gains and tax-avoidance (both legal and less legal)—including covenants, benefits in kind such as free accommodation and cars, expense accounts, 'top hat' schemes, private superannuation and large tax-free sums on retirement—which are available exclusively to those in the higher income groups. Fringe benefits are estimated (*The Times*, November 2nd, 1966) to amount to 31 per cent of salary at £7,000 or more a year. Their prevalence is increasing rapidly: the *A.I.C. Annual Survey* of 1966 reveals that 36 per cent of executives now have 'top-hat' supplementary pensions, and as many as 16 per cent—a four-fold increase in the past five years—have their houses subsidized.

The case against firm redistribution would be more respectable were there less likelihood of the inequities continuing; but while a minority are able to purchase grossly disproportionate educational, medical or housing opportunities—as, in previous ages, money could buy commissions in the services, acquittals in court or seats in Parliament—most of the families who are trapped in overcrowded classes or slums are all too likely to have their unfairly limited horizons perpetuated. (Anybody who chooses to believe there are no longer two nations in Britain is recommended to walk in London the few hundred yards that separate the City and Cable Street.) As money breeds more money, there is a continuing tendency in any capitalist society towards increasing inequality unless the state redresses the balance; but redistribution of opportunity is needed even more than redistribution of wealth. Some Conservatives may be sincere and altruistic in resisting government intervention on grounds of freedom; but this presupposes a society where every person first has the freedom of equal opportunity to all that his life could contain of earning-power, health, education, justice, leisure or the arts. Yet at present it is just those whose incomes are lowest, material reserves smallest and opportunities the most restricted who remain most vulnerable to unemployment, accident and illness, and who are invariably expected to bear the brunt of any deflation. W. G. Runciman has charted how the social inequality between clerical and manual workers is persistently reinforced by their differences in conditions and pensions, and in their opportunities for promotion, fringe-benefits and tax-avoidance. Under the Conservatives, the relative income of the salariat increased at almost exactly twice the rate of wage-earners: between 1957 and 1963 salaries rose by 57 per cent while wages went up by only 29 per cent. While we now have at one end of the scale 2 per cent of our adults enjoying 40 per cent of the country's assets there are, at the other, 71 per cent of adults who have assets of less than £1,000 each, and are therefore unable to change their environment or the quality of their lives by purchasing such things as better housing or private education. The scales of justice themselves are still weighted in favour of the richest people and companies who are able to afford the best lawyers; indeed the bulk of the population will remain ignorant of and excluded from their legitimate rights until there is a full-scale national legal service. The extent to which the electorate are aware of Britain's continuing inequalities is doubtful: how many people know that nearly *two-fifths* of all families and single individuals have to live on less than £10 a week, or that between 1953 and 1960 the number of people living at a standard no higher than the average family on National Assistance nearly doubled? It is a characteristic of society that the victims of inequality tend to be less articulate and less influential than those who already possess the advantages of affluence. Only strong action by the government, therefore, can change our national criteria from being determined by the power of traditional hierarchies into being ones related to need and merit.

Professors Abel-Smith, Townsend and Titmuss have recently exposed the fact that on several fronts the gap in this country between private affluence and public poverty, far from narrowing, is in fact widening. Insular complacency with having pioneered one form of welfare system has blinkered us to truths such as that the proportion of gross national product which we are now devoting to social security benefits is lower (while our taxation is also lighter) than that of any Common Market country; that our manual workers' holiday entitlement is among the smallest in Europe; and that, for example, in ratio to our wealth, we are spending £200 million less a year on our Health Service than Sweden. Six categories of people in particular continue to suffer indefensibly in our society: large families living on a low wage; the sick and disabled; fatherless children; the retired; mentally abnormal people; and those who are unemployed. None of these groups can organize effective political pressure: but the extent to which we share the benefits of our prosperity with them is a measure of the civilization of our society.

In the north and the west of Britain selective migration has, as Gerry Fowler shows in his contribution, caused accentuated social hardship. One of the principal difficulties of our economy is how to control the over-heating of London and the Midlands without chilling the rest of the country. In several fields—arts, transport, and urban renewal as well as economic development—we have only just started the necessary positive discrimination; and in the future even stronger regional correction will be needed to counterbalance the effects of the Common Market (irrespective of whether we enter) and of the Channel Tunnel. At present throughout the whole of Britain there are eight million people whose incomes are inadequate for a reasonable diet; the proportion of children whose diets are below the B.M.A.'s standards has risen from 36 per cent in 1960 to 43 per cent in 1966. But the flat-rate contributory basis of our current welfare system in fact only serves to intensify inequality, while it is the people with the largest incomes who are able to claim the most in tax relief. This has the extraordinary effect that the state is providing the most generous subsidies for those children who live in the richest homes, and the least for the families who find it hardest to make ends meet. It cannot make either social or economic sense to give, as we do at present, the most extensive social security to the people who are at least in need of it, the best education to those who are already most privileged, or to grant the most generous help from the state in housing-allowances to the best-housed owner-occupiers. It is socially regressive for our fiscal system to make the lowest income groups pay so much more, proportionately, in indirect taxes and flat-rate contributions than higher income groups do. The remedy must be to rationalize without delay the net effects of our tax and social security systems which are working at present in conflicting directions.

This is the background of the Britain for which several of these essays propose internal reforms, including the extension of industrial democracy and public ownership. The provision for workers' consultation in the new national Steel Corporation is a progressive move which should be extended to every firm and developed, by means of access to data, into a meaningful participation in decisions by employees. Socialists believe that economic growth is best achieved by allowing an employee his share both in planning and in results, so as to end the destructive friction between workers and management and to remove the fear of productivity's effect on employment. A Labour Government clearly should also develop assets such as the North Sea gas-fields for the benefit of the nation, rather than allow them to be exploited by a commercial oligopoly in the interests of a few shareholders. To finance comprehensive welfare and education the public should take into ownership industries such as oil, insurance, pharmaceuticals, gambling, natural gas-fields, and the banks—all of which are likely in the future to be highly profitable as well as, in each case, to benefit from responsible control. (For example, a state motor insurance scheme financed by a levy on petrol would be simpler and socially more desirable than the present system: it would at the same time obviate evasion, administrative duplication or any necessity for checking, while more equitably sharing the cost in proportion to the amount of motoring a policy-holder does.)

But the method of the change to socialism is seminally important; it is crucial for success that its development should be a democratic and not a bureaucratic takeover. We must carry with us the people who are the ends and the means of all our planning. Government must be concerned with the qualitative as well as the material development of society: with the proper function of the car in our environment as much as the opportunity of each family to have one. Every political leader today (other perhaps than Mr Powell) accepts the necessity for government intervention and planned economic remoulding: but socialism will succeed or fail by its ability to arouse in the public a conception of their community and of their right to participate in the private sector of the economy. In 1966 and 1967 the successive failure of several motor insurance and finance companies brought home to many people the limitations of irresponsible private speculation. Our task is to convey not only the moral rightness of reforms as an extension of democracy but also the potential benefits in human development, in order to enlist the nation in an active concern for its success: socialism is achieved not by passing laws but by convincing public opinion of the need to change the structure of society. In no country is this more true than in Britain, where a tradition of resentment at government intervention (except at times of crisis) dies hard. Our attainment of a new and better community depends on our success in conveying the realization that all our institutions, from our civil service and professions to the political parties, exist for our benefit rather than vice versa — and can be reformed accordingly:[1] in arousing a consciousness that the activities and interests of a democratic state are those of the public — not excluding its inarticulate and weakest members. From the rapid spread of the consumer movement to the recognition of the public's interest in profits made on public contracts, in the investigation of prices and in incomes priorities, there has recently been growing a consciousness (except in the professions) that the public's rights are paramount — and, where organized, irresistible.

There will be powerful and wealthy interests fighting at the next

[1] Parliament itself should be scrutinized by an outside commission to recommend reforms designed not so much to improve M.P.s' convenience as to provide the country with the best possible legislature.

election to prevent this evolution of a participating and cohesive society based on interdependence and inter-responsibilities. The Conservatives, under a guise of 'freedom versus planning', are likely to fight to put the clock back to the time when a few could enjoy privileges and economic power at the expense of the community. We must make plain our reply that socialism expands the realities of liberty, by making opportunity available to all and not merely to those with superior capital. At the same time we should reaffirm our belief in intellectual freedom — not least within our own party — and that democratic socialism respects this above all else. It is equally essential for success that reform in the public interest should be applied impartially to every sector of the country: few spectacles are less defensible than that of a Parliament, composed largely of professional members elected by trades union voters, rebuking the unions for their restrictive practices while the legal profession, for example, refuses to reform its own monopolistic restrictive practices. All the professions, as much as the unions, should be accountable in the light of socially desirable criteria.

If the present anomalies were exposed sufficiently clearly to the people of Britain, I believe there would be an immediate outcry for a change in our public values. At present we spend more money each year on military bands than we do on the United Nations, F.A.O., UNESCO, UNICEF, and I.L.O. combined; more on cigarette promotion than on research into lung-cancer; more on the fashions of car styling than on the improvement of car safety. It may be only a qualitative judgment that Britain spends over a hundred times more on horse-racing than on encouraging all the arts put together, but can it be right that a single soap company spends more on advertising than all our local authorities are able to devote to the problems of mental health which affect a tenth of our population? It is possible that if voters personally knew any of the 7,600 people who are homeless (let alone the 150,000 families waiting on housing-lists or the number still living in slum conditions) in London today, they would demand that they be housed in the offices, houses and hotel rooms that are lying empty.

The same widespread education, in human implications rather than in statistical terms, is necessary to transform the climate of public opinion about our foreign policies — and, in particular, about our aid for underdeveloped countries. At present we spend between 6 and 7 per cent of our gross national product on Defence, a far higher burden[1] than that of any other country in western or eastern Europe, and more than five times as much as we do on aid. The proportion should be reversed: even if a mortgaged gunboat were a credible weapon, the sinews of foreign policy today are grain ships rather than battleships. Since 1945 Britain has been involved in forty different armed conflicts: with what result? Although we must never again be caught in a Munich-type state of unpreparedness until disarmament is achieved on a universal basis, our continued attempt to arrogate to ourselves a self-appointed nineteenth-century role of policing the world is an embarrassment to our friends. The lesson of these last twenty years is that 'peacekeeping' is generally less politically suspect if it is effected through the United Nations instead of by individual powers seeking to protect their interests in—and at the expense of—Cuba, Aden, Hungary or Vietnam. The establishment of an international peacekeeping force would provide the umbrella under which nations might be persuaded at last to take the plunge and disarm. If the U.N. could stabilize the security of, for example, the Middle East or South-East Asia, the money being wasted there on arms races could be channelled into some much needed social progress. Instead there is every indication that Britain is involving herself in the Persian Gulf in the same type of morass as that from which we are painfully extricating ourselves in Aden. Whether or not we join Europe, the tragic result of our illusion of a neo-imperial world mission is that this prevents Britain from making the two great contributions for which she is principally fitted at this stage in history: it inhibits us from playing any effective role in promoting the *détente* between East and West, and in addition, the consequent economic burden prevents us from helping with essential development projects abroad as much as it limits our own capacity to change internally.

The funds that we do devote to development overseas and our volunteer programme would perhaps be administered better by an independent body who would be free from suspicion of being influenced by any national or political considerations, and could

---

[1] cf. (1965/66) Belgium 3.5, Denmark 2.6, East Germany 2.4, France 4.8, Italy 3.3, Poland 3.4, U.S.S.R. 4.6, Australia 3.7, Canada 3.0, Japan 1.3, and New Zealand 2.2 per cent. It is interesting that we spent (1965) 12.6 per cent of our G.N.P. on Social Security, whereas West Germany spent 15.7, Italy 14.3, the Netherlands 13.1 and France 15.9 per cent.

work on a multilateral U.N. basis solely according to criteria of development. The rapidly widening gap—ominously on lines of colour—between the standard of living in Europe and North America and that of the rest of the world, together with the decreasing likelihood of any amelioration (the number of illiterates, for instance, having increased by over 200 million in the last six years alone) is, as Frank Judd describes in his contribution, by far the greatest problem facing us today—by comparison with which our own internal economic preoccupations should be suspended in an ashamed silence. During the last six years, average annual incomes in the developed nations have risen by £75 to about £600, while the per capita income in the poorer nations has, despite all the programmes of international aid, increased by less than £3 to about £30 a year. This situation is as indefensible as it is inflammatory. It is a symptom of myopic insularity that so much of parliamentary debate is concerned with domestic trivia rather than with the real problems of mankind such as the United Nations, the development of world food resources or the peaceful uses of atomic energy. The population of the world is estimated to be likely to double by the turn of the century, with the speed greatest in the two poorest continents. While persisting in attempts to reform international systems of trade and liquidity, we should now be enlisting public opinion for what may eventually be inevitable: a voluntary restraint or even a cut in our own standard of living, as being the only solution to the problem of the hunger of a world population which is increasing by 200,000 people a day.

In 1647 Rainborough said, 'The poorest he that is in England hath a life to live as well as the greatest he.' His words are as valid across national frontiers as they still remain relevant in this country three hundred and twenty years later. If this book can make any contribution to the reappraisal and revision of Britain's values and priorities at home or abroad, it will have achieved its purpose.

© 1967 BY BEN WHITAKER

Europe

DAVID MARQUAND

British membership of the European Economic Community is now the declared aim of all three parties in the House of Commons. To judge by the Press and the opinion polls, it is also supported by a majority of the electorate—and an overwhelming majority of those in leading positions. The Confederation of British Industries is enthusiastic; most trade-union leaders seem to be in support. If British opinion were all that mattered, the deed would be as good as done. But British opinion is, of course, very far from being all that matters. In spite of the oversimplifications of some of the more ardent advocates of British membership, it is not possible for Britain simply to 'sign on the dotted line' and join the Community forthwith. In the first place, the Rome Treaty has no dotted line. The accession of a new member has to be agreed to by the existing ones. In practice, it is inconceivable that the existing members would agree to Britain's accession—no matter how enthusiastic Britain herself might be—without long and complex negotiations. This would be true even if President de Gaulle had never existed, simply because of the inevitable problems which the accession of a nation of fifty millions would be bound to create; the fact that President de Gaulle does exist merely makes that truth more obvious. Moreover, even if it were the case that Britain could join overnight merely by proclaiming her wish to do so, no sane British Government could contemplate such a course for a moment. Membership of the Common Market could—and one day almost certainly will—bring great long-term benefits to this country. But unless satisfactory transitional arrangements are made, the long-term benefits could easily be outweighed by the short-term costs. If Britain is to join, then, negotiations must first take place; and it will not be possible to evaluate the final outcome until the negotiations are well under way.

Yet it would be futile to spell out in advance what tactics the Government should adopt if and when negotiations begin. Complex haggling of the kind which will be necessary is best left to those on the spot. In any case, it is not possible to predict at this stage what cards the parties to the negotiations will hold, or how they will play them. A great deal has changed on the mainland of Europe since January 1963. The Common Market has become more cohesive in many ways, and shown even more resilience than its admirers expected; but it has lost some of its supranational mystique in the process. The power relationships of its members have changed also. The Franco-German axis, so beloved of Dr Adenauer, is no longer a significant factor: nor, for that matter, is Dr Adenauer. President de Gaulle is as intransigent and awkward a neighbour as ever; and his declared aims are even more disconcerting to his allies. But his hold on French opinion no longer seems quite as unshakeable as it was, and his intransigence has failed to bring his aims any closer to realization. On the other hand, the developing *détente* between Russia and the West has made Gaullist attacks on the sanctity of the Atlantic Alliance less dangerous as well as more plausible, and the increasingly costly, bloody and apparently futile American involvement in the distant jungles of South-East Asia may well have had a similar effect. These and other changes must surely have affected the political climate in which any negotiations between Britain and the 'Six' take place. How, and to what extent, however, it is impossible to tell.

But although it is not possible to predict the course of such negotiations, or to prescribe in detail the tactics which Britain should adopt, it is perfectly possible to examine the broad considerations which should govern Britain's choice of tactics and the broad implications of a British decision to embark on such negotiations in earnest. Indeed, it is not only possible, but desirable. One subsidiary, but nevertheless important, cause of the failure of the Conservative Government's attempt to join the E.E.C. was the lack of realism displayed by informed British opinion at that time. Advocates of British membership often underestimated the problems it would pose, for the Community as well as for Britain. Moderate opponents grossly overestimated the extent of the concessions the Six could reasonably be expected to make, and failed to recognize what was negotiable and what was not. Partly because of this, valuable time was lost in the early stages of the negotiations in a doomed attempt to secure concessions for the Commonwealth, which the Six could have granted only at the price of undermining one of the basic principles on which the Common Market was based. The same applies to the exaggerated — and sometimes almost metaphysical — fears expressed in the House of Commons about the loss of 'sovereignty' which British membership of the Common Market would entail, and the crippling effects which European 'federalism' or 'supranationalism' would have on Britain's ability to conduct her own foreign policy or plan her own economy. These fears were related only in the most superficial way to what was actually taking place on the Continent. Nevertheless, they had a damaging effect on the negotiations. Partly because of them, the British Government consistently underplayed its commitment to the political unification of Europe, at least in those of its pronouncements which were designed for domestic consumption[1]. This in turn almost certainly damaged its credit with the 'Europeans' across the Channel. All this, of course, is not to say that the advantages of British membership of the Common Market are so self-evident that debate is unnecessary. But if the debate is to be worthwhile, it should focus on real problems rather than on imaginary ones. The real problems, after all, are serious enough.

The most fundamental of them is that the benefits of British membership of the Common Market would be long-term, and are to some extent a matter of speculation, while the costs would be immediate and are to a much greater extent a matter of fact. This applies, not only to the political benefits, but to the economic benefits also. Two important economic benefits seem likely. In the first place, membership of a market with a population of anything up to 280 million, depending on how many of the EFTA countries join too, should make it possible for British industry to profit from economies of scale which are not available to it in a home market of only fifty million. This is particularly true, moreover, of the most technologically advanced, capital-intensive industries like computers or aircraft, which will increasingly have to operate on a continental scale if they are to operate at all.[2] Secondly, British

---

[1] See, for example, the difference between the tone of Mr Macmillan's speech in the House of Commons in August 1961 and Mr Heath's statement to the E.E.C. Council of Ministers at the start of the negotiations in October the same year.

[2] Opponents of entry sometimes point out that British industry does not

exports could benefit enormously from tariff-free access to what has been, for most of the last fifteen years, the fastest-growing market in the western world.[1] It is true, no doubt, that if Britain joins the E.E.C. she will have to impose the common external tariff on imports from the Commonwealth, and therefore lose the preferences she now enjoys in Commonwealth markets. But even without joining the Common Market, the proportion of British exports which goes to the Commonwealth has fallen by about a quarter since 1955 (from about 40 per cent to under 30 per cent), while the proportion which goes to the E.E.C. countries has gone up by about a third (from 14 per cent to 19 per cent), and the absolute total going to the E.E.C. has increased from £300 millions to over £700 millions. Again, although it is true that membership of the Common Market would expose Britain to tougher competition from continental exporters, British industry seems confident that it can meet the challenge. In any case, it is worth noticing that for the last ten years, Britain's balance of trade with the Six has been consistently favourable. Both because of the economies of scale, therefore, and because of easier access to a rich and rapidly growing market, the economic benefits of membership are likely to be substantial.

They are, however, impossible to quantify or even to predict with any precision. In the end, moreover, the expectation that they will arrive at all rests on an act of faith — of faith in the capacity of British businessmen and workers to respond to the challenge of more intense competition, and to seize the opportunities it would bring. That faith, however, may be misplaced. Societies do sometimes become decadent, and incapable of adapting themselves to change; it may be that Britain has done so. Indeed, many of the most vociferous opponents of her entry into the Common Market base their case on the tacit assumption that she has. Thus, it is frequently pointed out that British exporters might fail to take advantage of the opportunities which membership of the E.E.C. would bring, that the structural reforms which would be necessary

profit from all the potential economies of scale which are already available in a market of fifty million. But although this may weaken the argument in favour of economies of scale for much of industry, it does not do so for the crucial sector of industry which operates on the frontiers of technical progress.

[1] British exports to the United States have, of course, risen faster than British exports to the Six. If the mirage of a free trade area between Britain and the U.S. had any substance, this might be a good argument against entry. In fact it has none.

for British industry to stand up to more intense competition might not be carried out, that the strong sectors of the British economy might therefore gain less than the weak would lose, that Britain might be to the dynamic centre of Western Europe what Northern Ireland is to the rest of the United Kingdom, or Sicily is to the rest of Italy. All this is true. It is equally true, of course, that if these pessimistic assumptions are valid, then the outlook for Britain is suicidally gloomy in any case. Even so, it is arguable that it would be better for her to decline slowly outside the E.E.C. than swiftly within it.

If the economic benefits are unquantifiable and speculative, moreover, the political benefits are more so. One's assessment of the political advantages of membership of the E.E.C. must depend, in the end, on one's assessment of its likely evolution. Any attempt to make such an assessment, however, is hazardous in the extreme. The crucial argument here is that the more cohesive the Common Market becomes, the greater its political weight will be. The more closely integrated the economies of the Six become, the more they will have to develop political institutions—and, more important, political processes—to match. One obvious example is of particularly painful relevance to Britain. In a fully fledged economic community, a balance of payments crisis of the kind Britain suffered in 1966 could not be dealt with by the member state concerned in isolation from its partners. Import controls would be ruled out. A unilateral currency devaluation would cause great problems for the rest of the community. So would deflationary measures of the kind which the British Government took. In a fully fledged economic community, in other words, the balance of payments problems of any one member would be a matter of common concern. The implications are revolutionary. For it means that in such a community, the member states would gradually have to harmonize, not only their commercial policies, but their fiscal and monetary policies and their economic planning. This would not be possible, however, until regular processes of harmonization were established. That in turn would entail the creation of institutions of some kind, no matter how loose and informal they might be.

The key words here are, of course, 'loose' and 'informal'. The development I have sketched is a long way off; and it is pointless to speculate on the precise form it might take. Even so, it is clear that in a fully fledged economic community, the Governments of the member states would no longer be completely free to regulate the working of economic forces within their own boundaries, without reference to their partners. But this would not involve a return to nineteenth-century laissez-faire. Such a return is inconceivable, if only because its consequences would not be tolerated for a moment by democratic electorates. Moreover, as Mr Andrew Shonfield has shown in his *Modern Capitalism*,[1] the principle of state intervention in the economy is now an accepted part of the landscape throughout Western Europe—even in that supposed bastion of rugged individualism, the German Federal Republic. In France and Italy, the principle is more widely accepted than it is in Britain, and its practical consequences more thoroughly exemplified. The fact that it will no longer be possible to carry out certain kinds of economic regulation on the national level does not mean, therefore, that they will cease to be carried out at all. On the contrary, it means that they will have to be carried out at the community level instead. The powers lost by national Governments will not disappear. They will be transferred to authorities capable of exercising them on a continental, rather than on a merely national, scale. This is not to say that economic integration entails political federation. The whole concept of 'federation'—with its overtones of nineteenth-century constitution-mongering—is probably out of place in this context. What seems likely is not the creation of a 'United States of Europe' on the pattern of the U.S.A. It is the gradual development of a network of agencies, with different functions, different jurisdictions and different methods of working, yet all serving the common aim of economic regulation and control on a community basis. The result would not be a 'federation' in the normal sense of the term, but a new kind of political animal, hitherto unknown to political zoologists, for which a new name would have to be invented.

For a Socialist, these are in any case attractive perspectives. The last two years have shown that it is much harder to carry out the kind of planning implied in Labour's 1964 election manifesto within the confines of a single nation-state than many of us had supposed. It is true, of course, that many of the difficulties which the Labour Government has faced are merely due to the legacy left by its predecessors. Others, however, seem more fundamental, and would be likely to face any Government which wished to plan an economy as sensitive to marginal shifts in world trade as the British

[1] Royal Institute of International Affairs, 1965.

economy necessarily is. It is equally true that planning on a European scale would present formidable technical and administrative problems. Even in Britain, the statistical raw material without which economic planning is merely a phrase is patchy and in many cases grossly inadequate: such difficulties are likely to be even greater in Western Europe as a whole. Again, sophisticated economic planning requires a bureaucracy of high quality. In France this exists; but in the rest of Western Europe it is doubtful whether it does. But although the problems would be considerable, the rewards are likely to be correspondingly great. The fundamental obstacle to effective economic planning in a single nation-state is that too few of the variables are even potentially under the control of the planners. If planning were carried out on a European scale, this would not be true to the same extent, and the whole exercise would be that much more likely to succeed.

This is only the first of the political arguments for British entry into the Common Market. The second is that if the E.E.C. evolves in the sort of way I have suggested, Britain is likely to suffer a steady loss of world influence if she stays out. The language of power is apt to fall disagreeably on Socialist ears; and the world would undeniably be a pleasanter place if no one spoke it. In the world as it is, however, the language of power is also the language of diplomacy. Governments without power, however virtuous they may be, have little chance of making their virtue effective. It is true, of course, that even if Britain stays outside the E.E.C., her absolute power will not be seriously affected by developments inside it. Her relative power, however, would be affected a great deal. At present, Britain is one of a number of second-rank Western European powers, on approximately the same level as France, West Germany and Italy. The development of a massive new power-complex in Western Europe, however, would transform this state of affairs. In such a situation, Britain would no longer be one of a number of European states, of approximately equal size and weight. She would be an off-shore island, facing a much more powerful neighbour across the Channel. Her influence—not only in Europe itself, but elsewhere in the world as well—would be bound to decline in consequence.

That is, in a sense, a negative argument for British entry. The third is a more positive one. Since 1945 Britain has become progressively more confused and uncertain about her role in world affairs. Immediately after the war, it was fashionable to talk of the three 'overlapping circles' of Europe, the British Commonwealth and the Atlantic Alliance; and to suggest that Britain's role was that of the intermediary and interpreter between the three. She had closer ties with Washington than any other European country; the Commonwealth gave her links with the most distant parts of Africa and Asia; in a Europe battered and devastated by the most terrible war in history she was easily the strongest and the most self-confident survivor. None of this is true today. Western Europe has recovered. It is now more united and peaceful than it has been since the fall of the Roman Empire, and more prosperous than it has ever been. The nations of Western Europe no longer need intermediaries or interpreters in Washington; they are quite capable of doing the job for themselves. The British Commonwealth, although its existence is a great tribute to the statesmanship of the post-war Labour Government which created it in its present form, is no longer in any significant sense a political asset to Britain. The three overlapping circles, in short, no longer overlap as they used to do; to the extent that they still do, London is no longer the place where they intersect. In this situation, Britain can no longer play the role she played with such distinction in the immediate post-war period. Instead she has to choose between a primarily European role and the role of junior partner to the United States.

For most of the time, she has chosen the second. There is much to be said for doing so. Britain and the United States share a common language, and to a large extent a common political culture. Englishmen and Americans read the same books, respond to similar myths, and discuss politics in the same kind of way. British travellers in the United States are at home there in a sense which is true of no other Europeans; and the same is true of British politicians and civil servants. Thanks to these cultural ties, British public opinion has usually been prepared to trust the United States in a way in which public opinion on the Continent has not.[1] In spite of

---

[1] There have, of course, been outbursts of anti-Americanism in both major parties. But they have been directed against the American Government rather than against the American way of life. Whereas continental anti-Americans fear that the United States would not defend them in the event of Soviet attack, British anti-Americans tend to fear that the U.S. would use nuclear weapons too readily rather than not readily enough.

all this, however, it is becoming increasingly clear that junior partnership to the United States brings costs as well as benefits; and there is growing evidence that the costs are becoming greater while the benefits are becoming smaller. Two obvious examples are British attitudes to the role of sterling, and Britain's defence commitments in Asia. It is clear that the United States regards the pound sterling, with some justice, as the first line of defence for the dollar. So long as the British Government treats its relationship with the United States as the cornerstone of its foreign policy, this is bound to limit the options open to it in economic affairs. The same is true of the so-called 'East of Suez' policy. It is, of course, a crude and vulgar oversimplification to believe that Britain's continued presence east of Suez is solely the result of American pressure. Nevertheless, there is no doubt that the present Administration in Washington would be extremely sorry to see Britain depart from the area. If Britain is first and foremost an ally of the United States, rather than first and foremost a European power, this fact must weigh heavily in the British Government's calculations. Yet there is no doubt that Britain's defence commitments in Asia contribute significantly to her balance of payments difficulties.

These immediate problems are important enough. Yet they are of subsidiary importance in the present argument. The really vital question is whether or not the role of junior partner to the United States is likely—in the long run—to yield this country more influence in world politics than a primarily European role would yield. The answer is surely clear. Britain's influence as a junior partner of the United States is that of a courtier or confidant. She is listened to in Washington so long as she says what her hosts wish to hear. When vital American interests are not at stake, or when the Americans themselves have not yet made up their minds what their vital interests are, she may well enjoy great influence. But it is a transitory and insecure kind of influence, since there is so little real power to back it up. It rests on the quality of British arguments, the ability of British civil servants, the personal relationships between British ministers and their opposite numbers in Washington at any given moment. Influence of this sort is a valuable asset, if one has it; and it would be silly to underestimate its value. But it is quite different in kind from the kind of influence which derives from independent political and economic weight. That second kind of influence is the only kind on which it is safe to rely for any length of time. Vis-à-vis the United States, Britain can never hope for much of that second sort of influence. Vis-à-vis countries of the same size and weight in Western Europe, she can.

All this adds up to a powerful case for British entry into the Common Market. Provided they can be obtained at a satisfactory price, it would be foolish — and in the long run it might even prove suicidally foolish — to spurn the advantages on which that case is based. But can they?

This is now the crucial question; and it is on the answer to it that the success or failure of the Government's present enterprise will turn. If it is to be answered satisfactorily, however, it is necessary to define the term 'satisfactory price' with some care. In particular, it is necessary to draw a sharp distinction between the effects of British entry into the Common Market, and its effects on Britain's connections with the outside world. Clearly, the Six ought to be prepared to make concessions aimed at helping Britain to adapt her economy to the new situation which membership of the E.E.C. would create. If they are not prepared to do so, Britain's experience as a member of the E.E.C. would be likely to be unhappy. In any case, she could simply not afford to join, even if she wished to do so. For whatever may be negotiable, it is clear that the basic principles underlying the common agricultural policy are not. If Britain is to join the Common Market at all, British consumers will have to pay higher prices for their food. More important, a new burden will be placed on the British balance of payments. Higher prices will have to be paid for food imported into this country, whether it comes from the Community, or whether it comes from the outside world and has its price brought up to Community levels. At the same time, levies will have to be paid to the Community's agricultural fund. This basic structure is fundamental to the Common Market, and cannot now be dismantled.

In the long run, of course, its effect on the British balance of payments is likely to be much less harmful than is often supposed. World food prices are likely to rise in any case. With Britain inside it, Community prices will probably fall. Thus, the gap between Britain's present prices and the Community's prices is likely to narrow in any case. Even if it is not, it is worth pointing out that the probable cost of that gap to the British balance of payments is less than one per cent of Britain's present national income. In the short run, however, even that would be a heavy burden. Thus, it is not selfish or insular or 'un-European' to insist on a generous transitional period before the British economy experiences the full rigour of the common agricultural policy, or to fight hard for generous terms so far as Britain's levy payments are concerned. These are vital national interests; and Britain has as much right to insist that her vital national interests are respected by her future partners as they had to insist that their national interests should be safeguarded when they negotiated the Rome Treaty.

This does not apply, however, to the effect of British entry on her overseas connections. Indeed, since one of the strongest arguments for British membership of the E.E.C. is the increasing emptiness of her world role, it is hard to see why she should want to jeopardize her chances of joining for the sake of maintaining it. In any case, she has no right to expect tenderness from the Six if she tries to do anything of the kind. The suggestion that Britain's links with the Commonwealth would be in some mysterious way an asset to the Community, which was frequently put forward by British Ministers at the time of the last negotiations, is likely to be greeted with derisive laughter on the Continent. This does not mean, of course, that Britain should pay no attention to the interests of the developing countries of the Commonwealth. To them, she has a clear moral obligation. So, for the matter, do the Six—in common with the whole of the developed world. The developed countries of the Commonwealth, however, are in a quite different category. There is no reason at all to expect the Governments of the Six to sacrifice the interests of poor peasants in France and Italy in order to safeguard the interests of rich farmers in the Canadian prairies. For that matter, it is hard to see why British Socialists should want them to. Laissez-faire liberals may see something sacrosanct in the notion of buying in the cheapest market. Socialists, however, do not.

An equally unsentimental view should be taken of the effect of British entry on her relations with the United States—and since this aspect of the whole equation may assume critical importance, it should be examined with some care. Two sets of questions have to be answered: the first concerned with the tactics which Britain ought to adopt if and when negotiations take place, and the second with the much more fundamental question of what a British commitment to embark on such negotiations in earnest would really imply. The two sets of questions are distinct, though related; and they should therefore be examined separately.

The first set of questions has so far bulked larger than the second in public discussion. Will President de Gaulle let us into the Common Market if we refuse to break with the Americans? How would the other five E.E.C. members react if we tried to narrow the gap between ourselves and President de Gaulle on this issue? Assuming that we are not prepared to break with the Americans in the sort of way that President de Gaulle himself has done, is there any other inducement we can offer him in order to win his support for our entry? If we cannot win his support, can we at least persuade him to be neutral? If we cannot even persuade him to be neutral, what are the chances that he will, in the end, be prepared to incur the odium which would result from a second veto? It is questions like these which have dominated speculation in the Press. So far, the Government's response to them has been non-commital. Nevertheless, a consistent pattern of reasoning has emerged from ministerial statements, which runs something like this. It would be foolish and self-defeating for us to try to smuggle ourselves into the Common Market by disguising ourselves in Gaullist costume; since it would alienate our friends without necessarily winning over President de Gaulle. On the other hand, we can offer the French a powerful inducement of a different kind. President de Gaulle has frequently proclaimed his desire to make Europe independent of the United States, both military and economically. If these proclamations are more than rhetorical flourishes, he must realize that technology is of crucial importance. Europe cannot be militarily or even economically independent of the United States unless she is first technologically independent. But in the most advanced areas of modern technology, Britain is far ahead of any other Western European country—so much so, that if Britain is excluded from the E.E.C., any attempt to make Europe technologically independent would be a labour of Sisyphus.

There is much truth in this. It would obviously be absurd for Britain to make some dramatic anti-American gesture, merely to impress President de Gaulle. Apart from any other considerations, it would probably not impress him. The suggestion that Britain should in some vague and unspecified way 'do a deal' with France over nuclear weapons is equally misguided. Apart from the risks of nuclear proliferation which such a deal would create, there is no reason to suppose that President de Gaulle particularly wants nuclear help from Britain at present—whatever he may have wanted in 1962. Moreover, the 'technological' argument outlined above is, in fact valid. It is in fact true that Europe cannot be independent of the United States in power terms unless the gap between European and American technology is narrowed. And if that gap is to be narrowed, British co-operation with the rest of Europe is indispensable. President de Gaulle's attitude to British membership of the E.E.C. has been self-contradictory. He has opposed it in the name of European independence. Yet by opposing it he has in fact helped to perpetuate European inferiority, and so to frustrate his own long-term aims. By exposing this internal contradiction in Gaullist foreign policy, or rather by focusing attention on the concrete issues it raises, Britain may indeed win if not French support for her application, then at least benevolent neutrality.

But although the Government's negotiating strategy seems sound, its answers to the second set of questions have so far been less satisfactory. Does Britain in fact accept the need to make Europe, however defined, more independent of the United States? Does she accept the proposition that membership of the E.E.C. is based on the tacit assumption that all its members have more in common with each other than any one of them has with anyone in the outside world? Does she accept the corollary that membership of the E.E.C. would imply a fundamental change in the Anglo-American relationship, and that in future the Anglo-American alliance would have to come lower on Britain's list of priorities than her relationships with her new partners on the Continent? Does she, in short, realize that membership of the E.E.C. is not primarily an economic question at all, but the most important political question which has faced this country since the war? To these questions, the British Government has so far returned a deafening silence.

Silence has, of course, something to be said for it. But although the Government is probably wise to avoid dramatic statements of its position, it would be highly unwise to avoid thinking out the long-term issues involved. In the first place, although it is true that President de Gaulle's attitude to the United States is not shared by the other members of the E.E.C., it is nevertheless equally true that they do share a common belief that Europe has counted for too little since the war, that it is time for the economic achievements of the E.E.C. to be matched by equivalent gains in political influence, and that the relationship between the United States and Europe should be one of equal to equal rather than one of leader to follower. These attitudes are widespread throughout Western Europe, and are part of the driving force behind the movement for European integration. If Britain is not prepared to come to terms with them, and in the long run to share them, it is hard to see how she could play an effective part in the E.E.C. once she had joined.

These attitudes are not, of course, 'anti-American' attitudes. In theory, they could be satisfied by the creation of a genuine Atlantic Community, based on equal partnership between Europe and the United States, of the kind which President Kennedy used to conjure with in his perorations. In practice, however, such an Atlantic Community has become increasingly remote since Kennedy's death. It could come into existence only if the United States were prepared to make a major sacrifice of national sovereignty, above all in the vital area of nuclear defence. As a minimum, the creation of a genuine Atlantic Community would entail the surrender by the United States of a major part of her nuclear arsenal to control by some Atlantic body. In the long run, it would entail American acceptance of a European share in decision-making, not only in the defence of the Atlantic area itself, but in American defence policy in the rest of the world as well. Even under President Kennedy, it is doubtful whether Congress would ever have been prepared to surrender American sovereignty on the necessary scale. Under President Johnson, it is surely clear that nothing of the kind is possible. The obstacles are no longer to be found only in Congress, but in the White House as well. The more the United States turns its back on Europe and concentrates on its struggle with Communist China, the more formidable these obstacles will become. With an Atlantic Community ruled out, however, it seems clear that the increasing pride and self-confidence of Western Europe, which helped to provide the fuel for the European movement in the first place and which seems certain to grow stronger rather than weaker as time goes on, will lead to a gradual loosening of the ties between the two sides of the Atlantic Ocean.

This is the second reason why the British Government, and British public opinion, would be foolish to avoid thinking out the long-term foreign-policy implications of joining the Common Market, more clearly and more explicitly than they have done so far. For obvious historical reasons, the dream of an Atlantic Community has exercised a hypnotic influence on the makers of British foreign policy. This is understandable, for membership of an Atlantic Community would undoubtedly be a far more attractive option for Britain than membership of a united Europe. So long as such a Community was on the cards, British Ministers and diplomats could be forgiven for hankering after an 'Atlantic' role and disdaining a primarily 'European' one. But although this was true in the past, it is not true today. The Atlantic option is closed. The choice lies, not between Europe and the Atlantic, but between equal partnership in Europe and junior partnership with America. Recognition of that choice does not involve public protestations of any kind. It does involve an inner realisation that if our proclaimed wish to join the E.E.C. means anything, it means that we now accept that our destiny lies on this side of the Atlantic rather than on the other.

© 1967 BY DAVID MARQUAND

The Reform of Parliament
JOHN P. MACKINTOSH

Almost every Radical and many Conservatives are in favour of something they call 'Parliamentary Reform' and recent public opinion polls show that a majority of the electorate are in agreement. But there is a wide variety of opinions included under this general heading and it is important to be clear about the reasons for reforming Parliament and the kinds of changes that are required.

In the left wing or progressive tradition in Britain there are two diametrically opposed views of Parliament and its functions. One view, taken by some Radicals ever since the time of Joseph Chamberlain and Randolph Churchill, is that the electorate is sovereign; it chooses a government in order to have a legislative programme pushed through the House. This remains the opinion of many contemporary Labour M.P.s. They regard the Commons not as a place where the Government should be criticized and controlled, but as the site of a struggle for power. The Government appeals to the public, explains its policies and proceeds to enact its programme; government back-benchers should do nothing to hinder this process. The Opposition's task is to put the counter-arguments to the public to try to discredit the Government and slow up its rate of progress. Reformers of this school want to get rid of unnecessary ceremony — two days for swearing in members, the re-reading of the Queen's Speech, the interruptions caused by Black Rod's visits, trooping through the lobbies to vote — but do not wish any changes which would allow the House extra powers to interrogate, delay or thwart the Government.

The other radical view is that there is an inherent value in government by discussion, in the participation of elected representatives, in the existence of checks which can force the executive to explain itself, to listen to other sides of the case and to win over parliamentary and public opinion. This school of thought has been alarmed by the increasing dominance of the Government, its ability and tendency to do without or ignore the House of Commons; and calls for changes in procedure which would allow the Commons greater powers to extract information and concessions from the executive.

Some authorities, notably Professor Bernard Crick and the Study of Parliament Group, have tried to argue that procedure can be reformed and the powers of the House of Commons to obtain information and debate policy increased without affecting the position of the Government. This is probably a sound argument tactically in that it minimizes the worries of those who value strong and effective government. It is also true in the broad sense that much can be done to restore the Commons' capacity to take a part in the decision-making process without returning to a situation where members could and would defeat governments and reject legislation in the fashion of British Parliaments in the 1850s or of French National Assemblies in the 1950s. But it is false in the precise suggestion that the balance of power between the legislature and the executive would not be altered by the kind of reforms advocated by either of the schools of thought just described. To tidy up the more ceremonial and anachronistic practices and give the time thus saved to the Government would, in some degree, increase the Cabinet's dominance over the House. To improve methods of extracting information, even to give M.P.s offices and secretaries, thus enabling them to put more time into preparing for debates and allowing them to devise more searching questions, would tilt the balance, however fractionally, in the other direction. It is hard to think of any reform of the House of Commons which would not in some degree have a marginal effect on the balance between Parliament and the Government.

There is, however, a further aspect. The delicate inter-relations between the various institutions which form the structure of British Government could be affected by parliamentary reforms in other ways than merely altering legislature-executive relationships. There has been little study of how far a ministry can ensure that its policies and attitudes are reflected in the actual conduct of administration by officials at the assistant secretary and principal levels in the various departments. This has not been studied because the Official Secrets Acts and the doctrine of ministerial responsibility make it virtually impossible. But there is no doubt that it is a problem and a system of specialist committees with powers to question civil servants might help ministers to know what is going on in their departments and to ensure that changes in policy at the top have some effect on the conduct of administration at all levels. This side effect of parliamentary reform would only come about if the reforms were of the second type, and included machinery by which the Commons could examine and observe the conduct of sub-sections of departments and even of individual civil servants.

There is no way of proving by factual demonstration that one of these two aspects of the radical tradition is right and the other is wrong. If efficiency is set up as the criterion it could be argued both that leaving the Government free to legislate rapidly aided efficiency and that insistence on proper scrutiny, the ironing out of defects before enactment and examination of the sources and reliability of official advice would likewise make the Government more efficient. There is evidence that when Parliament waived some of its rights in war-time, the British Government was able to mobilize the country for war with more completeness and efficiency than the totalitarian governmental machinery of Germany would permit. A case can also be made that the marked improvement in administration in the mid-nineteenth century was greatly aided by the powers of a far stronger House of Commons whose six hundred members shone their inquiring lights into every dark and cob-webby corner of the ancient structure of British Government. There have been many complaints in recent years, not about the probity or industry of the higher civil service, but of its inclination to continue with old techniques, of the failure to accept modern methods of data collection devised by social scientists and of the lack of emphasis on special training for those in the administrative grade. And in remedying these defects inquiries such as that of a sub-committee of the Estimates Committee under Dr Jeremy Bray in 1964/5 (H.C.308) certainly had an effect. It has been shown in Mr David Coombe's study[1] that the work of the Select Committee on the Nationalized Industries has helped clarify some of the unexamined assumptions in the running of the nationalized industries and in their relations with government departments. It could be maintained that another aspect of efficiency is the degree

[1] *The Member of Parliament and the Administration: the case of the Select Committee on Nationalized Industries* (George Allen & Unwin, 1966).

to which the community consents to or feels identified with the Government and that restoring the powers of the House of Commons might counter a tendency to regard the Government as a vast, inhuman, alien force, as 'them' always doing things to 'us'.

However effective and plausible these arguments, there is enough to be said on the other side to prevent the criterion of efficiency producing any clear-cut answer. In the last resort there has to be a value judgment. This essay is based upon the value judgment that government is better, that its tone and quality is more satisfactory, if the elected representatives play an effective part in the process of decision-making, if the House of Commons constitutes the main centre of debate about and source of information on issues of public policy and if there are genuine powers in its hands which the Government of the day cannot ignore or brush aside.

Parliament once had such powers. It has become fashionable to cast doubts on 'the golden age of the private M.P.', the period in the mid-nineteenth century when the Commons did exercise some real control over the Government, but the description was accurate. The House of Commons was able to remove ministries without incurring an immediate general election. It could and did re-write government legislation on the floor of the House, carry private bills in the face of government opposition, force the dismissal of individual ministers and compel the Government to appoint select committees and publish great quantities of information about the policies of the various departments.

These powers were steadily diminished from the 1860s onwards till by the end of the first world war, the House of Commons was reduced to its present powerlessness, though the situation has become worse as the complexity and range of governmental activities have increased in the last forty years. The root cause of the loss of power has been the growth of the party system. With a mass electorate returning loyal party members to the House, governments have become increasingly secure. The last time a ministry was placed in a minority by cross-voting on the part of its normal adherents was in the summer of 1885. As M.P.s' support could be relied on and as the volume of government business rose, the Cabinet's dominance over the House of Commons steadily increased.

The degree of executive control over a legislature can be conveniently measured in two ways, first by looking at the degree of control the legislature has over its own timetable and secondly by considering the amount of information it can force the Government to disclose. Thus the House of Commons in the 1850s disposed of its own time on three days of each week. On two only did government business get priority. Also the Commons could and did discuss matters for as long as members wanted and move as many amendments as members liked. There was no question of M.P.s being ill-informed, a common motion—and one that governments seldom cared to resist—being to request the laying of papers on a given subject before the House. Thus all the dispatches passing in and out of the Foreign Office relating to the origins of the Crimean War were published before the war was well under way, and before hostilities were over the House forced an inquiry into the conduct of the war.

Progressively in the last third of the century, standing orders were tightened till by 1902 the Government had assumed complete control of the timetable. By the use of closure, guillotine and selection of amendments, it was able to dictate what the House would discuss, for how long, and precisely when each Bill would be passed. At the same time the flow of information stopped. Fewer and fewer diplomatic blue books were published, the Government was able to maintain a secret clause in the 1904 Entente with France unknown to Parliament, and select committees of the House ceased to play any valuable part in the examination of problems or the preparation of legislation.

Since the second world war, the role of Parliament has been to enact legislation and grant the sums of money decided on by the Government, and to be the place where many, but not all, important statements on policy are made. The Opposition has virtually no influence over the Government of the day but is given about a third of the time of the House in which to make its case to the public so that it may have some chance of winning the next general election. Government backbenchers do sometimes have a little influence over ministerial policies but this operates on marginal issues only, and then infrequently. Because the Conservative Party is less committed to positive lines of change and because some of its backbenchers have a greater degree of independence, there may be a few more occasions when such influence can be detected under Conservative than under Labour Governments, but in either case it is a rare occurrence.

This backbench influence from the Government's own side may

THE REFORM OF PARLIAMENT 41

sometimes arise from the general atmosphere in the Commons, particularly the reception given to individual front-bench performances, but normally events on the floor of the House play no part in the process. Such as it is, this influence operates through party or informal channels. These communications may be by letter to ministers, or by chance encounters in the House; views may be conveyed through the Whips or at the party meetings — the 1922 Committee for the Conservatives or the Parliamentary Labour Party — either at full-scale meetings or in more specialized sub-committees.

Because this backbench pressure is exercised in private and is not evident to the public, and because the set debates and divisions, being predetermined, excite little interest, the Commons has ceased to be the forum of the nation. Ministerial announcements do matter to the public and receive widespread attention, but speeches in the House and the course of debates are seldom if ever mentioned in the popular Press. The public satisfies its considerable appetite for political argument and information by watching discussion on television and reading the comments of popular columnists.

Thus Parliament has become a machine which the Prime Minister and his colleagues use in order to pass a mass of highly complicated legislation and to explain and defend their policies — though this purpose is also achieved at public meetings and through the mass media outside Parliament. The House of Commons and its rank and file members have lost all control over the timetable of the House and therefore over the pace at which the Government's programme is put through. Apart from the work of three or four select committees (Estimates, Public Accounts, Nationalized Industries and Statutory Instruments) the Commons can bring no extra or specialized knowledge to bear in debates; members are no better informed than intelligent laymen outside the House.

At the same time, the importance of governmental activities in the life of the country has steadily increased, and to meet this groups of citizens with special interests have combined in unions, associations, councils and committees for the purpose of doing business with the Government. In most cases, the Government finds dealings with such bodies helpful both in forming and carrying out policies, and close relations have been established between such bodies and the departments of state. While major policies are decided by ministers and then elaborated and worked out in consultation with these groups, minor legislation and administrative changes often emerge purely from consultations between the groups and the civil servants concerned. In such cases there is nothing left for the House of Commons but to give its formal approval of the decisions reached. And if amendments are pressed in the House, it is usually because the interested group has failed to have all its proposals accepted in the original consultations, and it wishes, with far less hope of positive results, to remind the Government that it was not satisfied on these points.

As a result, membership of the House of Commons is not a completely satisfying career in itself for the ambitious and able man who wants to make a positive contribution to government. Parliament offers a ringside seat for great events, but membership is essentially a spectator sport. The weakness is cumulative for it is hard to utilize even the existing slight powers of the House of Commons to the full when the ablest 100 on the government side are in office and when almost all those with ability on the back benches are treating the House as an anteroom to office. Nor should such motives be condemned, for most of these men entered politics in order to be creative and this is only possible for those who achieve office. The same considerations apply with even more force to the Opposition, where front-benchers may be tempted away to important posts in industry or administration and where the loss of more than one general election has (in the case of Labour) and will (in the case of the Conservatives) lead to a sharp decline in the quality of men coming forward.

If the powers of Parliament over the executive are to be to some extent restored, there is no point in trying to recreate the conditions of the mid-nineteenth century. The social factors which produced the politics of that era have passed and attempts to prevent party pressures on M.P.s and to restore cross-voting are doomed to failure because both the public and members want parties and party discipline to remain. The electorate wants to vote for a Prime Minister, a Party and a programme and has convincingly shown this by defeating well-known and popular independents and replacing them with nonentities who carried the party label. And M.P.s cannot master the intricacies of each Bill and each amendment; they require the guidance of the party whip if their lives in the House are to be tolerable.

The real task is to decide the functions the House can and should perform if it is to be an adequate check on the executive in modern conditions and then to remodel procedure accordingly. The present procedure dates from earlier periods when the primary task of Parliament was to pass laws and grant moneys to the Crown. The standing orders were therefore arranged to ensure that every member had a chance to debate the principle of a bill, the merits of proposed taxation and expenditure and to amend these proposals in detail. Now that legislation is highly complex and carefully agreed with outside interests before it reaches Parliament, where the party system guarantees a stable majority, this form of procedure does not ensure — indeed it goes far to prevent — adequate control. Now that policy is determined at an earlier stage either in Cabinet (on major issues of principle) or in detailed negotiations with pressure groups, the task of Parliament is to intervene before decisions are finally taken, to isolate the factors affecting the formation of policy and to make its views known.

To do this, Parliament must restore its capacity to get at the information on which decisions are based, as well as check on the advice tendered to the Government by outside interests. In addition, it must recover sufficient control over its own timetable to be able to insist on debates on matters of policy when the House, as opposed to the Government, thinks that such discussion is necessary. Thus the Standing Orders must permit the House to consider general issues before or at the same time as the Government is making up its mind and on such occasions the Commons must be able to bring to bear knowledge comparable to that available to the Government itself.

For these purposes, the notion of Parliament as a maker of laws, framer of taxes and allocator of expenditure must give way to the idea of Parliament as a collector of information, an investigator of problems and a debator of major issues. The old doctrine of ministerial responsibility (which was designed in a previous era to make sure that the Commons disciplined the right person and has since become a shield for endless executive discretion) must be abandoned and replaced by the recognition that the minister is secure so long as he has the Premier's confidence but that he may be badly advised or have misjudged the weight of various factors in a problem. The view that Parliament can criticize and control without a small civil service of its own, that M.P.s can by themselves adequately collect enough facts or understand the working of a huge administrative complex which shelters behind the Official

Secrets Acts and the privacy of secret negotiations with pressure groups, must be dismissed as quite unrealistic.

Taking the procedure of the House of Commons as it now stands, the first change proposed is a minor one in terms of its impact on the government. It is advocated mainly for the convenience of backbench members, but logically it sets the context for the consideration of the day's business in the House. It is to move the start of each day's work forward from 2.30 p.m. to 10.30 a.m. with the normal time for adjournment being fixed at 6 p.m. rather than at 10 p.m. as at present. The object of this change would be to permit members a normal life in the evenings and to allow them to study and prepare material at home rather than try to work in the stale atmosphere of the anterooms to the House between 10 p.m. and 2 a.m. When committees were sitting these could meet in the afternoons while the House was in the middle of its debates, or in the evenings. In this way only some members would have to attend at the House after 6 p.m. At present some attend in the mornings for committees and all those who are not 'paired' have to be present till the late evening when the House usually adjourns. (The average time of rising in 1966 was 11.45 p.m.).

It is sometimes argued that this arrangement would be undesirable because the Cabinet meets in the mornings and because Ministers ought to be able to spend their mornings in their departments. But there is no reason why the Cabinet could not equally well meet in the afternoons. Only those Ministers who are actually speaking or are answering questions usually attend the House and these occasional absences in the mornings should not in any way disrupt the work of departments. By this arrangement, Question Time would begin shortly after 10.30 a.m. and the focal point of the day's business, the time when the Prime Minister answers questions, when personal and ministerial statements are made and the opening speeches from the front benches start, would occur before lunch rather than at 3.30–4 p.m. as happens at the moment.

Question Time is a much over-rated method of investigating and checking the actions of the Government and it has become even easier for Ministers to brush off critics now that questions have been speeded up and fewer supplementaries are allowed. Some Ministers only become accessible by being at the head of the list for oral questioning every five or six weeks. It would therefore improve matters if Question Time were expanded from its present fifty or fifty-five minute duration to nearly an hour and a half and if it occurred on five instead of four days a week. Then questions could begin shortly after 10.30 a.m. and cease at 12 noon when the business of the day would start (continuing through the lunch hour and up to 6 p.m.) and the Speaker could then go a little more slowly and allow more supplementary questions.

It is at the end of Question Time that members who wish to stop the normal course of business and debate 'an urgent matter of definite public importance' ask to move the adjournment of the House at 7 p.m. Coming under Standing Order No. 9 this procedure was intended to allow the Commons to debate unexpected but critical issues at short notice. In the ten years before the first world war the Speaker granted the request about five times a year but a series of restrictive precedents have so narrowed the interpretation of the Standing Order that permission has been granted only seven times in the last decade. There have been occasions when the House has evidently wished to stop and debate an unexpected turn of events and has been prevented from doing so; a humiliating situation when the entire Press and television coverage focuses on a particular problem but the Commons is not able to add its voice.

To overcome the difficulty, Speakers have been asked to disregard precedents and yield to 'the sense of the House' but the response has usually been that the Speaker does not wish to use his discretion. If the Government wants a debate, it can, being in complete control of the timetable of the House, arrange one, and requests under S.O. 9 only come when the Government is reluctant or fears embarrassment. This is precisely when the Commons should be able to insist on a debate, but the Speaker naturally dislikes being placed in a position of deciding such an issue. The solution is to take some control of the timetable back into the hands of the House. If an adjournment under S.O. 9 is claimed, the Speaker should then call for an immediate division on the question and if a majority of the House vote for a debate, this should then take place three hours later, that is from 4 p.m. to 7 p.m. on the same day.

In order to safeguard the position of the Opposition (who would clearly never muster a majority on their own) they should be allowed to claim four such debates each year even without a majority. To prevent this time being used frivolously or 'saved up' for the end of a session, if any of the four half days was not claimed, it could be counted as half a day when the Opposition could choose the subject for discussion and be added to the twenty-eight days already allocated to the Opposition for this purpose. These twenty-eight days (plus two full or four half days if S.O. 9 debates were not claimed) would be available for opposition motions and instead of being hitched to the old supply procedure which can involve formal motions to reduce a vote by a token sum, these days would be better left entirely free for the Opposition to raise any question it wishes to debate on a straightforward motion.

The procedure for enacting laws requires a major reform to allow members to acquire adequate information, to permit the discussion of principle and to remove the detail which at present takes too much of the time of the House. The first point to be made is that the House should have ample scope for discussing the issues involved in any important new Bills, an objective at present secured in the Second Reading Debate. But current procedure allows the Government to move the closure of such debates if it is supported by a hundred members, or to apply a guillotine. It should be made impossible to invoke these restrictions on Second Reading Debates if twenty members on each side of the House rise and indicate that they still wish to speak on the subject. Here again some control of the timetable would be taken back into the hands of members themselves.

For non-contentious measures there is no need to take the time of the full House and such Bills could be referred to a Second Reading Committee whose composition would reflect the party balance in the Commons. The remaining stages of Bills involve details and amendments which will only be carried if the Government gives way. It would save considerable time and involve no loss of authority if these stages were removed from the floor of the House. The one precaution necessary is that if amendments have been incorporated which in the opinion of the Speaker fundamentally alter the principles of the Bill, there would have to be a return to the floor of the House for a final or Third Reading Debate, when only the new additions or changes of principle could be discussed. Otherwise it would help if all further legislative stages were transferred to standing committees. Before describing these committees it is better to consider the other function for which a reformed House of Commons should be equipped: that of gathering information and checking on the advice put before the Government.

THE REFORM OF PARLIAMENT 47

The only way of achieving this is by establishing a sophisticated system of investigatory committees. A committee composed of fifteen to twenty members should be appointed to watch over each of the major departments of State. In economic and financial affairs there would need to be slightly greater elaboration, with an Economic Policy Committee, a Taxation Committee and the present Public Accounts Committee. The present Estimates Committee would be unnecessary as each of the subject or departmental committees — Health, Education, Housing and so on — would be charged with investigating the estimates for that department as well as examining the formation of policy and the conduct of administration. A committee of this kind, with its own full-time staff, with powers to summon witnesses and call for papers and with permission to hold hearings in public, if so desired, would then be able to build up a considerable body of knowledge and expertise on its own subject.

When the Government was putting through a Bill, say on housing, the members of the specialist committee on the subject would be able, in the normal way, to participate in the Second Reading Debate. It would clearly be ridiculous not to include them in the standing committee to which the Bill would then be committed. But the Minister of Housing would have to be present to explain and defend his Bill (Ministers would be excluded from the specialist committees) and the standing committee could therefore be composed of the specialist committee on that subject with the addition of an extra twenty members, including the Ministers. Standing committees of this kind would be able to conduct a searching examination of Bills. The specialist committee members could meet simultaneously or beforehand to hear evidence from the pressure groups concerned, from the civil servants who had drafted the Bill and from outside experts. The entire anatomy of the measure would be laid bare and the larger standing committee would be able to consider whether the purposes of the Bill were sound and whether its specific proposals were the best available for meeting these purposes. Once this procedure was developed, pressure groups would come back into politics, that is into dealings with the House of Commons, because it would be as valuable for them to put their case to the specialist committees as to convince the government departments.

By existing procedure when a Bill is through standing committee,

it returns for Report Stage and Third Reading to the floor
of the House so that members not on the standing committee may
have the chance of discussing any amendments that have been
made or of moving amendments themselves before the whole Bill is
re-considered in the final or Third Reading Debate. Both these
stages are time-consuming and usually involve the same members
going over the same ground. Any qualms about the removal of
Report Stage could be met by giving this stage to the same standing
committee, but allowing any member who had not been on the
standing committee but who wished to contribute to attend, to
speak and move amendments, but not to vote. The right to vote
would be left to the members of the original standing committee,
thus preserving the party balance. Third Readings would be taken
formally unless the Speaker ruled that amendments had altered the
nature of the Bill and the principles on which it was based, in which
case there would have to be a Third Reading Debate on the floor of
the House but confined to these new issues of principle. Should a
Bill be amended in the Upper House, these amendments would
also be considered by the original standing committee which had
dealt with the Bill.

The measure which takes most of the Commons' time and which
is least comprehended by its members is the annual Finance Bill.
After the Second Reading Debate, which could be considerably
extended in the manner described, this Bill could also be sent
'upstairs' for its committee and all subsequent stages, but the
standing committee should be larger—some 80 members—and
include all the members of the two relevant specialist committees,
those on taxation and on economic policy.

If these proposals were adopted the House would be saved some
26 days a session on public Bills and about 8 days a year on the
Finance Bill, all of which would be available for other purposes.
Two of these days have been awarded by these proposals to the
Opposition for its special adjournment debates and some time
would go on adjournment debates requested by a majority of
members. More time, it is hoped, would be spent on Second
Reading Debates, particularly on the Finance Bill; there would be
scope for more than the present meagre ration of two debates a year
on foreign affairs and on issues of importance not directly connected with legislation. Provision should also be made for debates
on reports from the specialist committees when they wished to draw

attention to the policies or administrative practices of departments where no new legislation or financial considerations were involved.

A final claimant for time are private members' measures. But often the real point of private members' Bills is not the enactment of a law but the drawing of attention to a particular problem, obtaining the support of the House and ensuring action which will end in a change in the law. For this purpose Bills introduced at the end of Question Time under the ten minute rule are the most effective in that they tend to be based on the views of the private member concerned. The other procedure, the ballot for the right to introduce a Bill, often ends with the Whip's office dumping minor measures on the private M.P.s who are successful in the ballot. So with the extra time made available by these reforms, it would be helpful to set aside four half days in addition to the present number of Fridays specifically for the Second Readings of ten minute rule Bills (in the last session, of 34 introduced only 2 received Royal Assent). The present adjournment debates which allow members to raise constituency matters last for half-an-hour. If the point affects only one M.P. then a fifteen minute speech with the same time for reply by a minister is enough. But there should be a provision allowing for up to six five-minute speeches if other members wish to add their voices. The adjournment would then last an hour from 6 to 7 p.m. and be a more effective way of pressing the Government.

The issue of televising the proceedings of the House of Commons must be mentioned here. The production of a balanced half-hour programme every day culled from the most interesting and important portions of Question Time, the major speeches and events in committee should not be too difficult. Of itself, this will not alter the balance or imbalance of power between the House and the Government. But as the Commons increases its knowledge of the options open to the Government and therefore its capacity to suggest alternatives, and as debates become more topical and searching, the public might well take a greater interest in Parliament and regular excerpts of the proceedings on television would help to stimulate this interest and make people turn to the Commons as televised for a major source of news and comment.

In order to take full advantage of these changes in the work and degree of influence of the Commons, there would have to be a radical improvement in the conditions for members. At present backbenchers are exhausted by the need for constant physical presence in a building without proper working facilities. Without homes or flats near by, they are unable to visit their constituencies at will and are generally lacking adequate help and finances.

The first task is to provide every member with a private office in the Palace of Westminster. This could easily be accomplished by moving out the House of Lords and all other persons and organizations (apart from the Speaker) at present allocated rooms (many of which stand empty). Then each M.P. should be provided with office equipment, a telephone, a secretary and a research assistant. If it is said that certain members do not need a secretary and would not know how to use a research assistant, the answer is that some could benefit enormously from such support and that soon other constituencies would come to expect the same service. Take the case of a member for a mixed agricultural and small town area with personal interests in foreign affairs, particularly in one part of the world, say Africa. An active member for this type of constituency will receive some twenty letters a day which will need replies and further letters to government departments pursuing particular complaints. He will make two or three speeches each week-end which have to be prepared, typed and distributed to the Press. In order to keep up-to-date, he will want the farming journals clipped and filed under the heads of the main crops grown in his area. Each of the boroughs and the county council in his constituency will require a separate file as well as a general coverage of the housing situation, local educational problems and the question of attracting or looking after existing light industry. Then the member's African interests can only be kept up to date by a watch on a series of papers and journals and another clipping service. Such a member will receive regular requests to contribute articles to British papers, he may write a column in the local weekly and be asked now and then to appear on television. To do this research, to keep up with the parliamentary side of these interests, to prepare questions, to use all the opportunities offered to the full would use all the time of the member, a secretary and a research assistant. Finally, if the specialist committees recommended are established, the work involved will add greatly to the pressure on M.P.s and make the need for a proper office and staff even more pressing.

Some reformers have discussed whether members should be part-time or full-time. This really is not a single issue but a series of points. It is not in the public interest that some M.P.s should have

THE REFORM OF PARLIAMENT 51

jobs (as does happen now) simply in order to earn enough money to finance their work as a member—to pay for their secretary or part of a secretary and for living accommodation in London. Some members, on the other hand, will always regard being in the House as secondary to their directorships or legal practices. It would not be desirable to force such people to give up their outside activities and Parliament does gain by having some members whose sights are not set on office and who can on occasion snap their fingers at the Whips. But these proposed reforms are designed to make membership of the House of Commons well enough paid and sufficiently absorbing and worthwhile for it to be unnecessary for even the ablest and most vigorous members to be distracted by any outside employment. To make the remuneration satisfactory and non-controversial, it would be better if it were made equivalent to that of the Assistant Secretary level in the civil service. In addition, all the costs of the M.P.'s office and staff should be met, including telephone calls, postage and free travel not merely to the constituency but to anywhere in Britain or abroad when the journey had a clear relation to the member's parliamentary interests or duties. Also a block of one-room flats should be provided, near to the House, for members whose homes are not in London.

A backbench member also faces the disadvantages of being tied to the Palace by the need to vote in person when far more important events may be occurring in his constituency or elsewhere, in or out of London. A simple way of overcoming this difficulty would be the introduction of proxy voting. At present ministers or senior opposition members can leave the House whenever they like by obtaining 'pairs'—a device which allows M.P.s to be absent while keeping the Government's majority at its normal level. But the system does not work so well for backbenchers, particularly those on the Government side. Voting under the present and the reformed system proposed here is not an important function in the sense that it requires the individual presence, since party loyalties render the decision virtually automatic. Thus it would be fitting and sensible if each member was issued with an identity card, which would permit him either to vote in person or to leave his card with the Whip with instructions to vote for him. Such a proposal usually produces protests that the M.P. ought to know what he is voting for. This is wildly unrealistic, as members often, under present circumstances, have no idea about the precise issue being settled by a division—they go into the lobby indicated by their Whip. Whenever the member was in any doubt or wanted to exercise any discretion, he could remain and vote for himself. The second objection to such an idea is that all the members would leave Westminster except the handful waiting to speak in the Chamber and the pointlessness of much that goes on in Parliament would be exposed for all to see. (This is like the pathetic objection to televising the proceedings in the House because that might reveal to the public that many debates are attended by only a dozen or so members on each side). But if members do not need to be in the House, it is much better that they should be free to leave and work elsewhere, though much of the urge to leave would be removed once late night sittings ceased and members had proper office accommodation in the House. Moreover it is hoped that these proposals would provide much more constant and worthwhile work for backbench M.P.s in the House. But when a member had a vital engagement in his constituency, his capacity to attend would no longer depend on his seniority or his good fortune in knowing one of the other side with whom he could 'pair'; he would be free to decide where his presence was most useful.

It is now generally accepted that the functions of tidying up legislation, permitting the Government to have second thoughts and allowing the introduction of non-controversial legislation and private Bills, make a second Chamber a useful if not indispensable adjunct to the House of Commons. A reformed Commons on the lines just suggested would still require this assistance and it would help and be in keeping with radical democratic views if the present House of Lords was reformed to enable it to be as effective as possible in performing these tasks.

Two changes are needed. The first is to abolish any delaying powers and to remove the Law Lords to a separate final Court of Appeal. This would strip away all ancillary functions and make it clear that the task of the second Chamber was a technical one, aiding the House of Commons, not in its new central functions of discovering the facts on which policy is based and commenting on the conduct of that policy, but in its old function of producing well worked out legislation. There would be no objection to the second Chamber debating policy also, but even less notice would be taken of such debates if the Commons were properly informed and able to take up crucial issues as soon as they arose.

THE REFORM OF PARLIAMENT 53

The other necessary change would be a reform of the composition of the second Chamber. With such a technical, precise, yet valuable role all members should be appointed on merit and the entire hereditary qualification be swept aside. A Labour Government should not only cease to create any new peers, it should refuse to recognize all such titles. Then the second Chamber could be recruited entirely on merit, the members being appointed for life and paid a reasonable salary. To provide proper facilities for all M.P.s in Westminster, it has been suggested that the second Chamber should be moved out into new premises, an arrangement that should in no way hamper the work of the new body.

In order to bring out the advantages of these reforms, it is worth concluding with two examples. Since the war, the main decisions in agricultural policy have been taken outside Parliament. The National Farmers Union played party politics before 1939 and reaped little advantage. Then the war and the 1947 Agriculture Act turned the Union into a body advising and co-operating with the Ministry of Agriculture, this relationship reaching its climax in the annual price review. The effect has been to present the House of Commons each year with a set of prices (which determines the health and direction of the industry) which M.P.s have not discussed or heard of till they are published. Then members on the Government side are committed to defending the policy while the Opposition members are free to criticize but neither group knows how the negotiations were conducted or what alternatives were considered, at what cost. M.P.s are only brought in if the N.F.U. is unhappy about the review for that year and encourages its branches to press members for rural constituencies to complain about the treatment of the industry. But farmers' leaders are reluctant to take such action and far prefer to keep the issues 'non-political' if at all possible.

A specialist committee on agriculture would not take over the process of settling prices or determining policy. But it would question the civil servants, economists and union leaders so that the ingredients of each review and the possible alternatives were made clear. The committee could press the Ministry to answer questions about the possibilities and cost of import substitution, about the effect of food agreements and the cost of administering different kinds of support. Then members for agricultural constituencies would be able to estimate the possibilities in a forthcoming review and make their views known before the decisions were taken. Members for urban constituencies would know the effect of proposed or possible changes on taxes and on food prices and could put their point of view. When a new departure, such as entering the Common Market, was canvassed, there would be a body of knowledge and fact-based opinion already in existence instead of the almost total ignorance revealed in the discussions on the subject in mid-1966. Unusual occurrences such as the sudden collapse of livestock prices in the autumn of 1966 would be watched with the aid of accurate information and the resulting debate in the House might contain, instead of routine party propaganda, some positive suggestions which the Minister would have to treat seriously.

A second example is defence. The White Paper issued in 1965 gave more information to the House than any previous review, but even then much was not explained, and there was no account of the arguments which had raged in the Ministry of Defence before the White Paper was published. It was only when Mr Christopher Mayhew resigned that his speeches and writings showed some of the alternatives and raised some of the questions that should have been asked at a much earlier stage by the House of Commons. It is often said that to open these issues would endanger security, but the main alternatives are based on technical considerations well known to other powers — indeed, British defence problems are often more knowledgeably discussed in the foreign Press than in the Commons. A specialist committee could have heard all the evidence for and against a carrier force in the 1970s, it could have found out the cost of the bases east of Suez, the anticipated capacity of the F111A aeroplanes, and our precise commitments to other nations. Then the House would have been in a position to make its views known before the White Paper was finally drafted.

The Government, as the Prime Minister keeps saying, must govern, but these reforms would allow the Commons to exercise some influence, to educate itself and the public on the issues and to form opinion while problems were still under discussion. This could hamper Ministers but it could also help by making the Ministries explain the alternatives, it could lead to an earlier recognition of anomalies, and it could ensure that the policies finally agreed upon were carried out. The enthusiasm of the public for the democratic process, the quality of M.P.s, the standard of administration and the vigour of political life should all improve if Parliament is once again given a real capacity to exercise some influence over the Government, so that the House of Commons can become once again the forum of the nation.

© 1967 BY JOHN P. MACKINTOSH

Approaches to Industrial Democracy

ERIC MOONMAN

The British Labour Party, in spite of its name, has always been only marginally interested in industrial policy. Such debate as there has been over the years has been inadequate and spasmodic, perhaps because the routine of the factory floor and the tough-minded negotiations of collective bargaining lack the emotional satisfactions of crusading idealism and the glamorous publicity of international politics. A bed of nails is never the most tempting of resting places, and many a potential leader in the Parliamentary Labour Party and in the constituencies would sooner rise to be Foreign Secretary than Minister of Labour.

There is, today, very little to show for the enthusiasm for industrial democracy and workers' control that was fundamental to early socialism. It is now over sixty years since the Webbs[1] described industrial democracy as a major controlling process by the employees, by the socialization of many industries with union representation on the controlling boards of these industries and employee participation in the councils and committees which would be associated with their administration.

Why should industrial affairs have been so neglected in Labour programmes? There are two reasons. Firstly, the close alliance between the Labour Party and the trade union movement. Records of early debates among the founders of the Labour Party reveal a desire for an alliance which would result in greater sympathy for the workers' situation on the part of a political force in the Commons, but it was also expected that the Labour Party would help to organize and control the industrial front. This has not happened. The links between the two have grown and flourished in many respects but they have certainly not assisted a move towards a socialist philosophy in industry. On the one hand, the trade unions

[1] Webb, S. & B., *Industrial Democracy* (Longmans, 1962).

could well complain that the alliance with the Labour Party has hampered their attempts to assume a similar role to that of the American trade unions, which is, briefly, to make the capitalist system work more efficiently so that the unions can demand a greater share of an even greater cake. On the other hand, the Labour Party has hardly benefited in theoretical terms. Indeed, its relationship with the unions has, in some ways, deterred the Labour Party from formulating a continuous, intellectualized policy on industrial relations.

What, then, are the advantages of this alliance? Certainly the trade union movement has its lobby in parliament and can therefore affect legislation bearing on local and national industrial affairs. In practice, however, this lobby is not such an independent and powerful force as it might be because of the undertaking each Labour M.P. gives when joining the Parliamentary Labour Party that his first loyalty is to that body. The position of Labour M.P.s is made more complicated because, as candidates, they are expected to belong to a trade union (a very loose qualification indeed as an examination of a list of Labour candidates' jobs and their unions will show). Only a third of the present Labour M.P.s are eligible to attend the Parliamentary Trade Union Group, a term given to those who are financially sponsored by the unions. Money is provided by the unions for the Labour Party both between and at general elections. Committees at local and national level bring together representatives of both groups to discuss and work out programmes. However, in practical political terms all this does not add up to anything more than that the Labour Party has a greater compassion for and more personal interest in the individual worker's problems than the Conservative Party. No long-term planning of the roles of labour and management has been undertaken by the Labour Party because it has felt that this was a job for the T.U.C. Significantly, it was not until 1966 that a working party was set up by the Labour Party to examine the question of industrial democracy.

The second cause of the present need for a genuinely Socialist industrial philosophy is the lack of encouragement by the Labour Party to many activists inside industry who might have worked for a more democratic structure. They were distrusted, frequently because their militancy was not in line with Labour Party methods. In fact, many of the most effective shop floor representatives have been Communists who, now lacking any representation at Westminster, have concentrated on grass roots activity.

Besides the absence of a considered policy on industrial relations, there has also been some confusion in the Labour Party as to the meaning, the extent and the limitations of industrial democracy. The early socialist pioneers recognized the value of having a clear involvement in industrial organization. Workers' control, as a concept, was meaningful when it was still possible to think in terms of a Labour Government altering the economic order. By the time the seventh Labour Government took office in April 1966, there were only a small number of people in the Labour Party who imagined this to be possible. In the long term, the real integration of full economic planning and workers' control will be a feature of British society, but in the short term (a period which depends on how well the Labour Party educates the electorate) it is the job of Labour to make the capitalist system more efficient by control and planning to ensure a greater share of the benefits for the working classes of this country.

The forms of industrial democracy which exist in other countries will be examined later, but at this point a definition of what the term implies in the British setting should be attempted. It is a total sharing of decision making at all levels within an organization. If this is not feasible at present in Britain, how can we interpret industrial democracy for the present and for the next decade? My own research and the research findings of other workers in the field of management-employee relations as well as the experience of many people working in industry suggest that there are two elements of industrial democracy existing today: established communication processes and shared decision making.

Communication in industry between management and employees is much less formalized than most other communication in that environment, whether it is communication between management and the shareholders or management and the customers or clients. The rather casual nature of management-employee communication is the cause of much conflict and controversy. Hence George Evans of the National Union of Vehicle Builders spoke for many union leaders when he said in the *Guardian* (on September 14th, 1966) of the action of British Motor Corporation, 'We shall insist on the fullest possible consultations with the management and by that I don't mean a meeting at which the management will glibly tell us their intentions—I mean consultations where we can thrash the matter out in order to protect our members.'

Breakdowns in communication occur in all organizations and inevitably give rise to doubts about the efficiency of the body concerned. Management often fails to clarify its own role sufficiently so that its aims and objectives are not appreciated. Professor Tom Lupton expresses it this way: 'Communication cannot be adequate where organization is ill-defined.'[1] a view supported by important British research projects.[2]

Communication may be described as the capacity of an individual or group to relate ideas and feelings to another individual or group, and, where necessary, to evoke a discriminatory response. Within the interaction of business and industry, the process of communication and the way in which information is circulated is of crucial importance. More and more managers realize that the effectiveness of an organization is reduced if information between the various levels of authority is not accurate and relevant. There are two important reasons for the increasing emphasis on efficient communication: the growth in the size of organizations and the growth of trade unionism.

The creation of the functional departments in industry, such as personnel, time and motion study, data processing, etc., and the general increase in the number of management levels has brought about an acute need for an exchange of information between line and staff whilst during the last twenty-five years the political and economic power held by the unions has created demands from employees for more information about the methods of production and their hours and conditions of service. This places a responsibility, not only on the business enterprise, but also on the trade union.[3]

Due to the stress on the organization created by these two factors, those who work within it are anxious to get the most from their efforts and this is not to be measured in terms of money alone. Job satisfaction, status in the working community and good personal

[1] Lupton, T., *Industrial Behaviour and Personnel Management* (I.P.M., 1964).
[2] Burns, T., & Stalker, G.M., *The Management of Innovation* (Tavistock, 1961); Woodward, J., *Management and Technology* (H.M.S.O., 1959).
[3] Moonman, E., *The Manager and the Organisation* (Tavistock, 1961).

services, are items which employees are beginning to demand. In all this, the value of prompt and accurate information cannot be over-emphasized. Improvements in the flow of information are largely a company responsibility, and its success reflects the quality of management. The modern manager's responsibilities include liaison, supervision and co-ordination. If he fails to achieve a high standard under any of these heads, his communication links with his subordinates and superiors will suffer. Those employees who observe and experience the resultant breakdown cannot be expected to remain passive.

If good communication is desirable for industrial democracy, a share in decision making is essential. The term implies firstly, a control in the organization on matters that are directly related to employees' pay and conditions and rewards generally; secondly, an obligation to assist in the analysis which management should be making from time to time of the positive features of the working environment as well as the breakdowns; thirdly, the ability to put forward detailed proposals and to take the initiative for introducing items of policy that are less controversial but affect every class of worker, such as welfare facilities and refreshment arrangements.

Taken together these three factors would form a powerful step forward in industrial democracy in Britain. I should now like to examine the operation of industrial democracy in some other countries.

Israel: In Israel the Joint Production Committee was first introduced for those firms owned by the Histadrut, the central trade union body. In 1952, however, the J.P.C.s were extended throughout industry as a result of a national agreement completed between the Histadrut and the Manufacturers' Association as well as the Association of Engineers and Architects. The structure of the committees is the same throughout the country and in different industries. They operate on both national and local levels. At the national level there are several joint councils as well as an overall co-ordinating agency. When there is conflict or disagreement at the committee level, the co-ordinating agency will be brought in to provide guidance, interpretation or evidence.

The Israeli system goes fairly deep in involving the small firm in the decision-making process: all enterprises employing fifty or more workers must set up a J.P.C. It should be noted that the

APPROACHES TO INDUSTRIAL DEMOCRACY 61

committees are advisory although executive decisions can be taken if there is support from a majority of both management and employees.

Representation on the J.P.C. consists of equal numbers of managers and employees. In some industries, the workers' committees (which will be described later) make the nominations for their side, but in other cases they will nominate only a few of the places on the J.P.C. In any event, the employees are appointed for a year and then must offer themselves for re-election. Both sides provide the two chairmen whose job it is to agree the agenda and to discuss matters affecting the J.P.C. between meetings. Two features of the J.P.C. need to be noted. Its agenda will not include items relating to collective bargaining of wages and conditions of service although it will examine incentive payments in detail. Secondly, it has the authority to bring specialists and experts to its meetings. Properly used, this facility provides a great opportunity for intelligent management to have outside and independent voices explain and help to convince the employee representatives of the value of a particular course of action. It alerts or informs employee representatives, enabling them to use the meetings in a constructive manner. Sub-committees can be set up and the detailed points of a specific problem can be analyzed, to the advantage of both sides. For instance, one such sub-committee deals with the study of the works operations and with awards made to those employees who submit ideas for improvements. The advantage this has over the British 'suggestion scheme' technique is that the committee stems from the J.P.C. and there is therefore a better chance to follow through the proposals made. Several British firms, for example Glaxo Laboratories Ltd, also try to relate the two, with some measure of success.

To sum up, it may be said that the subject matter covered by the Israeli J.P.C.s is similar in some respects to the subject matter of the British works' councils, but the actual differences between the two are substantial. Additionally, the J.P.C.s are concerned with the organization as an entity with emphasis on the development of staff, the process of supervision and management and the interpretation of incentive schemes.

The workers' committee is often confused with the J.P.C. so it is as well to clarify the former's purpose and representation. Every business which is not run entirely by the family or which has more than a handful of staff, will have a committee of its organized workers. The actual number of the committees will depend on the size of the enterprise: two would cover a fairly large organization. The committee has either a one- or two-year life until it is re-elected by the employees. The size of the committee varies, but usually it will have about half a dozen members though it can have as many as twenty. Each committee has at least one secretary who will be engaged by the firm on a full-time basis and provided with an office on company premises with clerical assistance and general staff according to the amount of work. Meetings are held as and when required but usually once a week.

The main function of the workers' committee is to deal with those areas of inquiry not covered by the J.P.C., namely, to bargain with management on the grading of employees and to examine locally based contracts on wages and services which are usually more specific and detailed than national agreements.

The local labour council will also take part in such discussions. This body, similar to the local labour and trades councils in Britain, may be regarded as the political wing of the industrial trade union structure.

A new collective agreement will require, at the factory level, the involvement and agreement of employees both through the workers' committee and through the secretary of the labour council. It is the latter, though, who will exert the national influence if he feels that the award fails to meet or exceeds the standards of the Histadrut for that industry.[1]

The element of control in industrial relations is at the heart of the debate both here and elsewhere in the world. Should employers and trade unions be left alone to work out the services and the basis for work systems or should the State, either directly or through its agencies, ensure that a national standard prevails and that all groups of workers are treated fairly? In Israel, the enormous social and political change which has taken place since the creation of the State in 1948, has given the Histadrut the influence of a third partner in collective bargaining. Perhaps the Histadrut would reject this suggestion, wishing to prove that it is a federation of Jewish labour. (It is worth noting that the Histadrut is opposed to the use of the strike weapon.) Through its labour councils it is

[1] See Meir, Z., *The Labour Movement* (Israel Today, Jerusalem, 1965).

APPROACHES TO INDUSTRIAL DEMOCRACY 63

providing important support for any government policy on pay norms. As one member of the Knesset said to me, 'It's more than a union. It's a way of life.' The individual union has only modest responsibility in relation to the power of the Histadrut.

Sweden: The common purpose of management and labour in setting up works' councils in Sweden in 1946 was to increase production. The agreement signed by the Swedish Employers' Federation (Svenska Arbetsgivareföreningen—S.A.F.) and the Confederation of Swedish Trade Unions (Landsorganisationen i Sverige—L.O.) was to ensure a scheme for regular contact between the two. An important clause in the agreement revealed that employees were anxious to obtain a better insight into the management of an enterprise. Other clauses related to the promotion of security of employment, health and safety, and vocational training within the individual firms.

The structure of the councils rests on the fact that firms with at least fifty people are generally required to set up a council, which either side can ask for. According to the number of people on the payroll, the trade union is entitled to nominate three, five or seven members to represent the workers on the council. Salaried employees and supervisors nominate separately. The composition in a firm employing a hundred to two hundred people would be something like this: five employers' representatives, five employees' representatives, and three salaried including supervisory representatives.

Meetings take place quarterly and the employee representatives are elected for a two-year spell. No secretariat is provided, and the secretary is usually a member of management. The council is advisory, concentrating on the provision of information, consultation on a variety of matters not covered by collective bargaining and linking up with suggestion schemes. Although all this is a fairly modest approach to industrial democracy, the information provided by management is far in excess of that given in the majority of British works' councils. The items covered include operational and financial data, new methods and statements about the consequences of change. The employer also has to give the council information on the state of market trends, and on all matters dealing with security of employment. Meetings take place outside work hours and representatives are compensated accordingly.

It is necessary to make a distinction between councils which operate in industry, commerce and the civil service including nationalized industries and the armed services. These last two categories are not so well developed as the former and play a necessary role in establishing a team-spirit amongst staff. It is in the industrial section that the councils have been most effective and their approach to decision-making has influenced the other two areas.

The legal barriers to providing employees with information are raised whenever questions of employee participation are discussed. In Sweden, management gives information to the extent required by the Companies Act but in practice many firms take the councils into their confidence and provide extensive details of work and planning.

The latest revision (1966) of the 1946 agreement between the two parties provides that discussions must take place on manpower and related subjects before any decision is taken by management. The problems which affect the Swedish councils are similar to those encountered by committees in Britain: the need to have an informed worker representative, the difficulty of assessing the strength of the committee in the small firm and the ability of management to learn and understand its new role.

Yugoslavia: The Yugoslav experience of industrial democracy has aroused more international interest and comment than all the other schemes put together. The essential feature of the Yugoslav approach is that it is more far-reaching than the others due to the special circumstances which existed in 1945. After the war, Yugoslavia had been left in a crippled state and had to engage in a massive operation to become a viable industrial nation.

All working organizations are managed by the workers either directly or through the management bodies they themselves elect. On the basis of the right to self-government, workers organize production or some other activity by themselves, are responsible for the development of their organization and lay down the plans and programmes of its development. In addition, they decide independently questions affecting their products and services and resolve other problems relating to the functioning of the organization; they decide on the use of the resources and their distribution. The workers are also brought into matters of manpower: they decide on the employment and dismissal of staff, determine working hours in accordance with the general conditions of work, regulate and improve working conditions, promote safety at work and recreational facilities, and ensure the necessary conditions for their further education and training and the improvement of the individual and general standard of living.

A law passed in 1950 provided for a workers' council in each firm. In firms with fewer than thirty employees, all of them serve on the council. In larger firms the council is elected and varies in size according to the number of people employed. The council approves the 'plan' for an enterprise, makes general decisions about its execution and about the conduct of the firm, and appoints and dismisses the members of the management board. The latter body, of between three and eleven members, is responsible for the execution of the plan and the appointment of the senior staff apart from the director.

The unions have no direct part in the workers' council or the management board, but several important powers are granted to them. They have the right to present lists of candidates at the election of the workers' councils. Other lists may be submitted, but this happens infrequently and in the overwhelming majority of instances the trade union list is successful. Again, a number of decisions of the workers' councils require trade union approval, including decisions affecting wages and the allocation of surplus profit. Finally, all proposals for federal or state legislation on labour matters are required to be submitted to the unions. Disputes between the workers' council and the union may be resolved by the local authority. If not, they are submitted to a tripartite arbitration board representing the union, the local authority and the trade association to which the firm is affiliated.

An official Yugoslav publication sums up the peculiar situation between workers' control and the unions this way: 'It is through the workers' management bodies that the workers exercise their power, their right to make decisions. It is through the trade unions that they exercise their right to unite, to represent their own interests in an organized and uniform manner, to act, and to fulfil their socio-political functions independently.'[1]

This is not an entirely happy distinction and leads one to

[1] *Why there are both Workers' Committees and Trade Unions* (Belgrade, Govt. Publications, 1963).

suggest that there are advantages in having a single channel system within the factory.

Western Germany: The present workers' councils exist within the framework of the German system of co-determination based on a law passed in 1952. This in turn is based on a system of co-determination evolved during the occupation (in the period when the relationships that many industrialists had had with the Nazis gave the unions a strong bargaining position) and applied to the coal and steel industries by a law passed in 1951.

It provides for worker participation in two of the three governing bodies of German companies, the supervisory board and the board of management, but not the general assembly of the shareholders.

One-third of the members of the supervisory board representing both manual and salaried staff must be representatives of employees elected by them in a secret ballot.

Labour representation on the management board consists of a labour director, who is appointed by the supervisory board but must have the support of a majority of the employee representatives. He is the representative of the workers within the management of the company.

In firms with over one hundred employees a special economic committee subjects both management and workers to severe rules of secrecy even towards members of the works councils. Its function is to advise management. The size of the works council depends on the number of employees. All employees over eighteen years of age may vote; whilst those over twenty-one, who have been employed in the firm for one year and are entitled to vote in German federal elections, may be elected to the council. Elections are secret and are held every two years. The works council has a number of functions. It handles grievances; it concludes agreements on piece rates, wage systems and conditions where there is no collective agreement on these matters; it may conclude agreements on wages or working conditions, supplementary to existing collective agreement.

In the case of dismissals the council must be heard. It must be consulted if larger groups are to be dismissed or hired and it has a veto power against new engagements in a few cases: (i) if the new appointment violates a law, collective agreement, or plant agreement (for example hiring of female workers in plants which are not allowed to employ women); (ii) if the new employee is not qualified and has been selected for personal reasons only; (iii) in the case of discrimination for reasons of race, religion, nationality, origin, political or union activity; or (iv) if there are reasons to fear that the prospective employee would disturb the peace in the plant by antisocial or illegal behaviour. In all these cases labour courts have the ultimate decision if no agreement can be reached between the council and management. The council also negotiates work rules, starting and finishing times, breaks, time and place of wage payments, timing of holidays, training, good housekeeping, safety and health. It negotiates with the employer on changes in the plant, such as restrictions of activity, transfer of departments, merger, introduction of new work methods. A special mediation procedure is foreseen in the case of disagreements on these matters. It supervises the enforcement of the applicable labour laws and of the collective agreements, and it administers the social welfare agencies of the plant.

It will be obvious that the ways these countries have approached industrial democracy is a reflection of their political systems and the development of the economic and social forces within the country concerned. The elements of industrial democracy in Yugoslavia and Israel incline towards giving the employee a constructive share in decision making whilst the German experience, a statutory one, is far in advance of our own joint consultation. The Swedish approach is modest and is concerned with increasing production. It may be that the most we are likely to achieve in Britain in the short term is an adaption of the Swedish system based on their 1946 and 1966 Acts.

The problem of the role of the trade unions in these countries is not clear cut. The somewhat ambiguous position of the Histadrut in Israel and worker-control and the unions in Yugoslavia have been referred to, and there have been critics in Britain and elsewhere of co-determination in Germany. The argument is that German trade unions have lost their independence because of their position in joint control.

On the positive side it should be noted, however, that the position of the Labour Director is less ambivalent for the individual appointed than it may appear. There is also no likelihood of conflicting loyalties on the management board as trade unionists are not represented there.

I suggest that the difference between the Yugoslav/Israeli system and the Swedish/British is that the former is a more imaginative concept of active participation whilst the latter confines itself to protecting rights and interests.

Positive industrial democracy can bring together management and employees in planning and forecasting in all areas of a business. A study of other countries clarifies the practical implications of industrial democracy in Britain. The concept of pay and productivity committees first appeared in the 1966 Labour Party manifesto and was expressed in terms of astonishing vagueness. Despite questions by members in the House of Commons, there is still little clarification about their function and the methods to be used. One thing does seem clear; they are not likely to alter to any great extent the traditional system of industrial relations in Britain. Yet they could help to regularize many of the industrial relations practices and break through some of the barriers to co-operation. Traditional joint consultation has caused, over the years, confusion and suspicion among management and trade unionists—particularly among worker representatives. The new committees, if they are to be taken seriously, must have and appear to have a serious purpose. A secretariat on the lines of the intelligence department of a local authority should be available to supply background material between meetings so that all participants—not only management— would be properly briefed.

Items on the set agenda should include: long-term and short-term forecasting; the financial position of the company; the order-book, with reference to work competed for and gained or lost (with causes examined); comparative figures for safety and good housekeeping; plans and techniques for dealing with staff career development; labour turnover and absentee reports on a company and departmental basis; pay schedules.

Some employers will argue that because business statistics are confidential it is unwise to make them available to employees. Certainly, they could be misunderstood or misused but this risk is relatively unimportant. In a research project I conducted in 1965 in Lancashire on workers' attitudes to technological change, I discovered that, in spite of strain arising from changes, employees were anxious to play a constructive part in the company's activities because, they said, the company shared its ideas and knowledge with them. Briefly, if management wants to encourage a co-operative attitude in its employees, then efforts must be made to win the employees' approval of what management is doing.

The composition of the pay and productivity committees should include specialist staff as well as line management. There is often as much misunderstanding between the different sections of functional and line management as there is between the line manager and the operative. All sections of an organization need to be represented.

What about committees in relation to the size of the enterprise? Clearly, it is in the larger company that the greatest need for organized consultation arises. Twenty-five per cent of people in industry work in factories employing over a thousand people. Thirty years ago the percentage was approximately half this. Organizations with more than two hundred employees should have meetings at least monthly, and for the smaller unit a twice-yearly management reporting session to staff would be the minimum acceptable.

The Ministry of Labour will presumably have the responsibility for designing the structure of each committee and for maintaining standards. One way of doing this would be for a summary of the main points of the discussion and of the decisions taken to be forwarded to local Ministry officials. Questions and matters arising out of the report could be taken up, where necessary, by the officials with the committee chairman. Committee meetings would incidentally perform a training function. A cross-section of people from different levels of authority and responsibility, gathered together to discuss common issues, would provide a unique opportunity for individual employee development. Staff from local college departments of industrial relations and management could be brought into the meetings as a resource.

Pay and productivity committees are only the first stage on the road to meaningful industrial democracy. I should now like to suggest that there are several aims in the areas of communication and decision making in industry which it should be possible to achieve within the British political and social climate of this and the next generation.

A large number of firms have already accepted the need for better ways of receiving and providing information to employees. Within recent years, the Glacier Metal Company has set the pace in experimenting with methods of communication.[1] Dr Elliot

[1] See, for instance, Jacques, E., *The Changing Culture of a Factory* (Tavistock Publications, 1951).

Jaques began an investigation into the company's problems in 1948 and since then his findings have been taken up to improve the quality of management-employee relations as well as company and departmental effectiveness. Distinctions in work terms, almost in parliamentary terms, have been made in the Glacier Metal Company; the executive, the representative, and the legislative systems.

If the workers are to co-operate whole-heartedly they will have to be given a new charter, a new social status which Nicholas Davenport in *Split Society*[1] refers to as 'service contracts' (retraining being part of the improvement in status).

Companies in this country can and must learn from the efforts of research workers, as they have in the United States, where there is less suspicion of the social scientist. For every Glacier Metal study in Britain, there are some fifty or sixty examples of action-research in the U.S.A. of which the Harwood Manufacturing Company report is a good example. This company was concerned about the loss of production which resulted despite extra fringe benefits, when workers were transferred to new jobs. A controlled experiment with other employees revealed that when employees were allowed to participate in changes by suggesting how certain processes might be implemented there was no drop in production: indeed output actually rose above the normal standards.

Three important developments in company communication must take place in the next decade:

Government involvement in company consultation channels. Should a single channel system of communication not materialize in Britain then the pay and productivity committees will obviously enlarge the scope, if not the authority, of the earlier works councils. The nationalized industries and those companies which are keen to experiment will go further down the line towards industrial democracy than the majority of firms, and this in turn will clearly influence the spread of ideas and methods of consultation.

Action research. An increasing number of social scientists, industrial psychologists and other related researchers will continue to feed ideas to industry. Whether their brief is an assessment of human relations or the organization structure, an accumulation of know-

[1] *Split Society* (Gollancz, 1963).

ledge is being built up about the way that people behave and respond to others—the central issue in communication. Even here the Government can play a constructive part in providing facilities for research workers to write up their material in digest form to ensure that their findings have the widest possible reading public.

Managers' role. The role of management is being increasingly analyzed by the larger forward-looking firms. Improved selection methods, appraisal and training schemes are elements of the broader issue, staff development, which should be as of much concern to a company as its technical and financial resources. The work of the British Institute of Management, the Institute of Personnel Management and the Industrial Society should be encouraged by special ad hoc grants from the Board of Trade to be used for the application of research findings in certain companies that have bad industrial relations records. This could link up with the strike-ending work of the Scamp Committee.

To what extent will management accept a partner in decision-making and how far is the State likely to be involved? How can we ensure that employee representatives are equipped for their new role? Just as it is necessary for management to be properly trained for the pay and productivity committees and other extensions to industrial democracy, a major programme of training is required to ensure that every trade unionist makes the contribution of which he is capable.

Courses on the role of the committee member would need to be initiated by local college and technological institutions. The courses should cover the human and social changes in the work situation as well as company finances, marketing and production techniques. Senior training advisers to the Ministry of Labour would need to see that proper standards were maintained in the colleges and that the teaching material and lecturing staff were competent for this grade of work. At the same time, a plan should be formulated for long-term higher education of trade unionists.

Research, too, is a responsibility which the modern trade union cannot ignore. In a situation where the trade unionist is to become involved in decision-making with management, it is vital that he be properly supported by a department at headquarters (and regionally) where he can obtain the material which will enable him to know the management case as well as he knows his own. A number of unions, large and small (T.G.W.U. and P.O.E.U., for example) already have research staff.

The approach of Walter P. Reuther, the American trade union leader, is also worth serious consideration by our trade unions. He has on the staff of his union a large number of graduates who are equipped to visit firms and assess organizational problems with management specialists, thus enabling a careful check to be made on a company's efficiency as well as formulating proposals for its future development.

The present trade union structure will prove to be inadequate to deal with an increasing amount of worker participation in decision-making. Progress towards a less cumbersome structure is a little faster now than in 1955 when Dr W. H. Scott wrote, 'If stewards of the various unions having members in a plant cannot sit together on a joint shop stewards' committee, how can the unions be expected to reach agreement on their respective representation on a new policy-making body?'[1]

At the same time, the new demands within firms arising from the complexity of processes and growth add weight to the need to improve the democratic processes on the shop floor. In all sorts of ways new responsibility will be handled at shop floor level. As Allan Flanders said, 'Bargaining between management and the shop steward is more likely to increase than diminish.'[2]

Consideration must be given to the type of union structure which will best serve the future needs of the members and the requirements of the State. Two main developments should be encouraged. Firstly, the continued amalgamation of unions so that there is less chance of confusion of aims and objectives between men of only slightly different skills. The picture today shows an increase in the number of mergers that have taken place but the T.U.C. ought to be prepared to take a greater initiative than in the past in accelerating the process. Secondly, increased participation is best suited to an industrial union structure. This is less of a controversial subject than in the past and stems from the first consideration. In the printing industry, for instance, the merger of smaller unions to form two main groups, the National Graphical Association and the Society of Graphical and Allied Technicians must surely be the

[1] Scott, W. H., *Industrial Democracy* (University of Liverpool, Occ. Paper No. 2, 1955).
[2] *Industrial Relations — What is wrong with the System?* (Faber & Faber, 1965).

APPROACHES TO INDUSTRIAL DEMOCRACY 73

basis for a complete association to cover the work of the industry. As opposed to the dual participation system of the works councils and collective bargaining meetings, the single channel approach would seem to have outstanding merit. Indeed, the constant efforts to 'involve' workers in understanding productivity problems lead one to suggest that unless the workers can usefully do something in such discussions it is an error on the part of management to try to involve them. The success of the productivity bargains shows that the increasing of output cannot be left entirely to management. The single channel system would require regular and continuous week by week meetings at which the workers would have power and responsibility.

This would not mean a complete acceptance of the Yugoslav pattern of industrial relations, but the structure would go beyond that which was described in connection with the pay and productivity committees. Two levels of organization would operate: one for the department, and a council from the departmental committees. The subject matter might not differ greatly from that which I proposed for the pay and productivity committees, but the difference would be in the increased power and responsibility given to the representatives.

Some of the negative attitudes of both sides in industry can be overcome as most of the productivity agreements have shown. Such agreements testify to what can happen when management takes the initiative to improve the effectiveness of the business and the welfare of the employees. There are examples where the unions have proposed changes, even suggesting that work measurement techniques be installed to improve efficiency.

The further value of the single channel approach is that it takes recognition of the power of modern trade unionism within the place of work. Shop stewards have increased in number and authority. In practice, whether the procedure is acknowledged or not, they do bargain with management over a wide range of problems. Again, a great deal of negotiation takes place at the place of work by local and regional union officers. The existing councils, on the other hand, have not met their own original purpose let alone taken on new responsibilities.

An increase in both the quality and quantity of information which the representative at the meetings receives will be necessary. To this end we should recognize that changes in company law are needed, so that there should be no doubt about the information employees should receive. In Norway, for instance, the Parliament has recently amended the Companies Act 1957 to extend the right of workers to be represented on the managing bodies of enterprises within the public sector. In public enterprises where the Norwegian Government has provided the initial capital employees will now be represented both on the board and on the supervisory council. The council must have at least six members of whom one-third will be directly elected by employees. The council is entitled to all necessary information about the operation of the firm as far as conditions permit and has access to all books and assets and expresses its opinion on the annual reports, accounts, and auditors' comments.

In this country, to ensure that companies provide a full account of their resources and operations to the committees, the laws relating to employment, safety, dismissal machinery and company structure should have a condition incorporated in them which recognizes the right of unions to bargain with the employers. Such an amendment to the Company Act is essential and it should extend to all information which an individual member of a committee needs to have before he can make a positive contribution. For instance, in the specific area of manpower, the range of material which the employers should be obliged to give includes: analysis of the labour force; cost of labour as a percentage of total costs; morale indices such as absenteeism, labour turnover and sickness; staff development including selection methods, appraisal and reporting; development and training facilities; and manpower policies at times of redundancy and expansion.

Similarly itemized areas of inquiry should extend to other aspects of information such as finance, marketing and production.

A final consideration on the proposal for individual factory channels of bargaining is that it should have greater relevance to the needs and purposes of the individual plant. For instance, many companies improve efficiency by putting men on shifts (electricity supply) whilst other firms are taking men off shift work (Mobil Oil). It would seem sensible, therefore, to link the needs of the environment with pay and productivity in a way that is almost impossible by national wage agreements alone.

To establish a single channel participation system, it would be necessary to ensure that an experimental approach was adopted.

Rather than introduce the system throughout industry it would be sensible to start such committees for a two-year period in the nationalized industries — their establishment in private industries could follow later. Company and employment laws would need amending to cover the disclosure of information to the committees. Regular disclosure of basic material is essential if workpeople are to be totally involved in decision-making in the enterprise. The interests of the consumer also cannot be ignored. The democracy of an industry cannot disregard those who purchase the goods. Private industry does little or nothing to involve the consumer. The nationalized industries have a better record with their consumer councils which vary in scope. I suggest that a consumer council for each industry should be established, with a close relationship with the central Consumers' Council. The Labour Party must take the initiative and must not leave the question of industrial affairs entirely to the T.U.C. There is a political view to be placed alongside the wealth of industrial experience and know-how of the T.U.C. I cannot over-emphasize that the voluntary principle in collective bargaining is dying, if not dead. The 1966 wage freeze and the legislation associated with it has firmly established the State's involvement in industrial relations. It is now essential that Labour reconsider how the machinery of income-price control can be given a social purpose.

Finally, the dynamic of the organization itself should not be overlooked. All organizations, whether they be factories, hospitals, or trade unions, exert some control over their employees. They build up a pattern of behaviour which the group supports. Nonconformity to the pattern of behaviour would cause disapproval. Owners of businesses have long recognized this; hence the arrangement of material rewards and bonuses to gain obedience which can be relied upon to be effective in most cases until a breakdown occurs, usually as a result of abuse in the field of human relations.

We have seen the ways that communication between management and employees can be improved with the adoption of a more positive approach. The best way of achieving the sharing of decision-making with employees is to move towards a single channel system. Legislation and State involvement cannot be ruled out. The State is now a major partner in industrial relations. However, we would do well to temper our enthusiasm for worker control and extensive Acts of Parliament by appreciating that changes in administrative structure alone do not bring about changes in management and worker attitudes. Attitudes to authority and about authority are deep-rooted within the individual personality and are conditioned by experiences of abuse and neglect which are not easily forgotten. The approach I have proposed for industrial relations in the next five to ten years is neither a neat package solution nor a straightjacket, but an attempt to adapt the experience of other countries to the realities of industrial needs in Britain.

© 1967 BY ERIC MOONMAN

Overseas Aid and Development

FRANK JUDD

There is no convenient geographical limit to socialist responsibility. A concern for the quality of life, for the rights of all individuals within society, has global implications. The twin concepts of society as an integral and co-operative unit and of the right of every citizen to share in the resources and wealth of his community are derived from the Jewish-Christian ethical influences which have played a major part in the modern social and political revolutions of Western Europe. They are now shared by most developed nations, whatever their political systems, and are increasingly reflected in attitudes towards the world community as a whole.

The revolution in communications, the ability to move beyond the physical limitations of the earth, and the capacity for total self-destruction have all served in the past two decades to emphasize that the experiences and mores of the nation-state must speedily be applied to international society. Whenever the majority in any community, albeit through articulate minority leadership, becomes aware that a monopoly of economic and political power is enjoyed by a privileged elite it is only a matter of time before reform must come. Where resistance to change is hardest the record of violence is greatest. In Britain the Stuarts were the last to pay the ultimate price for obstinacy. What has been true within the context of national history is being repeated in a wider international context. In the age of nuclear warfare, with its attendant risk of great-power confrontation and subsequent escalation, we cannot ignore this. Two-thirds of the world population living in poverty and degradation will not rest content now that they can see how the rich live and how their own problems could be overcome. Tension and discontent are inevitable. In 1965 the West spent collectively £28,570 million on the negative military preservation of peace. It spent only £3,213 million on the positive fight against hunger, disease and poverty which so often provide the social and economic origins of conflict.

There is another grave dimension to this problem which deserves careful attention. The division between rich and poor is more than a numerical extension of Disraeli's two nations: it is a division underlined by colour and by race. This is the most disquieting aspect of all, and we should therefore be cautious of oversimplified reactions of relief to any apparent rapprochement between the Soviet Union and the United States.

Sound and durable ethical principles are usually founded on enlightened self-interest: thus we acknowledge that our overseas development programme is motivated by the desire for peace and world security. In a free-thinking society such as our own this sort of argument anyway cuts more ice than a reliance on authoritarian morality. At a time of deep concern about our own economic well-being it is also worth emphasizing that, as a trading nation, the growth of purchasing power in the developing countries will be to our own long-term benefit in the same way as the growth of working class purchasing power has expanded the economies of the industrialized nations. This is not to pretend that it can be achieved without reorganization of long established industrial patterns here in Britain, but at a time when just such reform is being proclaimed as a primary objective of the Government it would be absurd to ignore the universal perspective.

A recognition of economic, social and political interdependence, and a conscious effort by governments to formulate their policies accordingly, are on the one hand the best guarantee of human survival and on the other the basis of a new world-wide prosperity in partnership.

The precise problems of development vary from territory to territory. Sometimes within the same area, or even within the same country, there may be wide social, cultural and physical differences. This is illustrated in the problems of Nigeria or in the agonizing difficulties of trying to build a viable federation in the Cameroons from two regions which were until recently administered under completely dissimilar colonial systems.

Certain general characteristics are, however, broadly applicable to most areas. Basically, all developing economics are heavily dependent upon decisions made abroad; the first exhilaration of political independence frequently turns to bitterness at the realiza-

OVERSEAS AID AND DEVELOPMENT   79

tion that economic domination is as strong as ever. The population explosion is overtaking developments in education and welfare services. Agricultural progress has often been neglected and, even in good years, the growing community may no longer be self-supporting; consequently food accounts for an increasing proportion of imports. Large scale migration to the towns, particularly by young people, results in rapidly expanding slums and shanty towns, fertile breeding grounds for disease. The new phenomenon of urban unemployment is inevitably accompanied by widespread delinquency which all too easily results when a break with traditional values and family security is not replaced by the self-respect, discipline and structural support of new employment. Idle and demoralized, the unemployed provide a basis for social unrest and political instability. Tragically this same manpower could often be used in programmes of agricultural development: the young people who drift to the towns are those who could best adapt to new techniques.

Widespread illiteracy, now reaching a world total of between seven hundred and one thousand million illiterates, together with a desperate shortage of trained personnel have been reflected in the absence of administrative machinery adequate to cope effectively either with social and economic planning or with the implementation of established policies. Existing social structures also frequently hinder reform: obstacles may stem from religious traditions, class or caste divisions, attitudes towards women, or from the established methods of land tenure and taxation.

While it might be thought that industrialization should be an increasingly speedy process for developing countries, because of the opportunity to learn from the experience of their forerunners and thereby to eliminate many intermediate stages, the impressive refinements in current science and technology can actually prove a handicap. The premium is on research into capital-intensive and labour-saving equipment, whereas the developing countries are short of capital and have a plentiful supply of manpower. Commercial research is also directed to improving the production of substitute synthetic materials at the very time when the developing countries are concerned by the need for more extensive cultivation of their primary products as the chief source of export earnings.

Underlying everything else there is a depressing shortage of capital, and the developing countries have almost reached breaking point under the deadweight of loan and interest repayments. It is estimated that in 1964 thirty-seven of the major developing countries had to provide more than £900 million for such payments.

World trade is still organized from the point of view of the older and richer countries which first pioneered in this field, and the developing economies are more often than not relegated to the role of supplying one main primary product. The pitfalls of this situation are obvious. Export values can easily fluctuate by as much as twelve per cent per annum. Terms of trade can drastically deteriorate, creating a deficit where there was previously a surplus, and undoing in one year the progress made over several. Access to rich markets for processed products is often very difficult. All this makes exports a most unreliable source of income for the developing countries, and consequently undermines their capacity to plan intelligently for the future. The outcome of discussions at the United Nations Conference on Trade and Development (UNCTAD) and the addition of the new Part Four to the General Agreement on Tariffs and Trade (GATT) indicate that the developed countries are at least aware of these critical difficulties and of the need to introduce international machinery to ensure fair market play. What is now needed is action.

U Thant has stressed that while sacrifices are necessary from the rich countries if development targets are to be achieved, 'by far the greatest efforts and sacrifices will have to be made by the peoples and governments of the developing countries themselves.' Nobody should underestimate the hazards facing their political leaders in these circumstances: the wisest long-term course of action may not show dramatic results for some time; it may not at once produce the consumer goods and welfare services the people want to see; there may be no fine prestige projects. The retention of positive co-operation for a national plan in the face of continuing poverty is no mean assignment.

It was with all these problems in mind that the United Nations designated the 1960s the 'Development Decade'. Its purpose was to remind us of the dynamic process of social and economic development in which the entire world is involved, although at widely differing levels. It was intended to dramatize the gap in living standards between the developed and developing nations. The decade would provide a focus for action to lessen the gap, ease poverty, and relieve the tensions which result from human misery.

Specifically, the hope was that a five per cent growth rate per annum could be maintained by the developing economies while the richer nations would provide increased capital assistance to the minimum level of one per cent of their gross national product each year.

Midway through the decade it has become clear that its objectives are not being fulfilled. In 1966 we find no less an authority than Barbara Ward Jackson writing urgently on 'Aid in Distress'.[1] In *Foreign Affairs* of January 1966 George Woods, President of the World Bank, said, 'Unless the Development Decade, as President Kennedy christened it, receives greater sustenance, it may in fact recede into history as the decade of disappointment'. According to U.N. sources the flow of capital to the developing countries has levelled off since 1960 both absolutely and as a percentage of the collective gross national product of the developed countries. Eight thousand million dollars in 1961 (0·84 per cent G.N.P.) had fallen to 7,880 million (0·65 per cent G.N.P.) in 1964. Including private investment, Britain appears to have reached 1·45 per cent of her national income in 1961 but to have dropped back to 1·08 per cent in 1964; in 1967 the percentage will be even lower.

Undeniably the Development Decade was a bold and imaginative idea: the setting of specific targets as a yardstick by which to assess achievements has enabled the richer nations to see how poor their contribution often is and may well have prevented their doing worse. It is none the less open to two fairly serious criticisms. In the first place, the targets are rather misleading to the general public. A five per cent growth rate, allowing for a three to three and a half per cent rate of population increase, would provide a rise in income per head of only one and a half to two per cent each year. As the Overseas Development Institute has pointed out, thirty-five to fifty years would be required to double living standards, and in India this would still only mean an average annual income per head of fifty pounds. For its part, the one per cent goal for the developed countries smacks too much of the charitable approach. It is a convenient round figure, but there is no indication that it is based on any scientific analysis of the needs or absorptive capacity of the developing countries. And it is certainly too low. In the second place, the concept of a Decade suggests that this is a problem

[1] *The Round Table*, July 1966.

which, with goodwill and effort, we should be able to go a long way towards solving in ten years. It is going to be a much longer and tougher struggle than that.

Of course all is not gloom: U Thant detected at the UNCTAD Conference in 1964 a genuine growth in enlightenment on the part of the developed countries; the Indian Government is already organizing a massive campaign to curb its population explosion; George Woods has pointed out that the developing countries have moved rapidly forward 'in the ability to formulate and carry out development policy, in the number of institutions able to conceive and administer measures for economic progress, in the number of individuals able to direct private and public enterprise'.[1]

In the history of aid and overseas investment there has been a great deal of wastage because problems have not been fully understood. Expert knowledge is now well advanced and the accumulation of statistical and specialized information provides a basis for realistic planning and projects. This is one sphere which has seen intensified activity by the U.N. specialized agencies during the Development Decade. The need for planning and integrating national policies into regional and international programmes is now accepted by most developing countries. Much attention is now given to the need for adequate infra-structure to improve links and trade between countries in the same area. For this, the services of international agencies such as the World Bank are invaluable in overcoming doubts and suspicions about neo-colonialism and political strings. The U.N. Development Programme, formed as part of the Decade, and combining the functions of the Expanded Programme of Technical Assistance and the U.N. Special Fund, has become the most important source of multilateral, technical and pre-investment assistance. It has the complex but vital function of co-ordinating the work of the different specialized agencies in the field (covering some two thousand five hundred projects in all) and linking them with appropriate financing bodies. The essential inter-relation of pre-investment studies, pilot projects and financing is now recognized. Wherever possible, efforts are made to involve investors at the pre-investment stage as a means of eliminating unnecessary waste on research which is not subsequently exploited.

From these new disciplines of aid certain patterns of priority

[1] Presidential address, Annual Meeting of the World Bank, September 1965.

are now emerging. The full utilization of generous supplies of manpower, together with the promotion of agricultural improvement and reform, is seen as fundamental to development. Enough food must be produced to feed the growing population and as soon as possible to provide a small surplus of resources for investment in future progress. Industrial and prestige projects must frequently be expected to take second place.

Doctor Schumacher, in his theory of intermediate technology,[1] has made two observations about large capital-intensive projects. First, they leave the majority of the population untouched and emphasize the gap between a privileged minority and the overwhelming majority; the social and political consequences of this can be explosive. Secondly, they may in fact aggravate the plight of the majority; the sophisticated factory in an urban centre may throw out of work large numbers of local craftsmen, thus wasting still more of the main potential economic resource of skilled manpower. Backed by the example of China, he advocates well placed modest investments, spread evenly throughout the country, to provide imaginatively but simply improved tools and machinery which can be quickly understood and used by peasant farmers or craftsmen enabling them significantly to improve their productivity. Schumacher summarized this theory concisely at an Africa Bureau meeting in March 1966,

> If you want to go places, start from where you are. If you are poor, start with something cheap. If you are uneducated, start with something relatively simple. If you live in a poor environment, and poverty makes markets small, start with something small. If you are unemployed, start using your labour power; because any use of it, any productive use of it, is better than letting it lie idle.

Replying to the criticism that intermediate technology is second best he went on to say, 'Well is it? For whom is it second best? Is a bicycle second best for someone who has got nothing? No, it is the best for him, and the gift of a car would ruin him. Is a computer the best thing for the illiterate? Certainly not!' While everybody should obviously have the best, care should be taken to see that it is really the best for him. The impact of Schumacher's thought can

[1] See *Economic Development and Poverty* (the African Bureau, 1966).

be judged by the inquiries from all over the world pouring into his Intermediate Technology Development Group in London. He gave one example, 'Some twenty or thirty years ago there existed a bit of equipment which one could purchase for twenty pounds to do a particular job. Now it costs two thousand pounds and is fully automated and we cannot afford to buy it. Can you help us?'

Against Schumacher it is argued that it is essential to build up the surplus capacity and wealth with which to forge ahead; dissipation of resources should be avoided and concentration should be on capital producing enterprises. Some large scale capital projects are of course indispensable, as, for example, the development of natural resources. The exploitation of mineral deposits will obviously help to increase the wealth of a country. Water must be conserved and efficiently used for hydro-electric schemes, irrigation and industry, and where there are no rivers a desalination plant may be required or underground supplies may need to be tapped. The infra-structure of transport and communications is an early essential. To accept this is not to contradict the intermediate theory but to argue for balanced economic growth. The weakness in the large scale capital producing argument is that frequently too much of the capital is extracted by the overseas investing country or enterprise. Mastery of demand-management played a leading part in our own sustained post-war economic expansion, and in this respect as well Schumacher is obviously on the right lines.

For intermediate technology, for improved methods of agriculture, and for relatively complicated industrial techniques, the quality and relevance of education and training are important. They are also basic to sound administration and political leadership. Education has almost always been given full backing in national development plans, but too much of it has been a direct duplication of western systems. A concentration on formal school curricula with little or no relevance to the immediate needs of the territory, to local cultural and social traditions, or to employment prospects, has led to large scale waste of scarce resources. This has applied both in primary and secondary education. The parrot learning of early years has been magnified by the buttercups flown in [sic] for the G.C.E. biology examination, by a preoccupation with the history and geography of western colonial powers, and even by the study of classics for reasons of social prestige. The wastage of the system has been aggravated by a fairly high dropout rate. The population explosion and the regression—inevitable when for many, flocking to the cities in search of white collar jobs, education leads to nothing but unemployment—have meant that there has actually been an increase in illiteracy during recent years. Now much effort is at last being spent on the revision of syllabuses and on the adaptation of secondary education.

The variety of approach is evidenced in the mass education movements of Africa and the social education of India. The British have pioneered community development, with its emphasis on practical education and more effective organization through self help and co-operatives. The French have favoured *animation rurale*, whereby the local leaders have been sought out and involved in local training courses with experts, the experts then following up with advice the work undertaken by the local people themselves. The Americans introduced extension programmes as the method of popularising new techniques; starting with agriculture they now cover home economics, nutrition and health. The principle is the training of local personnel who then disperse throughout the countryside to spread advice and instruction. The Russian experience of correspondence courses in their own development areas could also usefully be adopted. Methods are not the monopoly of the country of origin and altogether there is a widespread new concern for practically directed adult education as a cheap and efficient means of furthering development.

The U.N. Educational Scientific and Cultural Organization (UNESCO) has given a great lead with its selective and intensive world literacy campaign, related to development programmes, and largely concentrating on agricultural education. It has also undertaken teacher, technical and vocational training programmes. The International Labour Organization (I.L.O.) has sponsored industrial training and the World Health Organization (W.H.O.) has helped with the training of doctors and medical personnel. Whatever the precise method selected the normal objective is a pyramidal approach, or system of acceleration, which ensures that the most highly qualified are used to maximum effect in the instruction of the less highly qualified.

There are still considerable difficulties: the nightmarish multiplicity of local languages and dialects, a large proportion of which are unwritten; the physical complications of climate, distance, and inadequate local communications; the lack of qualified specialists; the imperfections and limited abilities of local personnel; the chronic shortage of books and materials. Daunting as these may be they can almost certainly be outweighed by the dynamic interest in a drive for education which is integrated with agricultural and industrial modernization and which is everywhere geared to promoting greater efficiency. One cautionary note is appropriate: the developing countries are not immune to the brain drain, and care will have to be exercised to ensure adequate remuneration for the qualified.

With appropriately trained manpower the streamlining of agriculture becomes feasible, and the 'Indicative World Plan for Agricultural Development' of the Food and Agricultural Organization (F.A.O.) establishes terms of reference as a framework for joint planning by the investing and the developing economies. A proper balance between livestock and crops will provide the basis for sound nutrition. Supplies of protein can be improved through the better breeding and marketing of livestock and poultry, through dairying, and through exploiting new sources such as fish. The fishing industry is still in its infancy, and there is great potential both for increased sea and river fishing with the introduction of new techniques and for the establishment of inland freshwater fish breeding in lakes or irrigation canals. For crops, the aim is to increase yields through improved seed, by the use of fertilisers and irrigation, by pest and disease control, by efficient marketing, and by modernized storage and processing techniques to eliminate the present alarming wastage of stored food supplies (West Pakistan, it is estimated, loses £2·3 million per annum through deterioration in storage of her rice crop). Industry can also be planned to complement agricultural expansion, providing the tools needed on the land and the consumer goods which provide an incentive to greater production.

In a world of rapidly increasing population the vital importance of a balanced, efficient and economical agriculture is matched by man's urgent need to increase the present areas of cultivation. Two great unexploited food sources lie in the oceans and in the third of the earth's surface now classified as desert, and it is essential that much greater international effort should concentrate on research into methods of harnessing these resources.

There is now reason to hope that population control, without which it will be difficult to avoid regression, let alone achieve progress, will become a real possibility as more national leaders come to acknowledge the dangers of uncontrolled expansion and as the development of the cheap and simple uterine loop method brings control within the reach of the poorest government and the simplest people. Birth control also becomes more viable in a relatively literate society enjoying rising standards of living. It is not just that the technical aspects are better understood but that the evidence of social and economic development in the industrialized societies indicates that the will to limit family size and to enjoy the new opportunities of increased material wealth is an accelerating process. The newly accessible diversions for leisure hours are also valuable!

Baulking the smooth implementation of these development priorities are the harsh economic realities which face the developing countries. The world shortage of international liquidity hits them extremely hard and the French opposition to the creation of additional monetary liquidities is for them especially depressing. The bad, and still deteriorating, terms of trade for primary producing countries create grave balance of payments problems, compared with which the current difficulties for Britain are small indeed. Moreover the aid which they are compelled to accept is too often tied, thereby limiting their freedom of manoeuvre and involving the purchase of goods from the donor country at what are quite frequently non-competitive prices.

There is unlimited room for action by a Government which while still in opposition, claimed in a propaganda leaflet that 'a Labour Government will give a new impetus to the war on want in the world. We see it as part of our Socialist obligations to intensify the struggle against world poverty'. The Cabinet was fortunate to have as its first Minister of Overseas Development a formidable politician who had earlier, from the Opposition Front Bench, indignantly repudiated one per cent as too modest a target for overseas aid. It was a relief to see that, after eighteen months of demanding crises, the 1966 Labour Election Manifesto was still able to state 'A Labour Government will mobilize increasing resources — in money, expert advice, and voluntary effort — to make war on want'.

The World Bank and International Development Association Report for 1964–5 estimated that the developing economies could effectively absorb an additional £1,000 million of external capital per year over the next five years. This would be roughly half as much again as existing aid programmes. There is no place for smugness on our part in Britain. We can and must do more. To plead an economic crisis as an excuse for stagnation is highly questionable; commitments made now would not become operative for more than a year. Grants should be increased, and where loans —always a poor second best—are made, they ought to be on increasingly favourable terms. It was to our shame that the International Development Association report of 1962 stated: 'Although the needs of the developing countries remained high, their ability to repay and service loans on high rates of interest was nearly exhausted. It is hypocritical and foolish of countries like Britain in these circumstances to go on offering loans which everyone knows the receiving countries cannot service. It is like offering a starving man a tin of food and no tin opener. It would be better to offer less money on better terms, although, of course, the aim must be to offer more on better terms.' This past policy is best forgotten, and there has already been welcome and decisive action to pioneer interest-free loans and grants by the Labour Government.

Technical assistance, relatively less of an economic strain, should also be expanded by Britain. We already provide more technical assistance personnel than any other country but we could still send more teachers and agriculturalists. Ways could be found to persuade experienced and skilled personnel serving in developing countries to stay for the maximum possible period of time. We could consider means of providing larger numbers of middle-level technicians, craftsmen and professional people to give meaning to the theory of intermediate technology. The highly trained expert may, in some situations, prove helpless compared with the experienced technician accustomed to the improvisations and frustrations of practical action. To involve specialist organizations and institutes at home in backing up with advice and research the work in the field is also important. Before the 1964 election, we heard a good deal from Labour leaders about the possibility of using surplus capacity in railway workshops and naval dockyards to provide some of the simple tools and machinery essential to development. Little has been heard since. It may be that the railway workshop surplus personnel have all been satisfactorily redeployed. But at least some

OVERSEAS AID AND DEVELOPMENT   89

of the naval dockyards are a contradiction of government emphasis on the need for increased productivity. Straightforward engineering work for aid programmes could use up spare capacity without necessitating wholesale reorganization which might interfere with constant availability for naval priorities.

Continual vigilance is necessary to ensure that our personnel serving overseas are operating in the most efficient context. We need to look at terms of service and periods of service. The present volunteer programme, which is already making a useful contribution, will be made far more productive at very little extra cost when the minimum period of service is increased from the absurdly brief one year to two. Similarly, we need to take a critical look at the extensive training of overseas personnel and students in Britain. Information is lacking on the real results of such courses.

It would be hollow to describe all this as costly philanthropy. Human links with Britain are a good opening to future export markets.

A greater readiness to provide technical assistance to supplement capital investment and, where appropriate, to assist with consequent running costs, would be beneficial. There is little point in opening an agricultural extension college in Botswana unless there is the staff to man it and the wherewithal to enable the qualified students to tackle their work convincingly.

In co-operation with other developed countries tied aid should be discarded at the earliest opportunity. A general international policy of untied aid would ensure minimum disadvantage to ourselves and maximum advantage to developing countries which would be able to purchase solely on a basis of economic judgment. It would also be a sensible move to examine the possibility of our taking over from the former colonies the cost of paying the pensions of former colonial civil servants.

The Government has set up a population control working party, including research specialists from the universities and representatives of the International Planned Parenthood Federation and the Family Planning Association. It deserves every assistance in its activity on this crucial front.

Britain has a vested interest in the improvement of world liquidity, and from the concern of the Prime Minister himself and of the Chancellor of the Exchequer, as expressed to world bankers in Washington in September 1966, it seems that the Government will be pushing hard on this. In doing so they should see that the special needs of the developing countries are taken into account. Barbara Ward has suggested that

> It might be possible to evolve a scheme in which part at least of the world's reserves were provided not by gold, nor by currencies, but by some controlled creation of credit on the part of the world's embryonic central bank, the International Monetary Fund. If each year it were empowered to issue credit certificates to the value, say, of 5 per cent of world trade, and these were placed with the near-liquid assets of the World Bank, the Bank could then transfer an equivalent amount of capital to its subsidiary, the International Development Association, for investment in the developing world. Alternatively, to make such a proposal respectable to banking opinion, it could follow the French suggestion that new credit issued by the International Monetary Fund should be given to developed nations in the proportion to which they give aid to the underdeveloped.[1]

In addition we should ensure that, at meetings of UNCTAD and GATT, we are giving the lead in proposing more favourable trade terms for the developing countries.

A consistent aid and development programme demands care that there should be no contradiction between it and domestic policies. At present this is not true of the British programme. We recruit skilled personnel to participate in technical assistance projects overseas, and yet at the same time encourage the immigration into Britain of skilled personnel from the developing countries at the expense of the less skilled who are not so desperately needed at home. We encourage the jute industry in Pakistan at the same time that we restrict access to the British market for the same jute. Quota systems at all, as principally covering jute, cotton and sugar, are hardly in keeping either with enlightened aid programmes or with a spirit of ruthless industrial reorganization in Britain. Whatever our own balance of payments troubles we could surely afford to follow the United States' example by offering special incentives for investments in developing countries, or at least by

[1] *Space Ship Earth* (Hamish Hamilton, 1966).

exempting investments in developing countries from the disincentives on investments in developed countries.

There are as yet no easily discernable criteria by which the Government decides its allocation of aid and technical assistance. Even within the Commonwealth, in which we have a deeper traditional and political commitment than elsewhere, the basis on which priority decisions are made is not obvious. There will always be exceptions to principles, but if there is to be comprehensive and viable planning it would be reassuring to know what is the relative weighting given according to population size, proximity to the point of economic take-off, emergency such as famine or floods, absolute poverty, absence of natural resources, and political considerations. The last does not automatically imply political strings. With the approach of India's fourth Five Year Plan it would be interesting to know why Britain has not in recent years provided more than 8 per cent (£30 million per annum) to the India Aid Consortium, especially when India receives less aid per head (currently 2s.) than most other developing countries despite her urgent need and her proven ability to use it well.[1] It would also be revealing to know why Britain felt unable to provide for Botswana and Lesotho the limited additional assistance which would make all the difference between stagnation in new political independence as economic Bantustans of South Africa and genuinely developing and independent stable African powers in the midst of an area where nothing could be more important. Presumably other commitments elsewhere had higher precedence. Which, and why?

Great emphasis is now laid on aid management. Technical assistance, and the creation of modern planning services within individual territories, are vital in this respect. So also is proper international consultation and co-operation both between donors and between donors and recipients. Harold Wilson recognized this when he said in Connecticut, U.S.A., in March 1964, 'There is the beginning of the acceptance that the battle against poverty cannot be fought without international planning'. General recognition of this principle is evidenced by the increase in world aid channelled through multilateral agencies from six per cent in the late 1950s to some ten per cent today. The growing attention paid to discussions

[1] Hansard, June 29th, 1967. Cf. Malta £18 4s., or Gibraltar £21 11s. per capita.

at UNCTAD, GATT, the World Bank, the Organization for Economic Co-operation and Development (O.E.C.D.) and elsewhere also illustrates this. In order to share experience and knowledge, to avoid duplication, and to ensure effective action through proper co-ordination, the value of multilateral action is self evident. From the standpoint of the developing countries it is attractive because it can be seen to be objective, free from political overtones, and a genuine exercise in partnership in which they have an equal footing. At a critical stage of economic and political evolution it provides a way to reduce complexities and minimize the confusion and damage which can be inflicted by a variety of terms of reference, traditions, techniques and control reaching into the heart of the territory from different countries of origin, and which by their fragmentation delay any chance of firmly based social cohesion.

International action also has a wider significance. It can reduce the likelihood of great power clashes in areas of tension. Through the art and experience of working together, quite apart from direct practical results, the world community will be learning how to appreciate its interdependence and how to exist as a peaceful constructive entity.

From every logical standpoint the long-term future must be with the international approach; in the form of increased export orders it is likely to make a positive contribution towards overcoming the balance of payments problems, but still the position of Britain is ambiguous. On the surface are the fervent protestations that the United Nations is the cornerstone of our foreign policy. In official statements there is a frequently expressed determination to work through multilateral agencies, and the Labour Administration must receive credit for having increased our financial support to the U.N. and its Agencies. Yet, reading between the lines, carefully noting the sentences almost in parenthesis, there is the unmistakable impression that this is all really regarded as rather remote, idealistic stuff, and that as a practical down-to-earth nation we must concentrate on the straightforward bilateral work which really ticks. We cannot be expected to do more internationally, the argument seems to run, unless other nations do as well. But somebody has to take the lead. Simply as a Government which prides itself on grasping the nettle of effective planning firmly there should be a clear, unequivocal statement that we are switching our main emphasis to multilateral action through the Commonwealth and the United Nations as soon as possible, and that we are happy to find ourselves leading the world in this direction.

Some steps could be taken at once. There could be a far more active and positive concern for the work of bodies like I.D.A., UNESCO, W.H.O., F.A.O., I.L.O., the United Nations Children's Fund (UNICEF), the Universal Postal Union (U.P.U.), and the World Meteorological Organization (W.M.O.), reflected in more discussion about, and publicity for, the role of our delegates to them. At the moment their work goes almost unmentioned in Parliament. Members of Parliament are seldom involved in their operation as they are for instance in the activities of the Council of Europe. Imaginative practical steps like an ex gratia contribution — following the lead given by the Shah of Persia — to the UNESCO World Literacy Campaign would also be helpful.

There is reason to believe that ambiguity is not confined to multilateralism alone. The formation of the Ministry of Overseas Development, with a minister of Cabinet rank, was intended as an earnest of the seriousness with which the Labour Government regarded development. While it was a pity that the excellent principle of co-operation — as stressed by the title of the Department of Technical Co-operation created under the Conservatives — was dropped from the title of the new Ministry, the change in status was important. The appointment of committed people like Barbara Castle as the first Minister, and Bert Oram as the first Parliamentary Secretary, led to a refreshing and stimulating White Paper and early action towards rationalizing and reinforcing our aid policies. Had Barbara Castle not been there during the days of deepening economic gloom it is alarming to think what cuts might have been made.

But the White Paper was followed by the publication of the Five Year Plan, and after only a year Barbara Castle was moved to Transport and followed in quick succession, within little more than six months, by two other Ministers. The start to 1967 was still more depressing. The Minister of Overseas Development was removed from the Cabinet. For a government with any claim whatever to a policy of internationalism, let alone socialist principles, this was extraordinary, but it was perhaps a sadly logical step for an administration which had just decided to increase drastically the level of fees demanded from students from developing countries. This measure caused the outcry it deserved, being a sad blow not only to development but also to future expanded export markets.

Against this background it was little surprise when the second White Paper on Overseas Development proved to be a feeble shadow of its predecessor.

The freeze, which saw significant qualitative changes from previous freezes under the Conservatives, by the exemption of social services, hospitals, education, and development areas within this country, did not leave overseas aid untouched. The Five Year Plan had signalled the retreat from the optimism and purpose of the White Paper. Lip service was paid to the principle of aid, but the general thesis that we had been doing more than we could afford and that we would have to slow down the rate of increase, was underlined by the firm view that the foreign exchange cost of the programme must be strictly controlled. The likelihood that this would mean a renewed emphasis on tied aid was depressing at a time when a good number of developing economies would do better with less aid of the right kind.

The Plan was not only concerned with current economic policies but analyzed the distribution of the new social wealth to be created by 1970. Here if anywhere one would have hoped to see a socialist administration setting out international commitments as a leading objective. No such principle was evident; and if the Plan is really to be redrafted this is something which should certainly be rectified. To improve the theoretical status of overseas development work is no alternative to the will to see it strengthened. The cuts in aid programmes resulting from the freeze are depressing. At a time when enlightened leadership should have said that overseas development was to go unscathed for the same philosophical and social reasons that exemptions were to be made within Britain there is a nagging doubt lest these cuts were thrown as a placating sacrifice on to the altar of ill-informed public opinion.

The new Ministry has a potentially severe weakness. To put all the responsibility for this sphere under one roof could minimize the pressure for action and the amount of constructive thought devoted to it. If liaison for work in aid and development with all the U.N. specialized agencies is to be in the hands of one department of government it is arguable that our contribution will be less effective than if the corresponding ministries (e.g., the Ministries of Health for W.H.O., Education for UNESCO, and Labour for I.L.O.) had a greater share of direct responsibility. In the era of planning, when the integration of our own economy into a future international economic structure is at least as important as the integration of regions within Britain into a harmonized national structure, it is doubtful whether the new Ministry will have sufficient specialist staff or the authority to ensure that any domestic policies with international ramifications are shaped with an eye to their wider implications.

A prerequisite of consistently positive government action on aid and development is a widely based, articulate and favourably disposed public opinion. Vocal, even hostile, opposition has not been lacking either outside or inside Parliament. Less responsible sections of the press have joined the band waggon. Popular misconceptions and over-simplified reactions to political events in Africa, Asia and Latin America threaten to turn a growing flow of criticism into a flood.

In British political history, radical leadership was able to mobilize the weight of working class vested interest to press successfully for social and economic reform; but in the world community, although the stakes may be far higher in terms of political stability and future world prosperity, it is more difficult to bring effective pressure to bear. One of the more significant features of the 1964 UNCTAD Conference was the emergence of the united front of seventy-seven developing countries, indicating a new mood of militancy and a determination to achieve results through joint action. Yet it still remains true that those within our own community who are concerned by the need to increase overseas aid do not have readily available a larger body of public opinion to press for or support government action.

An exciting aspect of the present Labour Administration is its attempt to break free from the age of traditional crude conflict between different sectors of large-scale vested interest. The aim is to introduce a more creative era of objective government which will release frustrated potential and provide at last a steady economic expansion. The same long-term economic considerations (quite apart from the moral obligations of socialist philosophy) should compel this Government to give high priority to the education of public opinion to the point at which the need for more determined action on aid is generally recognized. For government action on the scale necessary would be difficult without popular understanding and support.

The White Paper stressed the value of non-governmental agencies, and the wiser activists within them would certainly like to see a large part of their work as popular education. The fund-raising bodies like OXFAM, War on Want, Freedom from Hunger and Christian Aid have done a great deal to publicize needs besides financing a significant amount of overseas work. The volunteer-sending agencies like International Voluntary Service, the National Union of Students, the United Nations Association and Voluntary Service Overseas, apart from sending young people to make a practical contribution, have helped through the experience of these volunteers to build up a body of concern in Britain. Generous government support has come for the volunteer programmes from both Conservative and Labour administrators. But there are still many problems. The archaic definition of charity, unchanged under the otherwise constructive Charities Act of 1960, hampers the genuine 'development' nature as distinct from the relief character of the work, and forces some organizations at times to sail legally pretty close to the wind. The impact of much of the striking public relations operation has unfortunately fostered a feeling of complacency in some people. 'Look at all that work OXFAM does for those blacks; it's about time we got an organization doing some work like that for us' is a sentiment too frequently heard. The picture of the starving child is essentially an emotional appeal, but so also is the picture of atrocities in the Congo or of tribal fighting in Nigeria. Emotion is perfectly acceptable as a means of making contact, but this must be followed by a great deal of education in depth. At the moment this is lacking, and the atrocities picture may have the more powerful impact of 'What's the use of trying to help them?' We would be a lot further forward if all the OXFAM street collectors knew at least the essentials of the story behind the starving child. One well-intentioned advertisement, 'the most shocking figure about world hunger is how little it takes to help' illustrates the pitfalls of mass communication.

Recognizing the potential for education and for field collaboration between existing voluntary organizations, the Labour Government helped them to establish a co-ordinating Voluntary Committee for Overseas Aid and Development (VOCOAD). The Ministry of Overseas Development provides half the cost of a small secretariat of barely half a dozen people. Comment would be superfluous. The inadequacy is obvious.

There are other initiatives. There is the Ministry's own Information Department, backed to some extent by the Central Office of Information, and at Sussex University a new Institute of

OVERSEAS AID AND DEVELOPMENT 97

Development Studies has been founded with government assistance. Outside government circles there is the high-powered work of the industrially supported Overseas Development Institute. The two institutes are primarily concerned with research and training at an advanced level. To gain wider public support for the implementation of their theories there is nothing but the inadequate channel of superficial services forced to 'sell' in traditional charitable terms.

Government spokesmen are on record as talking of aid and development programmes in terms of full-scale war mobilization. To achieve this, an effort will have to be made comparable with that used in educating public opinion to accept massive armaments expenditure year after year. Into the structures being evolved for our own economic efficiency there must be injected a concern for economic priorities within the world community. Trade unions, professional associations and civil servants in all the specialist ministries should be brought into active consultation. Formal education should be adopted to promote a questioning interest in world affairs. There should be international information centres in every large urban centre. We must go beyond the notion that you pay your subscription to the United Nations Association if you are interested in the U.N. or contribute to OXFAM if you are upset by hunger stricken children. These are vital as pacesetters, but there must be a drive to bring home to people in their employment and in the organizations to which they belong that, simply by virtue of being alive, they are part of a complex human society with interrelationships which literally extend into space. Comfortable isolationism can lead only to the downfall of us all. The ramifications of this, of course, extend beyond the subject of this essay into many facets of international life. To promote an effort on this scale a government initiative will be essential.

Problems within the Labour Party itself should not be underestimated. As recent incidents in the field of race relations have shown, there are limited pockets of something uncannily reminiscent of national socialism within the movement. Compromise on race strengthens the respectability of these pockets of opinion, and for precisely the same reasons we must avoid any compromise on international responsibilities. There is a fundamental difference between a pragmatic approach towards the full implementation of stated objectives and a modification of those objectives to cope with current difficulties. The patronizing attitudes of nineteenth century reactionaries towards the working classes can too easily be projected by us collectively on to the developing world. There is no more logical justification for such attitudes today than there was then.

There has been emphasis on the political stability which aid and subsequent economic development can help to promote. However, economic well-being will not in itself guarantee peace. Certainly there will still be need for a system of international collective security, but the prospects for that too will be improved by an atmosphere and tradition of positive international co-operation.

A progressive administration is always open to the criticism that it is failing to achieve the policies for which it fought and won election. The very fact that it is deliberately trying to change the existing order and to establish new priorities brings to the surface a host of difficulties which conservative stagnation may delay. These difficulties do not discredit the higher purpose, but they do demand a nerve of steel and a sense of dedication, not to be confused with dogmatic obstinacy, if the countless temptations to 'be realistic' are to be withstood. Labour leaders have declared their conviction that socialism is about priorities and that overseas aid and development are a part of those priorities. It would be foolish to underestimate the gravity of the economic situation which the present Government has inherited, and there can seldom have been more call for political courage and determination. What we still wait for is evidence of the will behind statements about our international responsibilities on aid: there must be a greater indication of their significance within a comprehensive foreign policy; they should be an essential part of our approach to Europe; they will have to be argued with at least the same intellectual force as our extensive military involvements, and with an even greater sense of commitment than that which enables us to press ahead with the Concord project, costing in excess of £500 million, despite its strictly limited social and economic value, or to embark upon the highly questionable adventure of the soaringly expensive variable geometry swing-wing military aircraft. If the will is faltering, or, worse, has failed, it must be quickly rehabilitated. Otherwise it would have been better never to have spoken.

In political history honourable failure can always be respected. Ineffectual sentimentalism is marked by ridicule and contempt.

© 1967 BY FRANK JUDD

Public Ownership
JAMES DICKENS

Why should socialists bother about public ownership when it appears that welfare capitalism has provided a moderate and rising prosperity in Britain? Would it not be more sensible to reform the worst excesses of contemporary society without troubling about who actually owns industry or services?

Many people ask these questions and this essay will attempt to answer them. For socialists have traditionally regarded public ownership as an essential part of political programmes designed to move Britain forward to an egalitarian society. As a concept it has developed from the experience of the great majority of people under capitalism. They found that such a society was unable to provide security, that it gave the wage and salary earner little chance to to show initiative or to exercise responsibility and that it stunted his human development. Moreover, acquisitiveness and economic individualism led to an insoluble antagonism of conflicting interests. The well-being of the majority was seen to be incompatible with private ownership by a few, whose function was primarily to increase their own wealth by gain. This minority control made work simply an activity which seemed to have little relevance to the individual's self-expression or to community life. Thus, to resolve the contradictions created by the private ownership of wealth produced by the community, proposals for public ownership were gradually formulated.

Throughout the thirteen years that Labour was in opposition prior to 1964 the future of public ownership formed a central part of the debate on the ultimate purpose of the Labour Party. This reached a climax in the redefinition of Clause 4 of the Party's constitution in 1960, but the period was one of confusion, much of it deliberately created by the party's national executive, whose pronouncements used the fullest resources of the English language to sound radical, while remaining committed to little or nothing specific. Threatening noises were made, from time to time, on machine tools, chemicals, pharmaceuticals and the aircraft industry. But the only firm commitments consistently retained in policy documents and election manifestos were the re-nationalization of steel and road haulage, and the public ownership of water and urban building land (from 1961). An imaginative proposal for local authorities to acquire privately rented housing was dropped after 1959. It is doubtful if the 1966 Parliament will go beyond this.

The Labour Party, indeed the labour movement, have always had an equivocal attitude to public ownership. There were, of course, generalizations on the Clause 4 pattern, but the detailed research necessary to launch a successful political campaign for an expansion of public ownership has not been undertaken. The peak was reached in the early 1930s with the work of G. D. H. Cole and the New Fabian Research Bureau. It did not last. The attention paid to public ownership in Labour Party programmes was already being reduced by the late 1930s. *Let Us Face the Future* (1945), was a truncated version of the policy of a decade earlier, and it produced nothing like the furious response provoked by *Labour Believes in Britain* (1949). Generally, individual measures of public ownership were not related to an overall economic plan, or even to the mechanism of economic planning. The proposals were not prepared in sufficient technical detail. In particular, the effect of charging heavy compensation to the newly nationalized industries was not thought out. Most importantly, perhaps, the immediate measures were not linked to an ultimate socialist goal. The case for public ownership was not pressed persistently enough. All too often, it was confused, urged only spasmodically, or totally neglected.

In any restatement of the case for public ownership it is, perhaps, relevant to examine the achievements and failures of the public corporations created by the Attlee Government. Contrary to popular myth, the technical success of these enterprises is impressive and compares favourably with the private sector. Take the record of the National Coal Board. After generations of incompetent private management and organization in an industry suffering from a life-time of bad labour relationships and chronically short of manpower in the most productive coalfields, the Board was urgently required to reorganize, modernize and expand in a few difficult years at a time when there was an acute world shortage of coal until an international surplus suddenly appeared in 1957. Moreover, as with other public corporations, the Nationalization Act imposed pointless restrictions and management was continually at the mercy of Government interference. In spite of this, output rose from 190 million tons in 1946 to 222 millions in 1956, the final year of scarcity. The improvement in productivity is also striking. In 1947, output per man year was 262 tons: by 1965–6 it was 380 tons. Over the same period, output per manshift overall improved from 21·5 cwt. to 36·1 cwt; and productivity at the coalface was amongst the highest in Europe. At the vesting date, mechanized output was negligible; it is currently (October 1966) running at 80 per cent of total saleable output and the aim is 100 per cent by 1970.

The electricity supply industry, despite its inheritance of heavily rundown plant in 1948, has met an increased demand for electricity of over 280 per cent, and output of electricity per employee in the industry has risen by 150 per cent. The cost per unit of electricity has gone up by only 47 per cent, compared with 77 per cent in the price index for all U.K. goods and services. In the gas industry, total sales were 50 per cent higher at 3,505 million therms in 1965–6, compared with 1948–9, the last year of private ownership; and this output came from seven hundred fewer works and twenty thousand fewer employees. Further big improvements in efficiency can be expected following the important discoveries of natural gas. Again, the Atomic Energy Authority, taken into public ownership by the Conservatives in 1954, succeeded in producing electricity from atomic energy before the United States (or any other country). This was a remarkable achievement when one recalls that it was originally a department of the Ministry of Supply starting from scratch and deprived of the benefit of the experience and know-how of the United States. It is unlikely that it could ever have been attained by private enterprise.

The public corporations began life with the initial burden of debt for compensation to the former owners. This totalled £2,100 million for coal, transport, electricity and gas. The new boards were required to treat this as a capital sum on which they paid annual interest. The method of arriving at the total amount of compensation paid for coal differed from that applied to the other nationalized industries. The pre-war formula of the Labour Party was used as a basis. A tribunal (two judges and an accountant) calculated the net maintainable income which the coal companies might have been expected to earn in the future and multiplied this by a certain number of years purchase. They arrived at a figure of £388 million, but did not explain how this was devised, so it is impossible to say whether it was, or was not, a fair amount. Many socialists regarded it as over-generous. The transport shareholders, the electricity and gas companies and, later, the steel shareholders all had their compensation calculated on the Stock Exchange prices prevailing on specified dates. Disregarding steel, which was later denationalized, some £1,200 million was paid for transport, £342 million for electricity, and £197 million for gas. These transfers were generally made in Government Stock, which the public corporations were required to treat as a capital sum incurring interest, to be paid off completely within fifty years for coal and ninety for the others. The stock carried on average a rate of interest of rather more than three per cent, compared with a yield on ordinary shares of four and a half per cent prevailing in the immediate post-war years. Thus, the incomes of the former owners probably dropped from £95 million to £63 million per annum, or less than £20 million after taxation, and the old private owners gave up little by way of capital gains. Gas and electricity prices were previously subject to regulation and the railway shareholders probably avoided making capital losses. Certainly, some colliery company shares would have appreciated, depending upon the extent of price control exercised by the Government. But lacking any clear redistributive aim, such as paying compensation as a terminable annuity (which H. N. Brailsford and Sir Stafford Cripps once advocated), the compensation arrangements of the post-war nationalization measures made only a modest contribution to income redistribution.

A fundamental weakness of the public corporations has been their pricing policy. The nationalization Acts prescribed that revenue should be 'not less than sufficient' to meet 'outgoings properly chargeable to revenue account, taking one year with another'. This is not a break-even rule, as is frequently asserted. It is a restriction on the accumulation of deficits, not surpluses. But the emphasis on revenue equalling outgoings persuaded the various Boards to devise pricing policies which generally covered operating costs, but which made inadequate provision 'for the replacement of assets used up in the production process'.[1] Since fifty-five per cent of the sales from the public corporations are made to private industry, this has resulted in a considerable subsidy from the former to the latter. Thus, the National Income and Expenditure Blue Book reveals that between 1949 and 1965 the revenue of all public corporations (but mostly on the nationalized industry account) fell some £2,010 million short of the amount necessary to cover operating costs and the depreciation of capital assets at replacement cost; or an average of about £120 million per annum. In effect, therefore, the revenue from private industry to the public corporations was £66 million less each year than the sum necessary to meet this minimum requirement. The effect of the 1961 White Paper which aimed at financing a larger proportion of capital development and depreciation from revenue, has improved the position (although it is being operated regressively for individual consumers). Yet in 1965 public corporation revenue was still £24 million less than this basic need. Over the seventeen years 1949-65 only £187 million of the total deficit (£2,010 million) was financed by capital transfers. The remainder had to be borrowed at rising rates of interest. Moreover, the corporations had also to borrow an additional £5,230 million to finance net capital formation. Taken overall, nationalized industries have been able to finance only 42 per cent of their gross investment from their own resources in recent years, compared with 78 per cent by quoted public companies. Thus, in the five years 1959–63, the gross investment of public corporations was £4,400 million, but savings financed only £1,850 million of this. In other words, their revenue should have been £1,600 million greater (or £320 million a year more after tax) to achieve the same percentage of self-financing reached by the quoted companies. On the basis of their own financial practice, those companies would have found themselves paying £175 million per annum more for nationalized industry products.

One important result of this hidden subsidy to the private sector has been the rapid increase in the debt burden of the nationalized industries. Their capital liabilities rose from £2,110 million in 1949 to £7,600 million in 1965. Interest repayments have gone up even more steeply. In 1949, they amounted to £86 million per annum. By 1965 they were £412 million for that year alone, or almost five

[1] *Financial and Economic Obligations of the Nationalized Industries*, Cmnd. 1337 (H.M.S.O.), page 5.

times the amount due for the original compensation, in spite of the 1961 White Paper and the recent capital write-offs for the railways, the coal industry and the airways corporations. Indeed, between 1949 and 1965 some £3,870 million was paid by public corporations in interest.

Thus, far from achieving any redistribution of income in a socialist sense, the pricing policies of the public corporations benefited their private customers. These customers were, for the most part, firms which were thus enabled to make higher profits and whose shareholders doubtless made capital gains. Some, at least, of this surplus income was then honoured, under state guarantee, by the public corporations whose pricing policies in turn simply added to the vast burden of debt. To be fair, the corporations were not entirely responsible for this. For example, successive Conservative Ministers of Transport intervened (in 1952, 1956 and 1959) to prevent the British Transport Commission from raising charges. But the overall consequences were to lower morale amongst the staff of public corporations and, by incurring financial 'losses', to make nationalization politically unpopular.

An important, and comparatively neglected field is the role and influence of purchasing. This is unfortunate: on scale alone, the public corporations occupy a position of considerable strength as purchasers from the private sector. In an average year they account for over 20 per cent of all fixed investment. The proportion varies between categories. For new plant and machinery it is almost 40 per cent. In some fields (e.g., generating plant, mining machinery) the purchasing power of the corporations is dominant. There is also substantial spending on current account. Overall, between 1949 and 1963 they spent £21,570 million on goods and services from the private sector, rather more than the amount devoted to wages and salaries. About £14,500 million consisted of purchases on revenue account made from outside the public sector; the remainder on capital account. The current rate of purchases from the private sector now exceeds £2,000 million per annum; this is virtually equal to our annual spending on defence. For many years after vesting day purchasing was a subsidiary function of production departments, and the nationalized industries had no generally accepted procedures on how to derive the best commercial advantage from their strong position. It was only in 1957 that separate purchasing departments were established in the National Coal

Board and the British Transport Commission. Even today, despite the growing awareness of the significance of purchasing, it still appears to be a function of senior production or engineering staff in some corporations. It is inadequately covered in most annual reports and accounts. There is also a good deal of confusion about which purchasing decisions should be taken at national and area level. Again, the size of the investment programme is such that the timing of buying assumes a crucial importance in the relationship with private suppliers, both in contract prices and subsequent operating costs. In the absence of properly organized purchasing departments, there can be little doubt that the heavy investment programmes of the 1950s were needlessly expensive: inadequate control meant high unit prices.

Genuine competition amongst suppliers enhances purchasing power. When faced with a cartel, however, the purchaser might well become a manufacturer himself. In this respect the nationalized industries were seriously hindered by government attitudes which forbade them to manufacture or so inhibited them with legal restrictions that they gave it up. The outstanding case was the railway workshops, prohibited from supplying anyone but themselves from 1948 to 1962, and then further restricted by being prevented from manufacturing certain items of equipment for road vehicles.

Nor is this all. Nationalized industries have frequently been prevented by Ministers from widening the range of competition by buying abroad, being told to 'Buy British' at almost any cost. The cost has often been a surrender to British private monopoly suppliers. This has been the case with the Central Electricity Generating Board over the nuclear power station programme, and with the Diesel buying policy of British Railways. It is shown at its most bizarre in civil aviation. B.O.A.C. and B.E.A. not only pay the high price of the early versions of aircraft but, by testing them and ironing out the faults found in service, they pay a part of the development costs too. The later models are available at lower prices (due to reducing marginal costs in the larger production run) to foreign airlines who are then better placed to compete with British built aircraft, against our own corporations. The private aircraft firms share the burdens of production with the airlines, but they keep the benefits.

How accountable are the nationalized industries? There are

several ways of measuring this, of which the most obvious is parliamentary control. There is, however, considerable ambiguity about the power of the Minister over the policy of the nationalized industry in his field of responsibility. Constitutionally the Nationalization Acts severely limit the Minister's authority; although when this authority is stated it seems impressive enough. Thus, he has the right to appoint or re-appoint board members. He must approve plans of reorganization and development involving substantial capital expenditure (except for the airways corporations). He may invite boards to remedy defects in production. He can make new regulations for pension schemes, and authorize training, education and research programmes. He requires the boards to publish annual reports and accounts which must be laid before Parliament. In practice, however, the Minister's powers are somewhat greater. During the 1945-50 Parliament it became clear that difficulties were arising between Ministers and the chairmen of nationalized industries. In 1949, Mr Gaitskell (then Minister of Fuel and Power) made the point that if it was thought that a board was proceeding on lines contrary to the Minister's view of the public interest he would give them general directions. This right of ministerial interference was subsequently used by Mr Aneurin Bevan in 1951, when he told the British Transport Commission to raise wages. By developing the practice of regular meetings with board chairmen, Ministers ensured that their views would be known. This helped to keep policies broadly in line. There is little doubt, however, that Ministers have exercised pressure on the boards of nationalized industries to restrain or postpone wage increases at certain times. And if the board has incurred a revenue deficit, requiring exchequer finance, it has little independence.

On the other hand, Ministers have not exercised their authority in other directions. No Minister of Power has sought to implement his 'general duty of securing the effective and co-ordinated development of coal, petroleum and other minerals and sources of fuel and power' as provided for in the 1945 Act, although Conservative Ministers meddled with the public corporations in matters for which they had no statutory powers. Members of Parliament found they were unable to question Ministers when they suspected that unwelcome policies were being foisted on the boards without proper disclosure to Parliament. Indeed, the degree of parliamentary accountability is largely determined by the attitude of the government in office. They allocate the time, in the House of Commons, apart from Supply Days and the twenty days provided for Private Members Bills and Motions. Three days are normally given each year to debates on the reports and accounts of the public corporations, although this can be reduced by the time taken up by General Elections, as in 1966. Clearly, the arrangement only provides for the most infrequent debates, as the following table indicates:

Public Corporation	Annual Report debated	Date of most recent Commons Debate
National Coal Board	1960	October 24th, 1961
Gas Council	1956/7	November 26th, 1957
Electricity Council	1963/4	August 4th, 1965
Central Electricity Generating Board	1963/4	August 4th, 1965
British Railways (British Transport Commission)	1961	November 29th, 1962
B.O.A.C.	1955/6	November 2nd, 1956
Iron and Steel Board	1961	July 27th, 1962

It should be remembered that although the nationalized industries are generally under an obligation to present their reports to Parliament, neither the House of Commons nor the House of Lords need debate those reports.

These debates have been supplemented by others concerned with the reports of the Select Committee on Nationalized Industries on the N.C.B. (July 1958), the Airways Corporations (July 1959), B.O.A.C. (July 1964), London Transport (December 1965), and by supply day debates which in 1964–5 covered the civil airlines (March 1965), broadcasting (May 1965), London Transport and the Post Office (July 1965). Conversely, there has not been a debate on the annual report and accounts of the B.B.C. since 1948, and the Bank of England seems to be a law to itself. Its annual report ceased to be a Parliamentary Paper in 1959–60 and the House of Commons has not debated the report since the Bank came under public ownership. This must surely be attended to. Backbenchers have further opportunities to debate public corporations during the Debate on the Address, by 'Ballot Motions' and in the daily half-hour adjournment debate. Apart from debates, members also have the right to question Ministers on general policy, but not on day to day administration. They may raise points (brought up by constituents and others) in correspondence with board chairmen. The work of the Select Committee on Nationalized Industries is, of course, more specialized. Since 1956–7, the Committee has produced eleven reports. They have proved invaluable and have made a real contribution to the role of Parliament acting as 'shareholder for the nation'. The Public Accounts Committee have also examined the accounts of the British Transport Commission and the N.C.B. Their reports made a number of useful points of detail, but the Auditor-General has stated that he could not conduct an audit of the nationalized industries without greatly increased staff. Other less obvious forms of accountability are to be found in the information obtained from boards by government departments, in the reports of the various consumer councils and in the text of the annual reports and accounts of the public corporations. These latter reports are generally admirable and represent a big advance on anything prepared by the private sector. We certainly know much more about coal and transport, for example, than we ever did when they were in private hands.

Overall, I think the public corporation was the best way of organizing the various industries nationalized by the 1945 Parliament. I reject the view that they have been badly administered and I cite in support of this the judgment of Professor W. A. Robson, perhaps the foremost authority on the public corporation in Britain. He concludes his massive study *Nationalization and Public Ownership*[1] by saying: 'Allowing for some teething troubles, which are still not entirely cured, the public corporation which we have evolved is an outstanding contribution to public administration in a new and vitally important sphere.'

My criticism is not so much of the form of the undertakings as of the manner in which they were and are subordinated to the private sector, in terms of compensation, pricing policy, purchasing and other matters referred to above. A first priority for the future must, therefore, be the reconstruction of the public corporations to make them more effective instruments of socialist planning.

The fact that nationalization has traditionally been part, if a somewhat ambiguous one, of a socialist programme is insufficient reason for its retention now. The role and function of public ownership must be analysed in relation to the problems of the

[1] Allen & Unwin, 1962, page 493.

rapidly changing society of today. In recent times and especially since the war a corporate economy has developed based upon increasing concentrations of private wealth and power. The joint stock companies and the financial institutions which service them tend more and more to combine in order to retain their interests and privilege. This is done in a variety of formal and informal ways resulting in financial, managerial and industrial control and ownership by oligarchic groups. These elites have often now abandoned competition. Their function is the perpetuation of corporate property. They are the most powerful vested interests yet developed under capitalism, and they are virtually free from control by the community. They are dominated by large shareholders and managerial executives who combine to ensure the success, the stability and the growing power of modern business. The complexity and scale of these concerns are now grouped together in massive institutions. The old ways of acquiring private wealth quickly have been replaced by new and subtler forms. The large individual shareholders now acquire wealth by dividends, capital gains or capital appreciation. Managerial executives derive their status from high salaries, expense accounts and bonuses. Moreover, it is certainly possible for a group of larger shareholders to determine company policy while owning less than a quarter of total voting shares. Professor Sargeant Florence has described this as 'Oligarchic minority owners control'.[1] Thus, power over the dominant sector of British industry is frequently exercised through minority blocks of shares organized by a pyramid of holding companies and manipulated by the interlocking directorates of the big private corporations. These bodies exercise the power of a new elite, who are not publicly accountable.

In Great Britain in 1963, the eight largest companies controlled 70 per cent of the vehicle (including aircraft) industry; in chemicals (including oil and petro-chemicals) twelve companies held 90 per cent of the industry; in metal manufacturing thirteen companies held 80 per cent. A similar pattern has developed in other industries. Share ownership in companies is also heavily concentrated. A recent estimate[2] states that one per cent of the adult population own 80 per cent of company shares and five per cent own 96 per cent.

[1] Statistical Journal, part 1, 1947.
[2] Lydall, H.F., and Tipping, D. G., 'The Distribution of Wealth in Britain' (*Oxford Bulletin of Statistics*, February 1961), page 90.

This heavy concentration of company formation and share ownership has taken place simultaneously with a number of other important factors which have distinguished the post-war years. In this country, and to a greater extent in other advanced industrial countries, we have experienced much steadier economic growth than in the past with a rapid increase in production. It is remarkable that in spite of the hindrances of stop-go policies, national production rose by 2·1 per cent per annum in 1956–61, compared with 1·7 per cent between 1913 and 1950 and 2·2 per cent from 1870 to 1914.[1] The development of new techniques of business management in the private sector has not only controlled and regulated competition but, by using new techniques of operational research and long-term forecasting it has steadily reduced the area of unpredictability. To meet the needs of rapid technological change and to protect heavy capital investment which may take longer to mature than before, governments (even Conservative governments in which men like Mr Enoch Powell held high office) seek to develop a form of economic planning by consent. They encourage firms to evolve broadly agreed policies on the basis of common long-term interests. The classic conception of competition between firms to the disregard of the market as a whole has gone for ever. Again, the more rapid application of science and technology to industry has led to an abundance of consumer goods and services. The benefits of this new prosperity are more widely distributed than ever before although grave problems of poverty remain. There has been a steady rise in social welfare expenditure, especially in education, and the real income per head of population has consistently risen.

One major contemporary problem for the private corporate economy is the management of automation. This is only a cloud on the horizon in the United Kingdom in the mid-'sixties, but it is already being described as a menacing nightmare by American authors. Thus, in 1964, ten men could produce as many automobile motor blocks as four hundred men in 1954; fourteen operators tending the glass-blowing machines manufactured 90 per cent of all the glass bulbs in the United States; two workers could make 1,000 radios a day, where it took two hundred a few years ago. Automation will significantly affect social habits, with the rapid extension of shift working. It will change the basis of skill and necessitate a

[1] Maddison, Roger, *Economic Growth in the West* (Allen & Unwin, 1964), page 28.

massive retraining and redeployment programme. Ultimately it will end payment by results for employees in favour of long-term wage agreements.

It is unlikely that a system devoted to obtaining the maximum profits will be able to resolve the problems created by the concentration of power in private hands or the questions of public accountability, of fairly-shared abundance, or of automation, without government participation in industry. Experience has shown that the forms of participation developed so far have resulted in a public sector which is subordinate to private enterprise. To avoid any repetition of this the time has now arrived to change this balance by altering the basis of ownership in commerce and industry and by promoting a new form of public ownership designed to achieve the following:

1. to make those in control of economic power accountable to Parliament and its agencies and thus responsible to the people as consumers, producers and tax-payers.
2. to move further towards an egalitarian society by substantially reducing unearned income, the inequalities of wealth and the subsequent class divisions thus created.
3. to facilitate central economic planning and control for the benefit of the nation.
4. to eliminate the restrictions on production created by private monopoly.
5. to establish social priorities which will end the Galbraithian contradiction between private affluence and public squalor.

These ends can be attained by reforming the existing public sector and by extending public ownership to new and important activities as part of a revised economic plan aimed at improving the material and cultural well-being of the people.

The reforms might start with pricing policy. Revised financial objectives should be prepared for each nationalized industry, based upon the principle that their prices to private industry and commerce should yield sufficient revenue to cover operating costs, depreciation at replacement value and the financing of a proportion of capital expenditure at least equal to the average obtaining for public companies. The increased cost to the private sector must be made a charge on current profits and capital reserves; the Government should not allow firms to inflate prices on this account and any consequential price increases must be justified to the Prices and Incomes Board. Price controls should be introduced where necessary. Where it is deemed to be against the public interest to increase charges to the private sector (e.g., in transport) or where the nationalized industry is conducting unremunerative services which can only be justified on social grounds, the Government should pay a subsidy to recompense it fully for the loss of revenue, or the operating loss. The 'break-even' principle should, however, be applied in the tariffs or charges rendered to the individual consumer as an essential element in a policy of price restraint. There is no social justification for asking the individual to pay a surplus over production costs; he is not able to make capital gains at the expense of the public sector as private equity shareholders continue to do.

We might then move on to purchasing policy, by making the public corporation more economically self-sufficient. A number of steps on these lines have been taken since October 1964. They include the following:

1. the Atomic Energy Authority is now able to diversify its activities under the Science and Technology Act, 1965.
2. the commercial vehicle manufacturing units of the Transport Holding Company are no longer restricted to manufacturing for nationalized industries only.
3. the statutory restrictions on the manufacturing powers of the publicly owned transport industries will be removed in the forthcoming comprehensive transport legislation. This will be especially important to the British Railways workshops.
4. the British Waterways Board has obtained authority to extend its manufacturing activities to the construction of boats.

Henceforth, all remaining restraints on the manufacturing and bargaining powers of the nationalized industries should be lifted. Indeed, they should be encouraged to expand whenever it is beneficial for them to do so. Where they are confronted by monopoly suppliers, as the G.P.O. are over telephone equipment and the gas boards are over gas making plant, they should adopt a policy of 'vertical integration' and either take over a supplying firm or establish their own new manufacturing subsidiaries. The Central Electricity Generating Board might also consider the same policy for boilers, switchgear and other types of electrical equipment. Again, the inordinate time taken over the construction of conventional power stations could, perhaps be overcome if the Board, in conjunction with the new Steel Corporation, established a constructional unit with a guarantee of constant employment to steel erectors, in place of the present employment of casual labour. In other cases, 'forward integration' is appropriate. For example, the National Coal Board should continue to extend its activities in chemicals and coal distribution. Assets taken over by existing nationalized industries in this way should be reorganized as part of the structure of the public corporation, to ensure an acceptable standard of management and uniform conditions of service for employees.

Finally, the market power of the public sector—nationalized industries, central government and local authorities—should be marshalled in a central purchasing agency, which would undertake all purchasing on behalf of the sector. This could produce significant savings for the public sector and raise the standard of goods and services supplied by private firms.

EXTENDING PUBLIC OWNERSHIP—PROPOSALS FOR THE 1970s

1. *Investment*

The rate of capital investment in the United Kingdom has been chronically inadequate since the war. In recent years, in spite of many inducements, it has only averaged about sixteen per cent of gross national product per annum, against twenty per cent in France and twenty-four per cent in Germany; and much of this has been wasted in soft-centre, 'candy-floss' industries. Moreover, we know very little about the investment policies of some of the biggest sources of capital, as Professor Titmuss has shown in *The Irresponsible Society*.[1] Indeed, the insurance companies and the pension funds he discussed 'constitute by far the largest single source of new capital, the net rate of accumulation of the funds of the two groups of institutions being now some £600 million per year.[2] They now

[1] Fabian Society, 1960.
[2] *Report of Radcliffe Committee on Monetary System*, Cmnd. 827 (H.M.S.O.), page 290.

exceed £1,000 million per annum. The need is clear: the Government should take control of the direction and amount of investment. This means a direct attack on the centre of the corporate society: namely, the joint stock banks, the insurance companies and the investment trusts. The banks should be regrouped under a reformed Bank of England, thus eliminating much of the present duplication between the 'Big Five' banks. The insurance companies should be placed under the government ministry most appropriate for their functions (e.g., the Ministry of Social Security) and the investment trusts might form the basis of a National Investment Board, which would also have wide powers of control over investment policy generally.

2. *Chemicals*

The fact that I.C.I. is the largest private monopoly, and one which is not publicly accountable, is unsatisfactory. The Labour Party should declare its intention to take I.C.I. into public ownership and proceed, in consultations with the trade unions concerned, to prepare detailed proposals to replace this private combine with a public corporation.

3. *Pharmaceuticals*

The pharmaceutical industry has been heavily criticized in the past for its very high rate of profit, and the anti-social character of its marketing. It is completely dependent upon the National Health Service for home sales. It should be incorporated within the Service under public ownership.

4. *Docks*

The case for nationalization is made out in the report of the Port Transport Group of the Labour Party (June 1966) and need not be repeated here. The present unwieldy structure, with four main types of ownership — British Transport Docks Board, statutory port authorities, municipal enterprises and private companies — should be replaced by a National Ports Authority.

5. *State Holding Company*

A state holding company should be established to deal with smaller, isolated extensions of public ownership (e.g. in B.A.C. or Hawker as recommended in the Plowden Report). It should also take over the present state shareholding in Short Brothers, B.P. and Fairfields, etc. The company would select new areas for public ownership and move into them. It could allocate capital investment to small state concerns and it would provide common finance, administrative and technical services. It would be subject to investigation by a body similar to the Select Committee on Nationalized Industries, as would be all private companies in receipt of public loans (e.g. Cunard).

6. *Compensation*

The important point here is the need to tie this to income redistribution. The formula of assessing compensation on the basis of the Stock Exchange prices prevailing on specified dates should be continued. But the stock offered should be paid as a terminable annuity to the former shareholder and, when he dies, to his dependent; thereafter it would expire on the death of the dependent.

7. *Management*

Two basic requirements are necessary, at all levels. Firstly, a determination to make public ownership a success. Secondly, a high level of knowledge and competence in specific functional fields. The appointment of retired service officers to senior positions must never be repeated. The existing recruitment schemes for graduates should be merged into a central scheme for all the nationalized industries. Training should be given at a public enterprise staff college and in the industries concerned, and they should be joined by staff promoted from among the employees. Movement between different Boards should be made easier.

8. *General*

If we are to start to dismantle the private corporate economy and replace it by something on the lines of the above proposals, it will require a sustained educational effort on a scale hitherto unknown in the Labour Movement. The proposals must be popularized, related to the everyday problems of ordinary people, and supported by research in depth. It will not be easy, but there is no other way: Clause 4 generalizations are not enough.

© 1967 BY JAMES DICKENS

Foreign Policy
EVAN LUARD

The term 'foreign policy' is ambiguous. It may mean the delectable end-situations we would like to bring about: disarmament, China's entry into the U.N., a better deal for the developing, peace in Vietnam. But it must also include responses to the existing facts of life, which are often very different: nuclear proliferation, the existence of Formosa, the weakness of the British economy, and the refusal of two conflicting parties to negotiate on mutually acceptable terms. While the former meaning is more exhilarating, the latter is indubitably more real. And reality will not be transformed into dream by merely wishing hard enough. The object of a successful foreign policy is the best possible reconciliation of the two.

Such a reconciliation is difficult enough for any power at any time. For example, other nations may not share the same dreams (they may not want to see China in the U.N.). Or if they do, they may dream them in a different shape (they may want disarmament, but only on their terms). Or some of the aims may be mutually incompatible (it may be economically impossible to play a significant role east of Suez and to expand economic aid to the developing countries at the same time). Or others may not think our views are relevant in any case (peace in Vietnam is for them to decide, they may declare).

The reconciliation is especially difficult for the medium-sized powers. These find increasingly in the modern world that the widening economic gap between nations applies as much between the very great and the medium as between the developed and the developing; and that this economic gap is mirrored inexorably by a widening military gap as well. Thus though in relation to the very small or the very weak their own power and influence may remain constant, or even increase, in relation to the very great it diminishes, and diminishes further all the time (as the increasing dependence of

Britain on the U.S. today not only for many missiles, but for military aircraft, air liners, machine-tools, and other advanced products illustrates). For Britain there has even been a diminution in relation to other powers in her own class as a comparison of the relative position of Britain at the end of the war — one of the Big Three, the mother country of a huge empire, and a victor nation — and her position today, for example in relation to Germany, France, Italy or Japan, will demonstrate. This conditions her attitudes to foreign affairs. It would be an exaggeration to speak of resentment and frustration. It is rather the bewilderment of the former grandee suddenly come down in the world, and not yet quite sure how he should comport himself in his new situation in life.

The reconciliation is also especially difficult for governments and parties of radical persuasions. Governments of this type are perhaps more likely than others to feel sure that the existing world is out of joint and that they themselves were born to set it right. But they find the facts of the world no less stubborn and recalcitrant than other governments. Some of them they will find particularly uncongenial. A Labour Government in Britain today, for example, will find that many of the governments which are Britain's closest allies are conservative, or even reactionary, in politics, while many of the more progressive forces in the world are uncompromisingly hostile to her. In the new cold wars of the modern world, it has been mainly those on the radical side — Egypt, Tanzania, China, Syria, Indonesia and others — that have been most hostile to Britain, while her own allies have been in the opposite camp. And many of the situations in which Britain is placed, especially over the Middle East, Rhodesia and the relics of colonialism generally, expose her particularly to the hostility of the more leftist forces. She is therefore placed in the unenviable dilemma of having to choose between her declared opponents on the one hand and friendly sheikhs, war-lords and military dictators on the other. The position is still further complicated by the fact that often it is the progressives that progress least. It is not only that capitalist West Europe develops faster than Communist East Europe: Jordan and South Arabia develop faster than Egypt and Syria, Tunisia than Algeria, the Ivory Coast than Guinea, Kenya than Tanzania, Pakistan than India, Malaysia than Indonesia, Japan than China, almost anywhere in Latin America than Cuba. Here is another of the facts of the world to which a left-wing government must adjust its policies.

Britain's adjustment to this new reality is made harder by other factors. First, for all her decline in power, Britain still has genuine commitments abroad that are a heritage of her imperial past. However irrelevant they may appear in Britain's new situation, and however costly to maintain, they cannot be merely wished away or shaken off like cumbersome garments. For commitments that were entered into for our own defensive purposes are now mainly transformed into undertakings for the defence of others. And while the former can be abandoned at convenience, the latter cannot be unilaterally abrogated unless some adequate substitute has been provided. Yet so long as they remain, they provide a perpetual temptation to think in terms of a 'world role', even of Britain as a 'world power', terms that no longer really have much relation to Britain's substantive position or capacities.

Secondly, the obvious recourse for a power such as Britain, to make common cause with her nearest neighbours of similar economic level and interests, and so find a new role in a united Europe, is inhibited in the short run by the resistance still raised by France; in the medium term by the genuine difficulties that entry on the terms of the present Treaty would present to us, especially in terms of food prices here; and in the long term by Britain's long-standing associations elsewhere. Yet so long as Britain continues to hover uncertainly on the fringes of Europe, she will continue to find difficulty in visualizing her proper role within the world scene.

Finally, even if entry is achieved, this ambivalence will remain by virtue of the very real, and very rational, attachment that remains to the Commonwealth. That attachment subsists not merely because it is a British creation; but because it brings together nations of every region, race, stage of economic development, political belief and religious creed; and therefore clearly has a uniquely valuable role to play within the international scene. The ambivalence is intensified by a certain very proper squeamishness about becoming exclusively the member of a rich man's club and turning our back on those who need us most. There would indeed be a very real reason for hesitation if it were a fact that the economic and political benefits to be gained by entry into the European Community could be obtained only at the expense of weakening or destroying this existing multi-national community of the Commonwealth.

All of these difficulties of orientation are intensified by Britain's perennial economic weakness. This aggravates some of the dilemmas: for example if Britain's balance of payments might be strengthened in the long term by entry into the Common Market, will it be critically threatened in the short term? It also distorts judgments on some questions: whatever is the correct decision about Britain's medium-term role east of Suez, it would be an act of flagrant irresponsibility if it were to be decided, as some suggest, only on grounds of short-term balance of payments difficulties. Finally, it crucially inhibits British freedom of action in a number of fields in which hard cash is of the essence: aid to the developing countries, more support for the U.N., and the maintenance of a resolute posture towards the problems of southern Africa.

Defence and Foreign Policy

The 1966 Defence White Paper declared the Government's proud resolution that defence policy should be the servant, not the master, of foreign policy. Such sentiments sound very high-minded, since we all like to think that foreign policy is idealistic and enlightened, and defence policy sordid and ignoble: we thus do not wish Othello's role to be usurped by Iago. They are also unfortunately purest rubbish. They could have meaning only of a nation having aggressive intentions, for here war might truly be only the extension of politics by other means. For any other power potential it is threats to national or international security which are the most basic data in the situation and it is these, and not foreign policy aims, which determine defence policies. Whatever other aims a nation may have, none takes priority over survival. Foreign policy must be adjusted in its turn both to the threat and the response required.

What then are the kinds of threat that mainly exist in the modern world? Some indication can be found by examining the list of wars or armed conflicts that have occurred since 1945. A number of facts emerge from this list. Of the total of fifty-six, only five could be classified as wars of aggression, involving the crossing of a recognized frontier or use of force against a foreign government (Korea, 1950, Guatemala, 1954, Egypt, 1956, Hungary, 1956 and Goa, 1961); and there were a number of special factors even among these. There have been nineteen wars or armed actions *about* frontiers, together with many smaller frontier incidents and disputes; nine colonial wars, as well as many other incidents and sporadic violence connected with colonies; and about twenty-five civil wars, including a considerable number in which outside states or forces became involved during the course of the conflict. On the other hand there have been no world wars. The super-powers have never been involved against each other. Most of the wars have been minor in character. There has been a very considerable degree of stability in Europe.

There is no certainty that this pattern will be maintained. But it seems probable that it indicates the likely shape of conflict over the next ten or twenty years: small wars rather than major ones, outside Europe rather than within it, within frontiers rather than across them. Major aggression of the old sort seems now, with the increasing firmness of frontiers and the clearer outlawing of aggression, to be an almost extinct form of activity. Even China, though her words are often bellicose, has been exceptionally cautious in her deeds; even in the areas immediately round her borders where other great powers have tended to allow themselves considerable freedom of action. Conflicts over frontiers may continue, especially where these are not clearly demarcated. Colonial conflicts will be rarer, though they might easily occur still in the remaining semi-colonial area of southern Africa. But almost certainly the main type of conflict, in the immediate future as in the immediate past, will be civil war, with or without foreign intervention. The instability of many new states, the revolutionary doctrines emanating from China and elsewhere, the extension of related political creeds over a large part of the world, all these foreshadow an era of global civil war in place of the old-fashioned national wars of previous ages.

What are the implications of this for defence and foreign policy? Firstly, if the main threat to peace today is civil war and subversion, rather than external wars and aggression, Britain's own defence establishment and military aid policies must be adjusted accordingly. One of the main needs in such a situation is rapid mobility: this is already partly accepted but more still could be done in concentrating on more and better transports and paratroops rather than artillery and infantrymen. But there is equally clearly a need for helicopters rather than supersonic bombers, vertical take-off aircraft rather than high-performance fighters, better machine guns rather than better missiles, guerilla training in jungle conditions rather than tank-manoeuvres on Salisbury Plain. But the implications for foreign policy and military assistance are even more important. Clearly prevention is better than cure. The best deterrent for conflict of this sort is often political rather than military. It is effective and honest administration, even in remote parts of the countryside: assistance in building this up may be worth many thousands of foreign troops, whose effect may sometimes be the reverse of that required. It is good communications and an efficient police force: help in providing these may be often of more military value than advanced weapons. It is improved standards of living: economic aid may be of direct defence assistance even when used only for civilian purposes. Even for other types of war intangible deterrents may provide a better defence than deterrence by armed forces. Action to demarcate frontiers exactly before conflict occurs may be worth a lot of military help after fighting has broken out over them. The despatch of inspectors to watch a troubled area may be worth many peace forces sent after conflict has already occurred. Prompt procedures for hearing disputes in the U.N., for verifying the facts, for appointing conciliators, may inhibit attempts to settle the issue by brute force. One test of defence policy over the coming years, therefore, will be how far it takes sufficient account of the intangible weapons of deterrence as well as the physical ones.

Secondly, because of the incomparably greater military mobility available today, assistance, even when it does require to be military in form, does not necessarily have to be provided on the spot. The development of a better air-lift capacity, enabling military assistance when required to be despatched within hours, or at the most in a day or two from Britain itself, should obviously be the overriding priority of current defence policies. To provide the availability rather than the presence of troops not only benefits Britain, above all the British balance of payments; but it provides the substance of protection, without the appearance of provocation, not merely in the receiving country itself but to its neighbours. And because forces are unlikely to be required in Britain, or even in Europe, long-range air-lift capacity is likely to be vital for the kind of situation we are most likely to become involved in. Certainly, some supply and servicing facilities may still be required on the spot. But these can be maintained best by the host countries themselves, if necessary with outside help, rather than in large bases virtually owned by Britain, such as Singapore. Such a system might not provide so much economic benefit for the protected states. But this is not the form in which economic assistance should properly be provided. The next test of British defence policy over the next few years, therefore, must be how far it makes us better equipped to provide the protection required of us abroad with the minimum of troops based outside Britain.

Thirdly, if the main dangers are likely to come outside Europe rather than within it, clearly the reductions to be made in British forces overseas should be made in the first place in Europe, rather than elsewhere. British governments have been chary of reducing B.A.O.R. in the past for political rather than military reasons. But the dangers of letting West Germany go unloved and deserted are considerably less now than they were, especially with the improvement of her own relations with East Europe. But any reductions made by the U.S. and Britain should be bargained, as far as possible, against countervailing reductions by the Soviet Union, above all in the twenty divisions in East Germany, representing something like three quarters of Soviet forces outside her own borders. One way of making this more acceptable to the Soviet Union would be if Britain were to join General de Gaulle in acknowledging the permanence of the Oder-Neisse boundary. Another test of British defence policy over the next few years, therefore, will be how far it reduces our existing inflated commitment in Europe, and does so in such a way as to increase rather than endanger stability there.

Fourthly, if the main threat is not in Europe, it is necessary to analyse where it is and how it can best be met. The isolationist argument that Britain is now primarily a European power, and, with the end of the colonial era, should abandon the rest of the world to its own devices, is not one that bears close examination. It is only comparable to the general sense in the inter-war era that Ethiopia and Czechoslovakia were small, far-away countries that were of little concern to West Europe. The world is far too small today for stability and security in one region to be a matter of indifference to those in others.

There can be no doubt that one of the main areas of danger is South-East Asia. This is where there are a number of nations with deep internal divisions, a number of local disputes on boundaries and other matters, the destabilizing influence of large local Chinese minorities, the dominating proximity of China herself, above all, the area where the spheres of influence claimed by China and the U.S. come into immediate contact. The British presence in the area, whatever its original purpose, is maintained now largely at the request of Singapore and Malaysia. Its immediate removal before these countries are strengthened would create genuine difficulties for them. This does not however mean that the form this assistance at present takes is that which is most appropriate. Clearly the aim must be to build up effective local forces to replace the British commitment at the earliest possible time. The development of the appropriate local defence organization should be an urgent aim of British policy. If it is necessary for the facilities concentrated at Singapore to continue to be administered by an outside body (and the present relations between Singapore and Malaysia indicate this may be so), the best solution would perhaps be to prepare the way for transferring it by, or soon after, 1970 to some regional, or even Commonwealth, organization of this kind. Naval re-fits and a rear base could be provided in Australia. Staging-posts could be secured by the west-about route. While there might be little harm in using airfields in the Indian Ocean purely as staging posts, anything in the nature of bases, with a permanent establishment, would be a retrogressive step, conflicting with the basic principle that should govern all overseas defence policies: that military facilities should be provided only directly at the request, and under the control, of nations of the region (and not always then).

Much the same considerations apply in the Middle East. This too is certainly one of the areas where the threat of instability may continue, in this case the cold war between revolutionary, republican Pan-Arabism and conservative, monarchist Pan-Islam, led by Egypt and Saudi Arabia respectively. Here too there are some areas, traditionally dependent on Britain, still threatened by one or other of these forces. But here too it is important to see that assistance is given in such a form as will best deter, and not exacerbate, conflict. It should be a basic principle that any assistance should be such as to maintain the balance of power and not disturb it, and that Britain should so far as possible remain neutral in the conflicts of the region: moves, therefore, which, in the name of defence against Egypt, involve building up Saudi Arabia to become herself an expansionist power are of no service either to the region or to Britain's own interests. And here too, an important aim should be to build up an effective joint defensive capacity, so that even the precarious and tiny Trucial Sheikhdoms are increasingly in a position to survive, preferably modernized and reformed, without British guarantees (though they may continue to need one from elsewhere).

What is essential in both these areas, and indeed everywhere, is that increasingly all the assistance policies of outside powers, especially assistance in arms, are co-ordinated, rather than competitive. The fact that the capacity to manufacture the most advanced weapons is more and more concentrated among the most advanced powers means that these are in a position to bring about by their assistance policies a balance within other regions such as has never previously been attainable. It is essential for this purpose that all the major powers (including, of course, the Soviet Union) should increasingly discuss together, even if only in confidence, the principles to be applied in their own assistance programmes, and should seek to balance the arms given to major antagonists, so that those available, for example, to Israel and the Arab States, to Somalia on the one hand and Ethiopia and Kenya on the other, are always kept roughly matched. By these means it may be possible to reduce the worst risks of conflict in the most unstable areas.

The Great Powers and their Relations

It is part of the conventional wisdom today that the old cold war has now been replaced by a new one, in which China takes the place of the Soviet Union as the main antagonist. In many ways this is a false analogy. It is not merely because, as we have seen, many other continents of the world have their own cold wars, between progressives and conservatives within each region, which bear little relation to the others. China cannot be regarded as the leader of a large scale grouping of nations within the international scene, comparable to the Soviet bloc in the late 'forties and 'fifties, which could represent a formidable antagonist in such a contest: even the communist countries which are her immediate neighbours, Mongolia, North Korea and North Vietnam, now seem closer to the Soviet Union than they do to China. China has not shown herself active, in a military as opposed to a political sense, in extending her power in border regions that she might legitimately regard as buffer territories (as the Soviet Union did in East Europe, and as the U.S. has done on occasion in Central America and the Caribbean). Even in such areas as Laos and Vietnam, which adjoin her border, and in which conflict has been endemic, even over Hong Kong and Macao, unreconstructed colonies of the most old-fashioned type with almost entirely Chinese populations, China has been till recently cautious in her policies. One of the main problems of the next ten years will be to draw China out into the international community. It is doubtful if this can be satisfactorily achieved by waging a global 'cold war' against her, or seeking to achieve the 'containment' of a nation that already feels itself perilously hemmed in by foreign bases and alliances.

It is true that Chinese words are frequently militant and aggressive. But, here as elsewhere, deeds speak louder than words. There is frequently talk of Chinese 'expansion', in South East Asia or elsewhere. This is a term that needs careful analysis. If expansion by *direct aggression*, that is military action across the borders of those countries is meant, the charge is almost certainly misplaced. China has, over the last ten years, of her own volition demarcated her borders and entered into frontier agreements with every one of her neighbours except India and the Soviet Union, hardly the action of a power with territorial ambitions (compare Germany's perpetual challenge to her borders in the 'thirties). So far as India is concerned, China's aims are now almost certainly satisfied: and many Western experts regard the claims China put forward there as well founded. It is true that China still occasionally utters territorial claims against the Soviet Union, but the Soviet Union has recently strengthened her defences in that area, and it is inconceivable that China would, for very many years to come, feel in a position to seek a trial of strength with Russia on this issue even if she wished. If expansion by *subversion* is meant, the charge may have more substance. It is very difficult to be sure of the direct Chinese influence in the sporadic guerilla activities in Laos, Thailand, Sarawak, and the Philippines, not to speak of Vietnam itself. It would be surprising if these did not receive some encouragement from China, but evidence of direct material help is harder to come by. If expansion of *influence* is meant, there is no doubt that this will be sought, perhaps more and more powerfully. But it is difficult to deny the legitimacy of such an aim in an area so vital to China's security and interests.

Western, and British, policy must therefore recognize this legitimate Chinese interest in South-East Asia, while at the same time refusing to allow domination, intimidation, or subversion of local governments or peoples against their will. Since the main objective of China and the U.S. is that the other shall not acquire a dominant position, whether in South Vietnam, or Indo-China, or the whole region, the only mutually acceptable solution is one that provides for neutralization (even this is marginally favourable to the West in an area clearly of so much closer interest to China). This was in fact the implicit assumption on which the Geneva Agreement of 1954 was based; an assumption which was subsequently disastrously overthrown so far as Vietnam, and even Laos for a time, were concerned. Such a solution would not necessarily place any constraint on the political freedom of such countries, since there is some evidence that this is what many of the peoples in the area themselves desire, and, given this single premise, they could still elect the government of their own choosing. As co-chairman of the Geneva Conference, Britain has a chance to contribute to bringing about such a solution. Certainly no offer of terms to North Vietnam and the Viet Cong is ever likely to be persuasive, unless it includes the promise of final neutralization; for it is the long-term foreign relationship and not the immediate political future of the country that is of most concern to them. Given a sense of greater security in these border areas (and this might involve the cessation of U.S. U-2 flights over China and the patrol of Polaris submarines off her coast) China might in time become ready for a more forthcoming attitude to the West, just as the Soviet Union has done during the years since 1956, given a similar increase in security.

What about relations between China and the Soviet Union and the communist world generally? It is difficult to foresee any change in the progressive deterioration of these relations in the coming years. It seems likely that China will in time break away from the existing Europe-based Communist bloc, and perhaps set up a new Communist movement of her own, based on her own interpretation of Marxism-Lenism and the thought of Mao Tse-Tung. She will continue to appeal to the imagined revolutionary sentiments among the developing countries of the world, and inveigh against the diarchy of the U.S. and the Soviet Union. It seems doubtful whether many of the governments of these countries will find such calls particularly enticing, compared with the more solid attractions of economic aid from the Soviet Union and the West. But it would be foolish to suppose that a campaign designed to appeal to the poor countries of the world against the rich will not have more influence among the populations of such countries, especially the students and intelligentsia, than the ham-handed Chinese propaganda of the last few years has succeeded in doing.

Unless Western, and British, policy succeeds in showing that the economic gap is being bridged more successfully through their methods than it would by the revolutionary doctrines propounded by the Chinese, these appeals will have a growing, not a diminishing, strength.

Relations between the western Communists and the West on the other hand are likely to be marked by a continuation of the general relaxation and drawing together of the past year or two. It seems certain that the East European countries will continue to welcome contacts, especially economic contacts, that serve to increase their bargaining-power with the Soviet Union, without imperilling their relationship with her to danger point. The example of Romania, even if not explicitly imitated, is likely in the long run to prove infectious; and it would not be surprising if some kind of Balkan grouping emerged for certain purposes, cutting across ideological lines. Conversely, France, Germany and other Western states will certainly continue, perhaps in competition, to seek closer relations with East European countries. Britain can play her own part by encouraging not only trading, but cultural, sporting, touristic and other personal contacts to help create a sense of wider European unity, and strengthen further the general stability already established in Europe. If British and U.S. reductions of forces in Germany could be matched not only by the reduction of Soviet troops in East Germany, but total withdrawal from Hungary and Poland, the only other East European countries where they are stationed, West Germany might accept that her own security was enhanced rather than endangered by the process.

Over the longer term future the relations between the superpowers as a whole, of which China will be one, and the rest may prove a more intractable problem than ideological divisions. The ever-widening gap between the very great and the rest has been to some extent masked by the cold war and the clustering of many of the smaller powers round the shirt-tails of the mighty. As tensions relax and this becomes less necessary, and as the U.S. and the Soviet Union grow closer together, the medium powers may begin to drift away from them and to become more conscious of their diminishing power. One response will almost certainly be increasing unity within continents. And the nationalism that has been a dominant force in international relations for the past two centuries may be increasingly replaced by a continentalism that might ultimately be even more potent. This is certainly one factor that Britain will have to take into account in considering her long-term future role.

Regional Organizations

British foreign ministers and prime ministers have habitually pronounced their determination to 'build up' or 'strengthen' the U.N. This is very commendable. But it might be equally idealistic, and more practical, to say the same about regional organizations. These have a vitally important role to play in filling the gap in the international structure between the national state and the world organization. One of the great problems of collective security has always been that of bringing about a consciousness that the preservation of peace, even in remote parts of the world, is of sufficient concern and immediate national interest to be worth the heavy sacrifice of war to preserve. The examples of Manchuria and Ethiopia show the extent of this difficulty. It is less where regional organizations are concerned, for the preservation of peace within the same continent often seems of sufficiently immediate importance to warrant such action. Regional organizations, such as the Council of Europe, the Arab League, the O.A.S. and the O.A.U. perform many other valuable functions. They have adjudicated or intervened in local disputes and frontier conflicts (as the Arab League did over Kuwait, as the O.A.U. did about the Algeria-Morocco war, as the O.A.S. have done over the years about a large number of local disputes). The actions of both O.A.S. and the O.A.U. in preparing plans for atom-free zones is about the only descernible progress in the field of disarmament for several years. The Commissions of Human Rights set up in Europe and Latin-America are perhaps the only effective institutions for this purpose yet established. It would be logical for Britain to seek to strengthen these and to encourage more where they do not exist.

The area where such an organization is today totally lacking is that in which it is most required: South-East Asia. There are many difficulties in achieving such an organization, in the divisions, national and ideological, that beset the region. The existing Association of South-East Asia is much beloved by Malaysia, being very much the brain-child of Tunku Abdul Rahman; but is not particularly beloved by anybody else. Indonesia, in particular, feels herself too important to come in as a junior partner in an existing organization. Because of her own strongly anti-Chinese sentiments, she is more attracted towards reviving the racially inspired Maphilindo (Malaysia, Philippines and Indonesia). But for this very reason both Singapore and Thailand are hostile to that idea, and it would indeed have many drawbacks. ASPAC (the Asian and Pacific Council) arouses the suspicions of Indonesia, Cambodia, Burma, and even Japan and Malaysia, as too militantly anti-Communist and blatantly U.S.-inspired. What seems to be required, here as elsewhere, are two types of organization. An overall, comprehensive, politically neutral, consultative body for the entire region (including perhaps Australasia) — say an Organization of South-East Asia and Australasia — corresponding to the O.A.S. or the O.A.U., joining all the nations of the area regardless of ideology, for discussion of matters of common interest and the adjudication of local disputes; and a new, more closely-knit organization linking perhaps Thailand, Malaysia, Singapore, Indonesia and the Phillipines, for political, economic, and perhaps ultimately for military, co-operation as well.

There is also need for some more effective body of this kind in the Middle East. The Arab League could have filled the bill if it were used for neutral rather than for the partisan purposes it often is today. The acute divisions that at present exist in the area, though they make such an objective more difficult, also make it more necessary. British policy should be aimed at making such a development more, rather than less, probable. The O.A.U. and the O.A.S., too, could be given encouragement to enable them to play a still more useful role in their areas. Britain could encourage their strengthening, for example, by supporting the remission of certain disputes to them; by encouraging the development of effective procedures for pacific settlement within them; the development of regional assemblies; the evolution of Common Markets and other instruments of co-operation; and the development of a Commission of Human Rights in Africa, where there is perhaps most need of such a body. There is at present a tendency to suspect such organizations as weakening the authority of the U.N. There is no need whatever for this feeling, so long as the principle is maintained that U.N. authority is superior, and that (as laid down in Article 53 of the Charter) such organizations can only undertake 'enforcement action' to settle disputes with the authorization of the Security Council.

The area where such organizations come closest to Britain is

Europe. The corresponding general organization is the Council of Europe. This loses a great deal of its potential value by excluding all non-'democratic' countries, with whom the others most need closer contact. However inevitable this may have been at the height of the cold war, it seems to have little logic today. Many of the most important activities of the Council are functional, increasing co-ordination and standardization, for which comprehensiveness is essential. At least, an associate status for the Communist states and Spain and Portugal should be established. Membership of the Commission and Court of Human Rights are distinct from membership of the Council, requiring separate ratifications. This need not, therefore, be an objection (though, if any Communist country were prepared to ratify these, nobody in the West would be likely to object).

But the European organization that Britain is likely to be most concerned with over the next few years is the European Economic Community. This is not the place to argue the case for or against British membership (the question is considered in detail in another chapter). Like most people in Britain today, I personally regard it as inevitable, as well as necessary, that Britain should belong, and as soon as possible. As has already been indicated, negotiating mutually acceptable terms may not be so simple as is sometimes assumed. What is certain is that the Community that comes into existence if Britain, with Denmark, Norway and Ireland, as seems probable, also join, would certainly be something different from the Community as it is today; and still more different from what was widely assumed four or five years ago. Fears about centralized control over foreign policy, or internal economic decisions, such as were expressed by Labour's die-hards in 1962, always seemed exaggerated; they are more than ever so now, in view of the loosening of the Community that has taken place over the past few years. In its economic forms, the Community is more closely knit than ever. But it is its economic aspects that are at present most damaging to Britain, and could be most beneficial. It is more than ever clear that, whatever the pains in the early years, Britain cannot afford to be penalized in her most profitable markets for very much longer.

Such membership is not likely to transform Britain's political or military relationships. In the long run, there is little doubt we shall grow closer to our European neighbours. But this would have happened anyway, and membership of the Common Market in itself will not affect it as much as is often believed. But within the wider organization that will come into existence, some may be closer than others. There would seem some advantage in Britain seeking to cultivate a close relationship with the Scandinavian countries and Ireland, with which, on many issues—the U.N., disarmament, the problems of Africa, East-West relations, aid and other matters—we share common attitudes. The emergence of a North European grouping within the common framework of European and West European institutions, perhaps aligned on some matters with the Commonwealth, might contribute something of value to the Community without seriously dividing it.

There has never seemed any good reason why membership of such an organization should be regarded as weakening, still less betraying, the Commonwealth. Many other members of the Commonwealth belong to local associations without being any the less members, sometimes enthusiastic members, of the Commonwealth as well. In the type of world we live in today, an organization such as the Commonwealth, bridging so many gaps of race, religion and region, is of especial value. But it is not something that can simply be taken for granted, for it could easily weaken and disintegrate almost before this was realized. While it has withstood the test of Rhodesia so far, this issue alone, if weakly or opportunistically handled by Britain, would be enough to destroy it. The truth is that, whether Britain had joined the Common Market or not, there would have been many factors serving to weaken the Commonwealth at this point in time. And whether Britain joins the Common Market or not, it will be necessary for Britain, with other members, to take special steps to strengthen it, if it is to survive effectively. Far from the existence of Europe making the Commonwealth superfluous to Britain, as a superficial view has suggested, it becomes more necessary than ever if Britain is to maintain a world vision.

There are a number of steps Britain could propose for making the Commonwealth a more living reality. She could propose the establishment of a Commonwealth Assembly of parliamentarians on the lines of the European Assembly, for more regular and formal meetings than the existing Conferences arranged by the C.P.U. She could seek to bring about a Commonwealth Aid Programme, or at the very least, a co-ordination of economic assistance within the Commonwealth; perhaps the establishment of a Commonwealth Development Bank, on the lines of the European Development Bank, to assist the less developed members. She could try to co-ordinate Commonwealth initiatives within the U.N., especially for example in developing the U.N.'s peace-keeping capacity, and pledging earmarked forces. She could seek to propose the development of some kind of Commonwealth peace-keeping, or conciliation machinery (even the proposed Indian Ocean island air-strips might be set up on a Commonwealth basis). Some of these proposals may sound far-fetched at the moment; but the proposal for a Commonwealth secretariat was considered far-fetched until the year in which it was established. Successful initiatives of this kind would establish Britain as a 'world power', far more persuasively and effectively than the maintenance of military bases in South-East Asia could ever do.

The U.N.

But British Foreign Ministers and Prime Ministers are right when they pay their ritual devotions to the U.N. For if a more harmonious texture of international relations is ultimately to be established, this can only be through expanding the role which the U.N. at present plays within the international community. And to carry due weight, efforts within this field must be not an incidental, but the dominant element within British foreign policy today.

First, there is a clear need to expand the U.N.'s economic activities. Few can doubt that the really major international problem of the next twenty, indeed fifty and a hundred years, is the widening gap between rich and poor. British foreign policy can thus legitimately be judged by the test of how much Britain is doing in this field. It was inevitable that the British aid programme, relatively low though it is, should suffer some damage from the present economic freeze. But much more could be done to prepare the public for the need of doing more in the future: indeed, a major public relations effort is needed here over the years.

The U.N. specialized agencies have a unique role to play in this. The slight expansion of the proportion of British aid channelled through these is a beginning, but the proportion is still lamentably low. Aid in this form is not only more acceptable to the recipients, but for this very reason often more effectively supervised and better co-ordinated with other programmes. The development of the role of the resident representatives (the U.N. Development Programme representatives in the field) might enable them eventually to play the part of U.N. economic ambassadors, instituting more effective co-ordination of the activities of the multifarious specialized agencies so often at loggerheads. But developing countries need more trade than they need more aid. Even more important therefore could be the exercise of British influence within the Common Market and other institutions in favour of more liberal trading policies towards the developing countries. There is no more vital cause for British foreign policy to identify itself with over the coming years.

It would be nice to make a clarion call for a British lead on disarmament. But realism must accept that there is little prospect in the foreseeable future for much advance in this field; certainly not towards general and complete disarmament. The most publicized goals, a treaty on non-proliferation or a complete test ban, even if achieved, will exert very little influence on the present situation. There has never been any great difficulty in getting haves to agree about excluding have-nots; and it is only the accidental complications surrounding West Germany that have prevented a treaty being signed by the existing nuclear powers long ago. It is an entirely different matter to expect the have-nots to relinquish all chances of joining the club unless they are provided with very real evidence of nuclear disarmament by the haves, such as these have so far given no indication of providing—and such as no system of control could anyway enforce. Similarly, even if the test ban were made complete, the wording of the treaty is such that any power seriously wishing to go nuclear could always claim a new situation to justify an exception in her own favour. By far the most hopeful field in the nuclear sphere is in the development of atom-free zones, for here the sacrifice is shared equally among all close neighbours, and may therefore seem less inhibiting. However, the areas where it is most needed, the Middle East and Asia, are the areas where such proposals have so far not been considered. Otherwise the most likely and useful chances for disarmament, or at least stabilization, is in the field of conventional weapons. Though disengagement in the sense once suggested is still unrealistic, there might be mutual reductions in troops in certain areas. There would be value in conventions for keeping troops and aircraft away from frontier zones (say ten miles on each side), perhaps under U.N. inspection; and especially about the stationing of missiles near to foreign borders. Here perhaps are opportunities for useful British disarmament initiatives.

One of the most important challenges for British foreign policy over the coming years will be the problems of southern Africa. This too is closely related to the U.N. For it is clear that joint action through U.N. organs is the only action likely to be effective, and could avoid the dangers of uncontrolled unilateral action. This will only be achieved if the African nations are satisfied that the U.N., and especially its western members, are steadfast in their attitude and are taking effective steps. The first stage will be that of Rhodesia. If sanctions are to be effective there is no doubt that they must be not only declared, but enforced, on a U.N. basis: this might provide the testing ground of a new and important instrument of U.N. authority. Over South-West Africa again, only U.N. action, for example by securing a new International Court of Justice ruling on the mandate and by enforcing it under Article 94, provides a satisfactory way forward. And only action through the U.N., whether through the Human Rights Commission and other bodies or through Assembly pressure, may provide the means of bringing effective pressure to bear for changes in the whole system of administration in South Africa and the Portuguese territories.

Finally, there is a clear need to strengthen the U.N.'s peace-keeping capacity. The Labour Government has already some useful initiatives to its credit here: in the earmarking of logistic units, the offer of financial support to overcome the financial deadlock, and now the proposal for a peace-keeping fund (a welcome advance over the non-committal answers previously given by Labour Ministers on this subject). But the real root of the problem in this field is of course not a financial but a constitutional one: how can peace-keeping operations legally be authorized and controlled, and how should members be assessed for them? There are respectable grounds for arguing that the first of these questions can never be satisfactorily settled: that there is no reconciliation possible between the view that only the Security Council can authorize such forces and the view that in some circumstances the General Assembly can; and that it may therefore be better to leave the issue aside, since in a crisis situation the U.N. can generally be relied on to find a satisfactory formula for taking action. Against this, however, it is arguable that the financial crisis itself cannot be settled unless the constitutional one is too. For the moment at least there would seem to be a strong case for Britain continuing to support Ireland and those many other small states who insist on the Assembly's competence in *peaceful* peace-keeping, even if it has to be accepted that financial contributions must be voluntary. But if this is so, it is of the utmost importance to ensure that representation on any supervisory body set up to control the forces (which will certainly be necessary if the Secretary General is not to be given an excessive role) is confined to those nations supporting and financing the forces.

At the same time Britain should support moves to expand and strengthen the staff of the Secretary General to enable them to coordinate arrangements for peace forces. Britain might even extend its offer of logistic support by offering the use of overseas facilities, airfields and supply stores, for their operations. It must be recognized, however, that the usefulness of peace forces is confined to those cases where conflicts have not already broken out, and the essential role to be played is that of an umpire (as in Cyprus), or a buffer (as in Sinai), or a face-saving neutral (as in West Iran), or occasionally as a policeman (as in the Congo).

For other cases it is prevention rather than cure that the U.N. may be able to supply. Often apparently small or even trivial steps can have large consequences. For example, the clear demarcation of existing administrative boundaries, while it could not resolve legal disputes on such issues, would make it more difficult for nations to attempt to resolve the issue by force, and would establish the status quo that was to be restored. The laying down of clear principles of international conduct on such matters as international waterways, shared water resources, lines of communication (such as the Berlin corridor) and other issues that are frequently the cause of conflict might lessen the likelihood of resolving such issues by war. Above all a clarification of the disputed legal position concerning intervention by outside states (including 'volunteers', or mercenaries) in civil wars would reduce the risk of conflicts that now sometimes arise in this way, perhaps the most potent source of conflict in the modern world. The encouragement of education about the U.N., its purposes and principles in schools everywhere, and a better U.N. information service would serve to prepare the next generation for a more peaceful world. Even the flying of the U.N. flag all over the world on U.N. Day might influence attitudes to the world organization. Such proposals seem trivial; but they are the type of triviality that ultimately transforms the universe.

© 1967 BY EVAN LUARD

The Welfare State: Reform and Development

CHRISTOPHER PRICE

Twice in the last twenty years a Labour Government has been elected on a tiny majority after a hard and bitterly fought campaign—but the key issues on which each election was won were very different. In 1950 it was 'Just look at the children' and 'Labour Gave you the Health Service'; in 1964 'Let's Go' and 'Get Britain Moving'. This progress from false teeth to technology, from soft hearts to hard heads, as has been evident from recent Labour Party Conferences, has set up very real tensions among the ordinary party members. The issue has been to an extent softened so far by the fact that the Labour Party is led by a Prime Minister who is firmly respectable on both counts; having resigned office to protect a free Health Service in 1951, he was almost solely responsible for launching and developing the modernizing technical stance on which the 1964 election was won. Since then, however, the flood of political technologists into the Party, the inevitable constant emphasis on efficiency and productivity in the ministerial and Party pronouncements, could endanger the delicate balance between heart and head which is essential to the Party if it is to survive. Policy statements there have been in plenty—but by and large the job of pointing out the gaps in the Welfare State and planning the future of social policy has been bequeathed to left-wing academics like Professors Titmuss and Townsend.

There is a real need now to relate the excellent analyses of what is right and what is wrong with our social services, to our basic political philosophy. We need the political will to bring our social services and our Welfare State up to date, and to ensure that generous social provision is a continuing high priority throughout the 1970s. When the vast majority of Labour M.P.s simply had to go to their homes and talk to their parents to be reminded of the crying needs that had to be met there was no danger that these needs would be forgotten; but with the changing social origins and living patterns of Labour Members of Parliament, all now themselves cushioned by higher salaries, this danger is becoming very real. For the Labour Party is dead, electorally, morally and in every other way, the day it is simply composed, at parliamentary level, of technologists and efficiency experts. Only a social policy which receives a constant high priority beyond the nicely calculated limits of exact electoral advantage will preserve for the Party that soul which, even though somewhat sentimentally dominant in the days of George Lansbury, is nevertheless the mainspring of work and effort for the strongest and loyalest of its supporters.

Moreover it is important to get the right and relevant political priorities in the development of the social services. When Labour went out of office in 1951, it was common to think the Health Service the best in the world, yet to be rather ashamed of the level of old age pensions; to be immensely proud of school milk and the school meals service, yet to feel that the level of sickness benefit was appallingly low: to show, in short, high regard for those services provided by the state to which everyone had access irrespective of insurance contribution, and rather less for welfare payments fictionally based on the principle of National Insurance. The average Labour supporter has always associated the Health Service, which is open to all without any qualification, with all that is best and most fair in Labour Party policy.

Too often in the 1950s the system that Labour bequeathed produced the worst of all worlds. National insurance that was compulsory but based on low flat-rate contributions, needed disproportionately large extra subventions from the state which, because it felt it was in some way 'subsidizing' the scheme, had no incentive to improve it or even keep up the value of existing provisions, while on the other hand family allowances fell far behind in real value. Similarly the Health Service, because of lack of planning, the imposition of charges to the patient, and a reduction in the number of doctors trained, also suffered a decline in standards. Moreover Labour Party policy, as laid down in 1963 in *New Frontiers for Social Security*, has always emphasized the raising of National Insurance benefits for unemployment, sickness, and retirement pensions up to a proper living-wage level; and it is obvious that, within the context of the present system, the only way of financing this is to change over to wage-related contributions.

But it is important to remember that it is very difficult to pursue any fundamentally socialist direction within this framework. It is primarily a Liberal concept by Beveridge out of Lloyd George; in Germany it has thoroughly paternalistic origins in Bismarck. It can be mildly redistributive to the extent that it is financed through taxation; it is also possible to bend any scheme in favour of the lower-paid worker. But the difficulties the Labour Government is finding at the moment in replacing the graduated pension scheme which the Conservatives introduced in 1962, and the absurdities created recently in the West Midlands by trying to redeploy motor workers receiving £16 a week wage-related benefit into £15 a week service industry jobs, simply highlight how intractable these schemes are when anyone tries to operate them in a socialist manner. It is almost impossible to get a scheme which at one and the same time is universal in its application, has a rate of contribution which lower-paid workers can afford and a rate of benefit which seems reasonable for the broad mass of the people. Someone, the poor or the rich, always either has to opt out or wants to do so, and the tendency is to end up with two nations in sickness and retirement, with lower-paid workers on a charity rate of subsistence (as in Germany or under the present graduated pension scheme) and substantial tax-relieved benefits for those who need them far less. Too many factors at the moment militate against a just national insurance-based scheme: in particular an absurd wages structure in which certain manufacturers pay three times as much as essential public services for the same sort of skills and a system of tax-allowances which structurally benefits the rich. Whenever attempts are made to keep the rate of contribution down and still produce reasonable benefits, the principle of universality always has to go.

This law applies in just the same way to any system of health insurance; when a group of Birmingham doctors in 1965 opted out of the Health Service and offered their patients a fairly cheap weekly insurance scheme, they immediately found they had to exclude a large proportion of their patients—the chronic sick, those with high drug bills, and many of the elderly—who needed their services most. The move towards wage-related benefits in Britain is an important and sensible move; but it should not now so obsess us as to make us think it will abolish poverty in the 1970s and 1980s. Fifteen years ago many people in the Labour Party were talking openly about poverty being abolished; now that academics have shown that it is very much still with us, and studies from the U.S.A. have shown the enormous extent of the problem there, it is clear that the specifically socialist task for the Labour Party in this field over the next twenty years will be to invent new and strengthen old methods of eliminating poverty from an increasingly prosperous society.

The strategy should now be to put as much social energy and expenditure as possible into building up the 'universal' parts of the Welfare State, financed out of taxation and open to all. This goes clean against the 1966 Conservative line on the social services which advocates means-test-based benefits to the poor in order to avoid wasting money on the rich. But the problem is not of course as simple as this; as the insurance-based sectors of the Welfare State have been developing, the areas of greatest need have been subtly and in many ways imperceptibly changing. Professors Townsend and Abel Smith have now shown us how it is large families, and therefore in particular the children of low wage earners, who are now suffering. These are the people who, of course, ought to be benefiting from the new social security supplementary payments and wage-related benefit, but very often do not even receive the full benefit which their contributions have paid for, because of the operation of the wage stop. It is now estimated that about three-quarters of a million children are living below Ministry of Social Security subsistence levels. The long-term answer here is a minimum wage for those in work and a guaranteed income (based on a universal tax return) for those on benefit. But since the minimum wage is in limbo and the Treasury appear uncooperative over using the income tax return for a guaranteed income, a considerable increase in family allowance — not substantially increased since 1952 (and then only to mask the abolition of food subsidies), is the only chance of offering some immediate help towards the elimination of poverty among large families. The better-off families would pay nearly half back in income tax anyway; and if the operation were linked with the abolition of child allowances on income tax, the allowance could be more than trebled at no extra cost to the Exchequer and the argument that tax-payers' money was being wasted on the rich who did not need it would hold no water at all.

The real point is, however, that family allowances are now established on an almost institutional basis, as a payment which, since everyone receives it, is wholly free from the 'charity' stigma. It is a payment which at once both goes where the need is greatest and acts as a unifying factor in society. It is not endowed with the grudging charitable aura of the supplementary pension and national assistance which hundreds of thousands have hitherto not taken up, an aura which even the advent of the Ministry of Social Security will not ever wholly remove. The Ministry have still elicited successful applications from only about half the estimated 700,000 who are eligible: the whole problem is far better tackled by ensuring that adequate welfare payments which do not bear a means test are both paid universally and hold their value in step with the growth in national prosperity.

The same goes for the non-insurance-based services of the Welfare State, primary and secondary schooling, the G.P. and hospital services and the local authority health services. The fact that these services are avowedly financed out of taxation and the rates, with no rebates and allowances for parents of public school children and patrons of private nursing homes, makes them genuinely cohesive social forces, knitting society together.

The day the country accepts voucher schemes for education and tax rebates for private health insurance, of the type which the new wave of right-wing academics are assiduously trying to inspire, the 'two nations' immediately become even more sharply defined and crystallized than now, with all the inevitable and patent social injustices that follow — one nation bathing in the private affluence of its select schools and nursing homes and the other thrown on the public squalor of an impoverished state system.

Many would, of course, say that this is the situation into which we are moving today. To the extent that we are, the responsibility is twofold. The growth of private institutions is partly due to general affluence but largely to the substantial tax advantages which these private institutions receive at the moment. To a really determined government the quality gap between the public and private sectors in health and education can be just as wide or narrow as they want it to be: the law relating to charitable institutions, the freedom given businesses to finance health and education benefits out of tax relief, the industrial fund for the public schools, (until recently) covenanting by grandparents and cross-covenanting between families, rating relief and many other methods of tax avoidance have been shown by Professor Titmuss and others to have made a substantial contribution out of public funds to the 'public' schools and private nursing homes. The successful pressure over the S.E.T. indicated the power that these so called 'charities' have to maintain their tax-exempted status. If we want to maintain truly national health and education services which tend to unify rather than divide the nation, we must use all the fiscal control we have to build up the state scheme and keep private ones down to the minimum. The principal effect of giving tax advantages to private schemes is to divert essential and scarce national resources — doctors and teachers, national wealth and building labour — away from those who need them most and towards those for whom they are often an extra luxury.

But of course the Government has a more important duty: to tackle the second and more substantial cause of private individuals opting out of the Health Service. It must ensure that the services provided reach the standard which many discriminating people in the country respect. B.U.P.A. and Nuffield Foundation money is not being poured into the development of private nursing homes, simply because of the tax relief available to the very rich, but because in the eyes of many people the treatment they receive at their local G.P.s and hospital is so poor, and contrasts so glaringly with all the instances of purchased affluence with which their lives are surrounded, that they decide to purchase this too. No one can blame them; one can only blame a series of Conservative governments which allowed the Health Service to become so overloaded that frequently it cracked under the strain. When a service like the Health Service is financed from national taxation the task of keeping up standards is always difficult; the temptation always is to save money by stealth, asking the wrong questions. 'How much extra can we afford this year?' is a far more common question than 'How much extra is needed to improve upon and maintain existing standards?' The result is the stories we read in the press towards the end of each financial year, of wards standing empty and nursing posts unadvertised because the hospital board has overspent on its revenue account for that year.

Part of the reason why the hospitals and the general practitioner service have been so consistently starved of funds is that, administered as they are by appointed rather than democratically elected committees, they are not nearly susceptible enough to consumer pressures. The contrast with the education service is illuminating; the schools and colleges have increasingly attracted a much greater amount of public money, because they have democratically elected committees to administer them and fight for them. Of course parents do provide a much more vocal pressure group than the sick and the elderly, but it is more than this: in the fight for more money for education the teacher and parental-consumer pressures roughly balance each other out, so that the professional interest is never over-influential. The money goes to the children and their new schools as well as to the teachers in increased salaries. The hospital and general practitioner world is far more rooted in the grip of the doctors; what it lacks is a substantial body of consumers pressing for more money to be spent on the right things. For as a result of successful pressure for better provision for education there has never been an opting out movement to parallel the growth in private health insurance. Private medical insurance has nearly trebled in the last ten years: over the same period the number of children in independent schools has barely kept pace with the natural increase in population.

These points lead to two conclusions. First, some of the sensitive apparatus of local democracy needs to be injected into the administration of the nationally financed parts of the Health Service. In his book *In Place of Fear*[1] Aneurin Bevan admitted that the lack of democracy was one important mistake made when the service was set up; to correct it should be easier in the future. The new enlarged local authorities soon to emerge from the Royal Commission on Local Government will not, one hopes, possess the stigma which existing local authorities had in the eyes of the medical hierarchy in 1948 and which resulted in the birth of those unnatural twin offspring—the Regional Hospital Boards and the Local Executive Councils.

Secondly, any government, but especially a Labour one, should always remember that the Health Service needs more positive government protection and development than the other public services, and that a policy for health should always spring from a constant reassessment of needs: it is not enough simply to fight for small improvements in an out-of-date structure; there must come a radical reorganization of health service administration about which more will be said later.

My purpose in drawing this contrast between politically neutral

[1] Heinemann, 1952.

insurance-based financial benefits and specifically socialist services provided by the state is not to imply that one group deserves a higher priority than the other. It is simply that most Labour thinking over the past ten years has gone towards rescuing National Insurance benefits from the pathetic depths to which they had sunk and introducing machinery to keep them at a realistic level; the problem of the next ten years will be to rethink the 'services' side of the Welfare State. This rethinking will come at a time when all the Tory pressure will be to dismantle these services, leaving them solely for the elderly, low-paid workers and the chronic sick. They will produce arguments which from a purely economic standpoint may appear to make sense, and instance the social security systems of many E.E.C. countries, notably West Germany, to back up their case. Their 1966 election campaign was only the beginning. The case has now been restated in a far more extreme form in a Conservative Political Centre pamphlet by Dr Wyndham Davies. It will be left to us not only to put the arguments for a comprehensive national service based on social justice and social cohesion, but also to show how existing services can be reshaped so that they do not remain the victims of perpetual financial stringency. As we have seen it is never easy to finance a social service out of taxation; English employers resent far more a forty per cent corporation tax which goes towards maintaining the Health Service than do their German counterparts the comparatively far heavier burden of social service payroll contributions which they have to bear. Yet the principle of national taxation for a service with national standards is important; and it is not the method of finance which is responsible for the broken down state of the service at the moment.

A great deal can be done to solve many of the problems of the social services by a basic rethinking of the role of their scarce personnel and the methods by which they are administered. The problem is as much about manpower as it is about money, and severe organization and methods treatment is called for from top to bottom. I can do no more than suggest the sort of direction which reorganization and reform should take.

First, the doctors. Are they trained in the right way? Are they used in an efficient and rational manner when they are trained? Have we got enough of them? The answers to all these questions are obviously 'no'. The doctors have firm control of training in their own hands and only make pathetic tiny adjustments to the deadweight of the study of anatomy and physiology on the one hand and that of obscure rare diseases which they will never meet on the other. These clog up a course which is hardly long enough for the future specialist but yet too long and ill-balanced for the future general practitioner. Half the patients in hospital are in mental hospitals, yet time devoted even to elementary psychiatry is minute, while all the sociological aspects of medicine, which are more essential than anything else to the future general practitioner, are virtually ignored. Once in general practice they have to spend too much time as service clerks for the hospital and National Insurance systems and too little practising medicine. Old-fashioned trade unionist pressure from the B.M.A. on the Willink Committee in 1958 has ensured that even without the present emigration we would still have an overall shortage of doctors which, unlike the teacher shortage, cannot be cured within the foreseeable future owing to the extreme length of the training course. Clearly we have a situation where everyone suffers, the doctors as much as the general public, and now that the targets of the National Plan are dwindling, there is little hope that the problems will be solved by a massive injection of public money.

What is needed is thorough-going reform in the shape of some form of package deal—a Doctors' Charter that really means something. We need agreements to rationalize and make more efficient the use of a general practitioner's time and the content of his course of training, matched by a promise of a substantial increase of his status vis-à-vis the rest of the profession by giving him, if he wants it, full access to facilities and some right to practice his medicine within the hospital service. General practitioner involvement within the hospital service is growing; nearly ten per cent of the patients who use the diagnostic services are sent by their G.P. But when it comes to actually practising medicine the picture is not so good. Only ten per cent of all G.P.s are involved in General Practitioner Hospital Units like those at East Birmingham and Queen Elizabeth Hospital, Welwyn, where wards are specially set aside for them: and with the amalgamation of hospitals into larger units the problem will grow more acute. But it must be tackled, for though to most medical politicians this sort of package seems a pipe dream, it is generally agreed that general practitioners' present complaints concern quite as much their isolation and inability to practise good medicine as their rate of remuneration.

The real stumbling block in the way of reform of this kind is not so much monolithic obstruction by professional bodies or indifference in Whitehall, as the vicious circle within which any government is caught up whenever it attempts to reform any part of the social services. To satisfy general practitioners it would be necessary to recast the system of granting medical certificates (which would involve the Ministry of Social Security), to bring together general practitioners with regional hospital boards (which would involve consultants and hospital administrators), and to offer them the services of Health Visitors as auxiliaries (which would involve local authority health committees and nurses' organizations). All these pressure groups in turn would demand their particular reform (always costing public money) as the price of any compromise, and the great danger would always be that a mountainous operation would end up by producing a mouse of reform. The modern sacred doctrine of consultation is often carried to absurd lengths.

Moreover where doctors are concerned there are special difficulties: it is a profession in which both power and financial rewards are absurdly orientated towards its senior members. Single general practitioners exploit their assistants, partnerships their junior members. The recent formation of the Hospital Doctors' Association and the unrest of the university clinical teachers are manifestations of the extent to which the juniors feel dominated by their elderly well-to-do big brothers. A Labour Minister carrying out this sort of reform would need to be a sort of super-Bevan, willing to tread on innumerable toes, someone knowing where he wanted to go but with a healthy disrespect for the top echelons of the medical profession. I once unwisely mentioned a consultant in a tone of some awe to a former chairman of a regional hospital board. 'Consultants?' he said, 'I've appointed them and I've sacked them. They don't worry me.' A useful sort of attitude to have in an operation of this kind.

For the problem of reorganization of personnel does not end with the doctors. The Seebohm Committee is at the moment struggling with the problems of redeploying social workers on a rational basis, and coming up against its own set of departmental jealousies. In this field (with the aid of some solid socialist prodding from Lord Longford in *Crime a Challenge*[1] and Peggy Jay in her Fabian

[1] Published by the Labour Party, 1964.

pamphlet[1]) thought is being applied to this new profession just in time to prevent the sort of structural hierarchical arthritis from which the medical profession suffers. Social workers are essentially the service engineers of the Welfare State: they are there to make sure that opportunities are not missed and that benefits go to those who need them, not solely to the wide-awake middle class who know how to apply for them. They have a clearly defined job to do which should cover the whole range of the social services, but they are in danger of slipping into all the hierarchical and departmental divisions from which the doctors suffer. Already child care officers are on a pay scale considerably in excess of other social workers doing comparable jobs and are well on the way to becoming the 'consultants' of the profession, while their poor relations, the 'general practitioner' education welfare officers, feel their inferior status acutely. Training is developing, but along separate tracks with little chance of sidestepping from one department into another. Moreover with the supply from the various forms of training not nearly great enough, we have all the elements of a crisis in the social work field in the future. As with the doctors, the only solution lies in strong government action which plans future needs, ensures an adequate supply of trained workers and co-ordinates functions and administration to prevent overlapping. The fact that three Ministries, (the Home Office, Health and Social Security) are all angling for the responsibility does not increase the prospects of positive action in this field.

Co-ordination of the functions of professional workers, then, is one important priority over the next decade; but there is little hope of making progress on this front unless co-ordination of the whole administration of the Welfare State goes hand in hand with it. Nor should this be seen as a mere tidying-up operation, a procedure to be dealt with administratively on an *ad hoc* basis over the next decade. The Welfare State, because it grew up under radical pressure against bitter opposition, exists in fragments, the result of a series of hard fought compromises. It is a positive socialist task to weld it into an efficient and cohesive whole. The first and most obvious reform is to unify the tripartite division of the Health Service at local and regional level. As we have seen, the regional

[1] *The Family and the Social Services* (Fabian Tract no. 359: the Fabian Society, 1965).

hospital boards and the local health executive councils were created by Aneurin Bevan in his efforts to play off against one another and finally to appease the consultants and the general practitioners. The regional boards, some of which in the first place were given Labour chairmen and a reasonably representative composition, have now drifted back to being very much the preserve of the leisured 'do-gooders'. Their job is basically to allocate scarce resources and settle quarrels between the hospital administrators (another underdeveloped profession) and the doctors. Being appointed rather than elected, they have not the means and often not the will to exert loud public pressure when they feel the service is being starved. So the hospital service gets the worst of nearly every world: no public representatives to fight for more money and give some social direction to policy; aggrieved consultants who feel that the board is always siding with their natural enemies, the hospital secretaries and administrators; a great shortage of junior hospital staff in the teaching hospitals, caught between the university and the hospital and usually exploited by both (while in the non-teaching hospitals almost all are people coming from the Commonwealth who are getting experience before going home); and finally bewildered consumers who do not know who to complain to about rudeness, appointment systems that do not work, and endless waiting.

Wholly divorced from this system of control and administration are the general practitioners, who negotiate their contracts direct with the Ministry, but have health executives as their nominal overlords, set up in 1948 as the only formula they would accept. As we have seen, their principal aim was to avoid being employed by the local council—rather like the public school headmaster who, when opting for direct grant from the Ministry rather than from the local council, said he did not mind being swallowed by a lion, but was damned if he was going to be eaten by the rats. Finally the rest of the Health Service, public health, preventative work, midwives, health visitors and ambulances are run by local authority health committees. The answer is to form area health boards, with elected members and associated in some way with the new larger units of local government which will emerge from the Royal Commission. Bringing together the administration of these different sectors would produce nothing but good; and the elimination of blatant overlapping and the introduction of more medical teamwork should enable valuable resources to be diverted to the improvement of the quality of the service.

The current dissatisfaction among general practitioners, who ought to form the hub of the Health Service, is not wholly concerned with money; they feel frustration at having to spend their time on trivial details while being compelled to refer any interesting cases which crop up to their hospital colleagues. There are three major reforms, conditional on administrative unification and co-operation, which would all bring major benefits. The first is that the new Ministry of Social Security should greatly extend or even perhaps do away with the period within which a doctor's note is required for sickness benefit. The number of people who would take advantage of this would be by and large those who do so already—most general practitioners are far too busy to look closely enough into alleged illnesses; if responsibility were taken off the general practitioners the Ministry could strengthen its own machinery for keeping malingerers in check, and this would also eliminate the bad blood caused between doctor and patient when the National Insurance doctor after a full examination is forced flatly to deny the certificate issued by a general practitioner after a cursory one. General practitioners are overworked anyway; there is no real reason why they should also have to bear the brunt of running the National Health Insurance scheme. Freeing them from this sort of chore would allow them to get on with the job of getting people well more quickly and sending them back to work.

Secondly, administrative reorganization ought to be able to involve a certain number of general practitioners in hospital work. The shortage of hospital doctors is in many ways far more critical than that of general practitioners, especially in the smaller outlying non-teaching hospitals, many of which are staffed entirely by Commonwealth or other foreign doctors; quite apart from the language problem which this poses there are now distinct signs that the Commonwealth Governments are changing their attitude and are ready to take drastic action to prevent their nationals practising on such a scale in Britain and other overseas countries. If they all went home tomorrow the Health Service would collapse; the only alternative auxiliary supply lies among the more highly qualified and energetic of the country's general practitioners. Increasing efforts must be made to use their talents within the hospital service.

Thirdly, the medical manpower in the public Health Service would be enabled under unified administration to play its part in freeing the general practitioner from some of his less appropriate tasks. This would need give and take on both sides: the general practitioners would have to accept the principle of teamwork and put genuine trust in the health visitors and social workers on whom might devolve much of the signing of certificates and the solution of personal problems with which the doctors are overburdened at the moment, while at the same time the public health hierarchy of doctors must shed their suspicions of general practitioners and the tendency towards personal empire-building to which some of them can be prone. With goodwill, the concept of the medical team should be able to replace that of the lonely doctor with the Gladstone bag, just as in scientific development the research team has long ago taken over from the slightly mad professor, alone in his laboratory, peering at his apparatus through his spectacles.

It is easy to see the advantages which a unified Health Service would bring at ground level. How would it work at the top? The great objection of all general practitioners to submitting themselves to reform on these lines would be one of falling into the hands of their twin ogres, the 'ignorant' non-medical local councillor, and the Medical Officer of Health. Doctors in public health are commonly looked upon (quite mistakenly) by their practising colleagues in much the same light as army officers who have taken refuge in Staff College; men and women looking for an easy, quiet, undemanding, nine-to-five existence. Administrative control of a reformed general practitioner service there would have to be; but it would be of the greatest importance to find someone quite new to take charge who had solid experience of general practice and commanded wide support in the area. The other great fear— democratic control—should recede a great deal with new enlarged area authorities. We have also seen how much in pure financial terms education has benefited from local democracy. The post-war school building rate is immensely more impressive than that for hospital building; and general practitioners are likely to obtain better equipped premises to work in from local councils with some responsibility for what they do, than they will ever achieve in the future by negotiating the necessary increase in their contracts. Indeed a contracted rather than a salaried service was one of the most dubious advantages which the hierarchy imposed upon general practice in 1948, as the emphasis on fringe benefits both in the Doctor's Charter and in the new contract is making clear; and quite apart from an increased programme of Health Centres which new enlarged responsibilities would encourage local authorities to build, they already possess in their school clinics and welfare centres much equipment which is not being adequately used and from which tax and ratepayers deserve an economic return.

To unify the Health Service under democratically controlled area health boards in this way would involve an administrative upheaval quite as drastic as that which took place in 1948; but the little-by-little Fabian approach has failed: co-operation, in areas where it should take place, is often non-existent, while a few scattered isolated health centres make a mockery of the high hopes for the future which existed when the Health Service was launched. Moreover revolution in administering the Health Service on an area level begs all sorts of questions about the administration of the whole Welfare State at national level. At present, as we have seen, the Ministry of Health is in charge of the Health Service, the Ministry of Social Security controls welfare payments, and the Home Office is making a strong bid to take responsibility for all personal social workers. This tripartite division has sensible historical origins but its disadvantages are beginning to become apparent. A merger between the Ministry of Health and the Ministry of Social Security is a prerequisite of fundamental reform, with the new Minister promoted to Secretary of State with the right to speak for the Welfare State as a whole, both in the country and in the cabinet. This clearly cannot come just yet; the Ministry of Social Security has only just swallowed National Assistance which it will need some time to digest, but this merger must be the next step if Britain's Labour Government is going to create in the Welfare State an adequate standard of provision which continues to improve with the growth of the gross national product. The Welfare State has plenty of passive supporters within the cabinet; what it needs is an enlightened apostle dedicated to its expansion and development.

Rethinking and reorganization at every level can bring great benefits; but we must not simply be animated by the vision of the restoration of standards which increasing efficiency can bring. We also need a vision which both looks ahead towards the development of the Welfare State in the light of changing social and religious attitudes, and also has a wide enough angle to notice how much other government action impinges on its services. First, development: many of the gaps in the Welfare State exist in areas which are heavily overlaid by religious dogma and spurious assumptions that they are in some way connected with morality. We have at last brought ourselves to distribute welfare benefits to those who would once have been classed as 'the undeserving poor'; we have got away from the nineteenth century idea that helping them makes them lazier. But when it comes to putting contraceptive provision on the Health Service, or liberalizing the abortion laws or generally increasing the money available for homes for unmarried mothers or counselling about personal relationships and family planning in our schools and colleges, there are still far too many people who imply that helping people in this sphere makes them more immoral or even more promiscuous. In particular these moral overtones rear their head in the Ministry of Social Security rules about cohabitation, which often cause great injustice to separated, divorced or unmarried mothers and prevent them from settling down gradually again into a more stable relationship. The Welfare State must go on developing into a truly comprehensive service; we must over the next decade shake off the last Victorian vestiges of a service which dispenses charity to the morally and spiritually deserving. It is quite as important to help to promote the quality of personal life as that of physical health.

Secondly, we must not only continue to develop personal services, but we must do everything in the context of the whole developing social life of the community. If we ever do get a Minister of Social Welfare, it will be his job to see that all decisions taken in other spheres—housing and planning in particular—tie in with his own policy. At the moment the incidence of housing subsidies— both the direct Exchequer and the rate subsidies for council house tenants and the tax relief on mortgage interest for owner-occupiers —are unplanned and often indiscriminate. The owner-occupier on low wages and the council tenant with a large family in an area with no sort of rent rebate scheme come off particularly badly. These subsidies are part of the Welfare State and there is a duty to make them as fair as possible; the Government's option mortgage scheme will help, but to solve the problem completely, it will be necessary to recast the whole system of subsidies both to tenants and to owner-occupiers.

Another area where a policy is urgently needed is the housing of the elderly. A very few are in the comparative luxury of recently built old people's homes, while others are kept in barely smartened up former workhouses; some are in specially built old people's flats or bungalows, far more live on their own in a three- or four-bedroomed council house which a family desperately needs: some live in old privately rented property, others (before Labour's introduction of rate rebates) struggled to pay their rates on their own house out of an inadequate pension. Although some get the benefit of a warden system or Meals on Wheels, others do not. Admittedly the old National Assistance and the new Social Security supplementary payments make some attempt to equalize the gross disparities in rent, where the old people are able to swallow their pride and apply for them; in spite of this, there is not enough effort to ensure that each degree of need is matched by appropriate provision, and there is often a sharp inequality in the amount of public subsidy which different old people receive.

A policy is also needed for 'problem' families. Spasmodic and occasional payment of rent by such families can cost the housing department, and through them the community, between £100 and £200 a year, and for this reason evictions take place from time to time. The fact that, once evicted, the family in care can cost the community anything up to £2,000 a year tends to be ignored by some of those in authority. All these anomalies spring from the fact that housing departments are there to administer houses not people and are tied down by rigid rules about keeping their accounts in balance. Housing is now such a substantial element in any family budget, that subsidies connected with it and methods of financing it need far more scrutiny from a social point of view than they receive at the moment.

The policies of the planners also impinge far more upon the Welfare State than they often realize. The allocation of land for housing as between the council and private builders, the distribution of old people's houses and flats throughout the community, the planning of communities with proper provision for neighbourhood activities are all decisions which can make or break the Welfare State in twenty or thirty years time. So, too, are the problems of areas of high immigration from Asia and the West Indies, the integration of these immigrants into both council estates and hitherto white owner-occupied areas to ensure their even distribution throughout the whole community and the avoidance of Chicago and Los Angeles type ghettos. When an area of a city becomes depressed and is left with only two or three general practitioners, each with lists of five or six thousand patients, or has discipline problems in its local secondary modern or comprehensive school, the unperceptive start to talk of our health and education services breaking down. In fact these services are being asked to bear the burden of the failure of the nation to plan the development of that particular community many years earlier — a burden it is often quite unreasonable to expect any service to put up with. A Social Welfare Minister with the resources to point to the exact consequences of planning decisions in terms of social expenditure, and able to give information and instructions to local councils on these lines, could enormously raise the social (as distinct from the general aesthetic) quality of planning in Britain. Town planners tend to be drawn from the ranks of architects, geographers and economists; like the medical profession they need a solid dose of social science both to remind them of their obligations to the community and to help them get their social engineering right. The Conservatives, after two election defeats, are not wasting time in recrimination; they are trying to build up a new philosophy of the 'hard' competitive state. It is up to us in the Labour Party, not only to clear our minds about the compassionate Welfare State in which we believe, but to show how it can be financially viable and be linked to an expanding economy, before the General Election in 1970 or 1971. For if we fail, especially with the standards and quality of the Health Service which is our own especial creation, if 1970 and 1971 see a further vast growth in B.U.P.A. schemes and private medicine (as many people believe they will) then we shall be doing nothing more than preparing the ground in which the New Toryism will flourish. If we are going to deserve to win the next general election we must begin as a matter of very real urgency to put the inner sanctum of our own house in order.

© 1967 BY CHRISTOPHER PRICE

Planning for the Population of the Future

GERRY FOWLER

1. The Problem of An Expanding Population

> In the last 70 years . . . the birth-rate has fallen to the point where the population now shows little growth . . .
>
> Unless the birth-rate suddenly shows an entirely new trend, a decade of high spending would leave the position here [in social investment, including housing] very much eased.
>
> C. A. R. Crosland, *The Future of Socialism*.[1]

In 1956, the year in which Mr Crosland published his book, the birth-rate in Britain suddenly began to rise from the plateau on which it seemed to have settled after the peak of the immediate post-war years. It has continued to rise ever since. The Government Actuary's forecasts of future population have moved up with it; his 1964 estimate of the increase in population by 1981 was already twenty per cent higher than the one he had produced two years before. It now seems likely that the rate of population growth for the rest of the century will be two-and-a-half times that of the past thirty-five years. The 1965 estimate of the Government Actuary for the total population in the year 2000 was 74,660,000 — an increase of nearly 20 million above its present level. Even if the birth-rate were to fall again, a large part of this growth is now bound to occur, merely because there will be a rapid rise in the numbers of those of marriageable age from the mid-1970s onwards.

Many of our past plans have now been overtaken by the rise in the birth-rate. Thus, Abercrombie's Greater London Plan of 1944 and the post-war Green Belt policy were based upon the assumption that the problem lay in the distribution of a *static* population. Even

[1] Jonathan Cape, 1956.

the North-West Study, published in 1965, used 1962 estimates of future population, and to this extent was out-of-date when it was published. Douglas Jay, in his book *Socialism and the New Society*,[1] published in 1962, devotes a chapter to the problems of world population growth, but says nothing of the British situation. He does at least suggest that we need many more new and expanded towns. Crosland did not, and his suggestion that a decade of high spending would 'very much ease' the need for heavy social investment is now palpably false. Here then is perhaps the greatest problem of domestic political planning facing us, and one with which too few socialists have yet come to grips — how to cope with a rapidly rising population.

The difficulties are further exacerbated by a steady decline in the size of households. Between the 1951 and 1961 censuses, the average size of private households inside the London conurbation fell from 3·02 to 2·85 persons. Over the same period, throughout England and Wales, the population rose by six per cent — but the number of households went up by twelve per cent. Thus the National Plan[2] estimated that for the next ten years the number of households in the country would increase by about 140,000 a year, and the South-East Study[3] that up to 1981 a further 400,000 dwellings would be required in the London area to account for declining household size and population growth alone, while only 150,000 would be needed to eliminate overcrowding in London. Both forecasts may well prove an under-estimate, but they give some indication of the scale of building required, not to deal with bad housing conditions, but merely in order to stand still. It may be that in the short term the decline in household size will be apparently arrested, or slowed; the increasing numbers of small children should ensure this. But the tendency for young people, on marriage or even before, to set up a separate establishment from that of their parents, and for the retired of all classes to maintain a separate home from that of their children will no doubt continue.

At the same time, there is a continuing demand for higher housing standards. Too many local authorities and private builders still regard the Parker Morris standards as a maximum rather than as a minimum; but steady governmental pressure is bound to lead eventually to almost universal conformity to these standards. If we are to take account of people's preferences, we cannot aim at a

[1] Longmans, 1962. [2] Cmnd. 2764 (H.M.S.O., 1965). [3] H.M.S.O., 1964, page 32.

maximum housing density of more than thirteen or fourteen dwellings per acre over any sizeable area. Most people still prefer a house with a reasonable garden space to a flat or maisonette, and there is little doubt that such dwellings provide better family living conditions. Thus, as standards rise, building costs will also rise, and we shall also find that the demand for housing land cannot often or for long be restrained by a policy of high density building.

It is well known that for a long time now the proportion of people above retiring age in the population has been increasing, as the average expectancy of life has risen. But it is young people who move most readily. Thus, as the population rapidly increases, especially from the mid-1970s onwards, there is a danger that without careful planning we shall produce an increasingly sharp difference between the age-structures of the population remaining in older housing areas and that moving to newer areas, whether they be new or expanded towns, or estates on the periphery of the big cities. Such social imbalance is not only undesirable in itself, but also places a heavy burden on the local authorities responsible for the newer areas, since it is they who must provide all the community facilities required by a young population, notably in education. At the same time some such facilities in the older areas will become under-utilized.

Because of migration from the less to the more prosperous areas of the country, this same phenomenon can also be observed regionally. The Economic Planning Review of Yorkshire and Humberside (1966) points out that the net loss of population by the region, running at about 7,300 persons a year from 1951 to 1965, was mainly a loss of people of working age. This means not only a sad loss to the region of manpower often skilled, but also that the region retains a higher proportion of the retired than the nation as a whole. The higher the migration from a region, the more marked is this tendency likely to be; in the North-West region the population aged between fifteen and retiring age actually declined by two per cent from 1951 and 1961, although it rose by two per cent in Great Britain as a whole. This is undoubtedly one of the reasons why average family incomes were in 1961–3 fifteen per cent below the national average in Scotland and the North of England.

Continuing migration between the regions clearly makes more difficult any rational solution to the problem of distributing an expanding population. Between 1951 and 1965 the civilian population of Great Britain rose by nine per cent. But the proportion of them living in Scotland fell from 10·5 per cent to 9·8 per cent and in the North-West from 13·2 per cent to 12·7 per cent. Unemployment in the cotton areas of the latter region was relieved almost entirely by migration; this resulted in a lower rate of natural increase here than in the country as a whole. Migration thus has a cumulative effect on population distribution. The population of mid-Wales is only 200,000; but it is falling by nearly a thousand a year.

There is nothing to suggest that this drift of population would cease of its own accord, or without more powerful government intervention than we have had hitherto. A far higher proportion of the industries showing fast growth rates are situated in the South-East than in the less prosperous regions. The congestion caused by this drift in the cities of the South, especially London, is notorious. But what is in many ways a more sinister phenomenon has recently appeared. In the decade between the 1951 census and the 1961 census the South-East as a whole gained 600,000 jobs, while the rest of England and Wales gained only 400,000. But the number of jobs in Inner London scarcely rose at all, and the number in the whole of Greater London rose much less than the national average. The dramatic rise was in the rest of the South-East, beyond the Green Belt, where the increase was nearly sixteen per cent compared with an average for England and Wales of five per cent. Even towns as far from London as Bournemouth, Ipswich and Cambridge have been showing very rapid growth, as also has the Southampton-Portsmouth urban complex. In Oxford, that onetime city of dreaming spires, there was a rise in employment of about seventeen per cent in the five years from 1959 to 1964 alone. Even if the Green Belt remains totally sacrosanct, the possibility now arises of 'conurbations beyond conurbations', first beyond London and at a later date in the West Midlands. Dr Peter Hall's vision, or nightmare, of a super Los Angeles, spreading from Southampton to Northampton, and embracing most of the land to the east of this line, may be nearer to realization than most of us care to think.

Whatever the deterrent effects of congestion, it is unlikely that migration will ever 'work itself out' naturally. One reason is that modern manufacturing industry is increasingly 'market-oriented'. Electricity has replaced the older sources of power, and the raw materials used are decreasingly those supplied by the older extractive industries. Thus, industry gravitates to the regions of heavy market density, and in this way migration to such regions naturally tends to multiply itself. This process will be given an extra boost if Britain enters the Common Market, where proximity to the markets of north-west Europe will become of prime importance. Even the construction of the Channel Tunnel will have a marked effect; already there is a proposal for a rapid build-up of population in the Ashford area.

Further, the most rapid growth in the post-war period has been in the service industries. But services expand most rapidly where population and income are increasing fastest. Significantly, the rate of employment growth in the distributive trades in the North-West fell well below the national average after 1959, although it had been slightly higher earlier. Each family which migrates creates a new service need in the area to which it migrates; again migration multiplies itself. Provision may even out-run demand in expanding areas, on the expectation of further growth.

Finally, a deterrent to the expansion of industry, both manufacturing and service, and an incentive to continued migration, is the depressing environment, especially the urban environment, of many of the less prosperous regions. Even if a manufacturer is willing to move to such an area, his key workers are often less willing, especially since such a move usually entails a drop in the standard of social and cultural amenities as well.

The answer to this problem does not then lie solely in increased financial incentives to manufacturing industry to move to the less prosperous regions. Nor does it lie in an old-fashioned new-town policy, operating purely on an intra-regional level; it is now clear that the first generation of new towns, developments of the 'satellite town' concept, were sited much too close to London. Nor, finally, is a satisfactory answer possible in the present fragmented structure of regional planning. To give an example: while the South-East Study assumed that the tendency of the South-East to attract the population of other regions would be largely arrested[1] and the West Midlands Study that there would be no net immigration, the North-West Study[2] assessed the needs of the region on the basis of a continuation of the average rates of net inward and outward migration obtaining from 1956 to 1964.[3]

[1] H.M.S.O., 1964, page 22.   [2] H.M.S.O., 1965.   [3] H.M.S.O., 1965, page 20.

Further, unless migration is arrested, an incomes policy is unlikely to succeed for any length of time. 'Wages drift' is very largely a result of the tremendous demands on the labour market in the south of England. We are all familiar with the proposition that wages in the motor-car industry are very high; but many are unaware that they are *not* strikingly high in car factories situated outside the southern half of England — at Linwood, say, or Bathgate. Failure to operate some sort of incomes policy successfully would have the most severe economic consequences for Britain. When the enormous and rising costs of congestion and delay are thrown into the balance, it is clear that there are sound economic reasons for making every effort to arrest regional migration.

Even within the regions, too little attention has been paid to the problem of rural depopulation. Except in South-East England, there has been steady movement of population from the rural areas most remote from the cities and increasing development of once-rural areas within commuting distance, immediately beyond the Green Belt. The West Midlands Study[1] proposes deliberately to speed up the latter process; it calls for 'a wide range of infillings and modest expansions which are within commuting range of the conurbation'. This process is called the 'thickening up of the settlement pattern'. Yet there is no attempt to see this 'thickening' in terms of transport generation, shopping facilities, recreational needs, social and welfare services, or its implications for the Green Belt.

It has become customary for politicians in recent years to speak of improving 'the quality of life'. We shall not do this if we permit ever-increasing sprawl — sometimes ugly, always adding to congestion and discomfort — in the South-East and Midlands, while other regions make strenuous efforts to run on the spot, or effect relatively marginal improvements. Nor shall we do it if we permit the life-blood to be sucked out of our genuine rural villages. It is time to show that such phrases are not merely political propaganda. Faced with a rapidly increasing population, we must make the decisions now which will determine whether or not this is a tolerable country to live in for Britons of the twenty-first century.

2. *The Solution*
(i) Some of the growth in population over the next thirty years can no doubt be accommodated by 'infilling' in the large cities and

[1] H.M.S.O., 1965.

towns, and more may have to be by a 'thickening-up' of the pattern of settlement in the commuter belts. More again may settle in relatively small developments in country towns and villages if the right conditions for growth are provided. But the rest must be settled in new towns or in large expansions of existing towns under the Towns Development Act. My own guess would be that we should cater for at least 10 million people in this way — that is to say, provide $3\frac{1}{2}$ million or more dwellings. We have made a late start; there has always existed a case for more new towns on social and economic grounds, and the rise in the birth-rate was apparent at least by the late 'fifties. The long gap between the designation of the 'first generation' of new towns and the inception of the second in the mid-sixties has greatly increased our problems, not least because it always takes several years to get a new town 'off the ground', while the basic plans are drawn, and the drainage and water systems and road pattern are established.

We should not be deterred by the cost of such schemes. Even a moderate-sized plan may cost many millions of pounds in direct public investment over a twenty-year period. But this may well be cheaper than any alternative: extensions to already large cities, and even extensive redevelopment schemes which include too many shops and offices designed to yield a rapid apparent financial return, usually lead to the need for more complex traffic and car-parking systems, which are often very expensive. Further, new towns are proving an ultimately profitable form of investment; the accumulated revenue surplus of the present new towns is now about 3 million pounds, and that of the 'first generation' is increasing rapidly. There is rapid appreciation of invested capital too; the government's investment of 17 million pounds in industrial and commercial development at Crawley and Hemel Hempstead has produced assets now valued by the New Towns Commission at about 27 million pounds. We should, in calculating cost, take our new towns as a whole, and regard the profits from the established and successful towns as a cushion for any transitional losses elsewhere.

There are certainly cost advantages in building much bigger new towns than we have done so far. What studies have been undertaken indicate that the cost per person decreases as the population of the town approaches a quarter of a million, and that in the expansion of a large existing town, it is relatively cheaper to double its size than to increase it by half. Where the existing communications of an area are good, but under-utilized, it is desirable to settle enough people to provide for heavy use of both roads and railways. When communications are bad, and new public investment is required in trunk roads or motorways, we must again ensure the fullest use of these expensive facilities.

There are, of course, dangers here. If, in order to satisfy these criteria and to provide a 'counter-magnet' to the nearest conurbation, we stimulate too large and rapid a growth in an area, we may find that subsequent 'natural' growth generates all those problems of inadequate social facilities, local congestion, and overstrained external communications with which we are familiar in our existing cities. A popular idea at the moment is the 'city-region', comprising a number of large and medium-sized towns within a region perhaps twenty-five miles across which complement each other's employment opportunities and shopping, social and cultural amenities. But we so far have little experience of 'sub-regional' planning, especially in transport; what will be the cross-traffic flows generated by such a pattern of towns? Nor has enough attention been paid to the danger that such a development will gradually 'conurbate', as the Black Country has done. In many regions therefore it may prove preferable to develop along radial corridors stretching outwards from the existing cities, often in a direction which will require new or improved transport facilities. But if this is done, the decision must be taken at the outset to build enough, sufficiently large, new towns, to justify the expenditure incurred in providing these facilities.

The new towns which have recently been designated or are likely shortly to be designated scarcely begin to form a national pattern of development. In the South-East, sites have rightly been chosen which will permit large-scale expansion at a distance from London sufficient to allow the new town to become a 'counter-magnet'. No one would quarrel with the choice of Ipswich, ideally situated if we enter the Common Market, and serving a large rural hinterland, or Peterborough, which may bring new life to the north-western parts of East Anglia. But Northampton and Bletchley, with their associated smaller expansions, are subject to the dangers just described. At its southern end this complex is not far from the ever-expanding London commuter-belt and when one remembers the other smaller developments already planned, or occurring unplanned, between this area and Southampton, itself probably the site of another very large city, the prospect of a Los Angeles megalopolis in the South-East may not seem too remote. In the whole of this region, as can be seen most clearly from the South-East Study, we are in danger of settling excess population anywhere and everywhere where the immediate disadvantages are not excessive, without regard to the long-term development pattern of the region or of the country.

There is still no new town in the South-West, despite the urgent need of the remoter parts of this region for new life and employment, nor in Yorkshire or Lincolnshire. In the North-West, new towns are projected at Leyland/Chorley (possibly of 500,000), and at Warrington (of 200,000), as well as at Runcorn and Skelmersdale. The first seems too close to Preston and some of the northern cotton towns, the second to Liverpool and Manchester. Here again we are in danger of so 'thickening up' the settlement pattern that ultimately a wide area of once separate towns will conurbate; the North-West as a whole already has the highest population density of any region.

The East Midlands Study[1] does not propose any new towns at all in the northern part of the region. But it points in striking fashion to the danger that by the year 2000 the whole of the Nottingham-Derby-Chesterfield area will have grown into one vast sprawling city. The parallel between the present settlement pattern in that area and that of Birmingham, Wolverhampton, and the Black Country in 1900 is so close as to be sinister. This time we must not shut the stable door only after the horse has bolted; we should plan now for population dispersal before an unmanageable and congested conurbation exists. The lesson is that such projects require a national rather than a regional decision.

In the West Midlands it is perhaps clearest of all that a national plan for population settlement is required. Decisions about the development of the Dawley-Wellington-Oakengates area and its future communications with the conurbation, must be made in the context of a wider decision whether or not to continue expansion along a 'western axis'. This entails a determination now whether and when to expand Shrewsbury, and to begin a new town in mid-Wales. The services provided by the former, if it is expanded, should complement those of Dawley. The latter is in a different

[1] H.M.S.O., 1966.

planning region, and a different minister, the Secretary of State for Wales, must decide whether it shall be built; yet the report of the consultants appointed to make recommendations to him makes it clear that a new town makes sense only in a West Midlands planning context.

It is clear enough from this interaction that a long-term national population plan is needed to prevent excessive concentration in already overcrowded areas, to make sure that developments in different regions marry with each other, and possibly to develop some of the more sparsely populated areas of the country—not just mid-Wales, but also, for example, the far South-West, and the Scottish Border country. The economic planning study of the Northern Region[1] suggests that the North could well absorb some excess population from other regions, but no other region has present plans for exporting people in this way. The South-East Study, indeed, saw large-scale developments in other parts of the country merely as efforts by those regions to retain population.[2] Even so, it has already been necessary to recommend big town expansions for Londoners outside the boundaries of that region, in order to ensure that they will be distant enough from London to be effective 'counter-magnets'.

It is arguable that in England and Wales at least, people live where they do in the twentieth century largely because of the pattern of past agricultural settlement disturbed only by movements dictated by the location of mineral resources during the Industrial Revolution. Industrial location decisions take a long time to work themselves out. National planning, or its absence, today will affect the pattern of settlement two or three centuries hence.

We have been promised[3] a special review by the Department of Economic Affairs designed to lead to the formulation of the requisite long-term plans, but it is not obvious that such an exercise can be successful within the present governmental and administrative framework. Most ministries are expanding their fields of vision, and employing more planning experts, but each jealously guards its own sphere of interests. The Department of Economic Affairs and the Ministry of Transport may each need their own central and regional planning units, but each should operate within a framework of agreed principles, standards and targets. Meanwhile, some

---

[1] *Challenge of the Changing North* (H.M.S.O., 1966), page 45.
[2] Page 66.   [3] *National Plan*, Cmnd. 2764 (H.M.S.O., 1965), page 97.

THE POPULATION OF THE FUTURE   165

government planning is still concerned only with the present population distribution, ignoring even decisions already taken. The Ministry of Health's compilation of local authority programmes for their Health and Welfare Services for the next ten years contains population predictions which are reached by assuming that, within each region, the change which occurred between 1951 and 1964 in the proportion of home population residing in each local authority area will continue at the same rate until 1976. Yet it is already clear that some of these areas will grow much more rapidly than they have done in the past, and it is hence impossible accurately to compare the scale of provision for different areas ten years hence.

It is perhaps in transport planning that there is the greatest need for co-ordination and foresight. It is pointless to plan new developments unless they are provided with good communications with their main markets from the outset: above all, it is doubly difficult to attract industry or people to them. The early development of Peterlee New Town was hampered by the inadequacy of both its road and rail links. The Ministry of Transport has now accepted the need to hand over a block grant to the New Towns Division of the Ministry of Housing for internal new-town roads; the same co-ordination is not yet apparent in providing their external links. Road congestion gets steadily worse. The number of cars on the road will double in the next ten years and is likely to treble in the next twenty-five. Increasingly, therefore, in siting new developments, the geographical distance from their markets and ports is less important than the time taken and cost involved in reaching them. But we have little information yet of the relief that could here be afforded by the development of new major ports, provided with new motorway links, or by the building of new motorways or trunk roads to and through areas at present less densely populated than others, in conjunction with the planting of new towns or cities along their route. (If we plan our new motorways to cater only for the present distribution of population, not only shall we thereby ossify that distribution but we shall probably find that we never quite keep up with the growth of traffic between ever-expanding cities.) The true cost of such schemes can only be calculated if we take account of the relief they afford to the road network elsewhere, of the delays and added transport costs they obviate, and of the duplication of existing motorways which they defer. But they must be linked to an adequate and planned population growth in the areas which they serve. The apparent logic of regional expansion can be changed by public investment in communications above all else; but it would be silly to build a motorway for a single new town. Hence a co-ordinated long-term plan is here the first essential.

What has been said of roads applies in a different way to railways also. Here the need is not to build new lines, but to decide on the basis of future rather than present population distribution which lines to close and which services to curtail or improve.

Although the case for co-ordination is clearest in the planning of communications, it is just as strong in matters under the control of other ministries. The siting of a new general hospital rests with the Regional Board and the Ministry of Health. But from the day when detailed planning begins (which may itself be years after the decision in principle is taken) eight years may elapse before the hospital is opened. At the rate of build-up required for a new town of 200,000 people, existing services will by that time be severely overstrained. With still bigger cities, they will fail. Arguably, the building of a hospital should begin before the first housing development.

The Department of Education provides an additional grant for areas of rapidly expanding population, but it provides it annually. Yet a new town of 200,000 people will need at least three new primary schools and one new comprehensive school for every year of fifteen years. Further education must expand *pari passu*. There is a strong case for building new nursery schools in such towns, since in the early years, when nearly all the female population are young mothers, there will otherwise be a shortage of female labour. What is needed here is an outline plan for educational development for fifteen or twenty years in each such town with the certainty that grants will be forthcoming for the fulfilment of this programme, whatever the variation in national provision from year to year. Without this the local authority dare not look far ahead in devising a programme for replacing inadequate facilities in other areas which may compete for scarce resources with the new development.

We might also profitably produce a sketch-map for future university building. In a rush of blood to the head stimulated by the Robbins Report, the then government sanctioned seven new universities; the former Colleges of Advanced Technology have also been raised in status. As a result there are likely to be no more new universities for several years. But the siting of future centres of higher education must be seen (as the foundation of some at least of the seven was not) as part of the regeneration of decaying areas and of the successful development of new cities. The social and cultural value to an area of a university may be as important as its direct educational impact; it may make a local theatre viable, it quickens local interest in the arts, it provides the organizers and the lecturers for a wide range of socio-educational activities. The universities have a vital role in the attainment of greater regional balance, and in the attraction of certain key workers (and hence of industry) to developing areas, as well as in producing scientists and technologists for such industry. A university may most economically serve in this way a population of between one and two millions.

What have traditionally been seen as purely local services will also affect the planning of population distribution. The prime example is water supply. The South-East Study revealed that at the end of 1963 there were no fewer than 130 separate water undertakings in the region. With such fragmentation, coherent regional planning becomes doubly difficult. One new scheme to serve one large new development may indirectly prohibit expansion elsewhere, through competition for scarce supplies. Hand-to-mouth planning inevitably leads to damage to amenities in areas whose scenic beauty is one of their principal economic assets, not just because of the tourist trade, but also in attracting immigrants. One region may seek to ensure its supply at the expense of another; how would the South-East Study's proposals for tapping the Severn catchment area fit in with the future needs of the West Midlands and Severnside itself? There is a strong case for a national water undertaking, with the resources to develop major bay or estuary schemes, and able to co-ordinate the activities of regional boards. Up to ten years may elapse between the inception of a scheme involving major works and the time when it first produces water in useful quantities. We cannot therefore afford any delay.

If inter-departmental co-operation is needed in all these fields, we must demand it also of that most independent and intractible of all departments, the Treasury. The correct fiscal policy is essential if we are to achieve regional balance; the free market has conspicuously failed to solve the problem of the distribution of population and industry over the available land. There is thus a case for regional taxes, through which the more prosperous areas would subsidize the less, or even for more narrowly local levies which would take account both of congestion and of the availability of labour. We do not seem to progress far in this direction. The Selective Employment Tax is certain to have an unintended regional effect, since it is heaviest in its incidence on those areas most dependent on services, often the most remote and least developed. Thus, it will bear hardly on the South-East, and properly so — but also on the remote South-West, increasing already high unemployment there, and encouraging migration from an area to which the government is trying to attract manufacturers with a 40 per cent investment cash grant. At the same time, it will draw relatively little revenue from the congested West Midlands. To develop some regional variation on this tax therefore seems essential.

The investment grant system is in itself excellent. Yet even here we ought to consider whether it might not be made more flexible by ranging on a scale over a much larger number of areas in which we should like new or more intensive industrial development; according to the area's position on the scale, firms would qualify for greater or lesser grant. But this cannot be done until we have a national plan for the distribution of population and industry. Flexibility is similarly needed in the Board of Trade's grant of industrial development certificates. Concentration on the development areas alone makes dispersal inside a congested region no easier. From 1945 to 1963 there was in the West Midlands a movement out of the conurbation into other parts of the region of only 20,000 jobs in manufacturing industry; at the same time, 100,000 jobs were moved from the region to other parts of the country. Certainly the less popular reception areas inside any region should be given some priority in their early years, until they can rely on their own intrinsic drawing-power. For such new towns the Board might consider the grant of certificates to one or two large firms of national importance and reputation in whatever region they are at present based, and especially if that is in the South-East. But all of this requires long-term co-ordination at the highest level, as does the steering of office development (particularly for government departments) not simply to those regions which have had less than their fair share of it, but also to the new towns and cities.

Finally, if we are to provide the 'pleasant human environment' of which the National Plan speaks,[1] both for its own sake, and to encourage the development or redevelopment of areas in which squalor and ugliness have hitherto contributed to emigration, we must make a national, and co-ordinated, effort to clear away the vile relics of our industrial past. Local authorities have not so far had much success with this task, even in the development areas, where governmental grants of 85 per cent of the cost are available for the clearance of derelict land. Outside these areas, virtually nothing has been done; in the East Midlands, clearance has scarcely begun, according to the regional economic planning council. Yet even on the most simple economic level, the use of such land for industry, housing, or recreation, avoiding the further erosion of productive farm land, would well pay the nation. Grants should be made available to any public body willing to redevelop such land, wherever it is situated. The Development Corporation at Corby, for instance, should be encouraged in its experiment of building on reclaimed iron-ore land. It would be sad if the higher cost of such building, resulting perhaps in higher industrial and domestic rents, were to deter people from moving there. But if grants are not enough, it is perhaps time that the Board of Trade made use — as it has not done so far — of its powers under the Industrial Development Act to acquire land and carry out the work needed to bring it into use or improve amenities. But so widespread is the dereliction and so long a task its removal, that it must necessarily be seen in the wider context of a national plan for the location of industry and people.

When the Department of Economic Affairs has completed its special review, we are promised long-term plans 'to ensure that new developments are planned in such a way as to make the best possible contribution to national growth and the improvement of living standards'. The last phrase is conveniently vague, and it is not clear whether these plans will be concerned solely with the economic gain to the individual (as well as the nation), or with the quality of his life, in a wider sense. Will he be able merely to buy a better house and a bigger car, or will his house be situated in an improved environment, with good communal amenities, and will he be able to drive his car on roads relatively free of congestion? We have long known that there may be some conflict between

[1] Cmnd. 2764 (H.M.S.O., 1965), page 95.

economists and planners; in this field economists must accept the occasional need for value judgments, for qualitative rather than quantitative objectives. At all events, there is an urgent need for a powerful co-ordinating ministry, administering and revising, if not now drawing up, the national population plan, building the framework within which other ministries can operate, and including among its staff not just economists and transport experts but also social planners. Such a ministry should be under a strong minister — possibly the Deputy Prime Minister.

(ii) It is certain that the very large new developments of the next thirty years whether they be formally new towns or not, will be too big for local authorities as at present constituted to handle. They have neither the expertise nor the money required for fast, large-scale projects. But it is not obvious that a large number of centrally appointed development corporations is the answer either. It may be that not only new town development, but also big schemes for urban renewal, should be undertaken by bodies with powers akin to those of the present development corporations. But the number of technically qualified and experienced staff will not multiply at the same pace as the number of corporations, if we create a separate corporation for each project. Such people are rare enough as it is; and there are increasing and competing demands for their services from local authorities, government departments, and centrally appointed agencies and commissions. Further, although the life of each of the present development corporations is fifteen or more years, not all of their staff are employed for that length of time. There may be an eight-year build-up, with an employment peak lasting no more than three or four years, followed by a period of run-down.

A case can be made for a national development corporation, perhaps springing from the present New Towns Commission, which would second working-parties for each project. But such a body would suffer from all the disadvantages of excessive size, and worse, it would be remote and insensitive to local needs and opinions. A much better solution would be regional development corporations, responsible for all save perhaps the very largest schemes in their regions. (Such projects as that for a city of 750,000 people on the Humber might still be entrusted to a separate corporation). Such a corporation would be able not only to offer continuous employment to its technical staff, but possibly also to keep together its constructional work-force, especially if the first houses in any new town were as a rule reserved for the building workers.

But the desirability of such corporations depends in part upon the future structure of local government which is at present being considered by a Royal Commission. While I do not want to anticipate its findings, something must be said about what type of structure would seem best suited to deal with the problems of population growth and regional regeneration. Certainly tinkerings with the present system will not suffice. There are too many local authorities, and most are too small. Councillors are often incapable, by reason of inexperience or insufficient leisure, of taking a long-term view. There are not enough officials of the right calibre. It is sometimes argued that all is well, since even the smaller councils in general employ 'qualified professional staff'. But what does 'qualified' mean here? An architect is not necessarily qualified as a social planner, and all too often the administration of housing is in the hands of a 'qualified' public health inspector. Further, the present boundaries separate the cities from their hinterlands, and the older urban areas from the zones of new growth which will house their overspill population. A unified approach to planning is thus impossible. An ever increasing number of services must be provided for an area larger than that of a single local authority. The only alternative to a radical recasting of local government structure is therefore the growth of more *ad hoc*, and probably non-elected, regional boards, themselves faced with problems of co-operation, or the transference of many local services to the central government.

The first tier of recast local government should cover a wide region, including both cities and their hinterlands. But such regions should not necessarily be as wide as the old standard regions, or their variants, the present economic planning regions, which often have a geographical but not a social unity. Thus, the present East Anglian planning region may be a viable unit of local government; but in the East Midlands, Northampton and its neighbouring towns have little enough in common with Nottingham and Derby, though much with Bedfordshire and North Buckinghamshire, at present in the South-East region. In the Northern region, Cumberland and Westmorland ride less easily with North-East England than they do with some of the northern parts of Lancashire, and even the extreme North-West of the West Riding. The Potteries are perhaps less at home in the West Midlands than with some neighbouring parts of other regions, and the remote South-West should not be administered from distant Bristol.

The concept of the 'city region', a city and the area which looks to it for services, both public and private, is perhaps more helpful. But even here there are difficulties. Coventry can perhaps be split from Birmingham, but not Derby from Nottingham, nor Bradford from Leeds. But there is a case for not including Sheffield with the last two cities — or Liverpool with Manchester — despite the overlap of their areas of influence, if only because the population and resources of such a region would be disproportionately large when compared to that of others. In some parts of the country there is of course no large centre; here a region, to be viable, would have to include several smaller towns and their hinterlands.

It ought to be possible to base local government for England and Wales on some twenty such regions, the greater number of them held together not simply by economic ties, but also by history and sentiment. Few need contain less than a million people, and few would be without some large centre of population as the headquarters of its regional services. But if such units are to be viable, we should be ruthless where historical boundaries conflict with modern social geography.

Regional development corporations could of course co-exist with such regional councils, acting as their agents for larger projects. But if such were the structure of the first tier of local government, it would be neater and more economical were the council to translate its own plans, and those of the central government, into action. This would have added advantage that the same agency would be responsible for new towns in the region, for developments under the Towns Development Act, and for large-scale urban renewal. In that case the council would need the wide powers which the present development corporations enjoy by the terms of the New Towns Act. There would be no greater danger to the rights of the individual than at present, provided that for any scheme where it was proposed to use such powers, it was required that a report by independent consultants be commissioned, a public enquiry held, and the sanction of the central government obtained.

No one has yet provided a satisfactory answer to the question of who should take over the physical assets of a new town when the development corporation is wound up. At present they are handed over to the New Towns Commission, but this body is inevitably somewhat remote, and must become increasingly bureaucratic as it takes over more and more towns. But to hand over the assets of a development corporation to the local urban district council would be tantamount to presenting it with an enormous Exchequer subsidy. If, however, all save the very largest new projects were the responsibility of the regional council, and financed from regional taxes, the problem would vanish since the financing authority could also be the administering authority in perpetuity.

A regional tax-structure in which a tax upon incomes replaced or supplemented the present tax upon property might have one further advantage. The collection of all personal taxes might then be handled at regional level, the regional authority acting as the agent of the Exchequer. This might do something to soothe the resentment of the working householder who is called on to pay rates *as well as* taxes. More important, if variations of up to threepence or even sixpence in the pound were permitted in the national component of regional taxes on income, we should be able to provide a powerful new incentive to industry and people to move into the less prosperous regions as well as a deterrent to over-development of the more prosperous.

In such a structure of local government the second tier might consist of 'sub-regional' councils, responsible for providing most public housing for local needs, for maintaining minor roads, organizing purely local transport services, and administering the more personal social and welfare services. The number of people in such a sub-region might vary from as few as 50,000 in sparsely populated rural areas to as many as a million in the big provincial cities. But the weaker authorities should always be able to call upon the regional council to aid them with, or act as their agents for, any scheme which was beyond the resources or expertise of their own staff.

Co-operation of this kind between regional and sub-regional authorities could solve the problem of rural depopulation. For while amenities in the villages and market towns and local transport services can be improved at the lower level, the crucial need is for new industry in the country towns. Only the regional authority would have the resources to build factories to let, to give incentives to industrialists to move, and to ensure that the communications of the area with the rest of the region were adequate. Such schemes make no sense unless they fit within the framework of a broad regional development plan, and they call for a combination of the skills of the physical and the social planner which is unlikely to be found at local level. Here too, then, a radical reform of the structure of local government seems essential, if we are to secure a sensible distribution of industry and population, and utilize to the full rare talents and expertise.

(iii) It is not my task to write of the internal planning of new towns, least of all to advocate some particular form or structure for them all. This will doubtless vary from town to town But the now fashionable 'linear' structure may often prove desirable, and not simply because it can reduce journey-time between home and work, ease the planning of public transport, and prevent the over-congestion of the city-centre which is almost inevitable when it is served by a ring of radial roads. The 'linear' town is also more easily expanded at each end; it is not subject to the same natural limit to growth as are most towns of the traditional pattern — without, that is, extensive and expensive redevelopment of the town-centre and the roads which serve it. Our population may continue to grow rapidly in the twenty-first century, and we should lighten where we can the burdens of future generations of planners.

Even in the nearer future, the population of a new town is always liable to relatively sharper increase than that of an older community by virtue of the high proportion of young people it contains. We should certainly aim to keep this proportion as low as possible. If no effort is made to ensure a more normal age-structure, the immigrants to a new town are nearly all young married couples. Some twelve or fifteen years after the birth of the town, there is a sudden rise in the number of school-leavers, which inevitably creates employment problems. A further twenty-five or so years on, there will be a decline in the activity rate, as the early immigrants reach retiring age. Thus at Crawley, one of the first post-war new towns, only four per cent of those living in houses erected by the development corporation are aged over sixty, while more than four-fifths are still under forty-five. It will never be easy to attract middle-aged couples to new development. But it ought to be possible to bring many of the parents of other immigrants into new towns as they retire, and in the case of some well-situated developments, other retired couples as well. Such a policy will only succeed if the right dwellings are available in the right situation. Hence, in any future new town, ten per cent of dwellings erected in the early years should be designed specifically for the retired (later the proportion might rise to fifteen per cent), and they should be sited close to shops and other community facilities. Until such time as there are enough elderly people to take them all, some can be used for childless couples. Any attempt to ensure a more normal age-balance in new towns implies greater public investment per working person, or per unit of industrial production. But such expenditure should have a double value—for it will also do something to check the growth of excessively elderly communities in the older urban areas.

If it is important to aim for a normal age-balance, it is equally important to create a socially balanced community in each area of a new town. Large families should not be clustered together merely because the developing authority has made no provision for them in the early years. Thus, about ten per cent of the houses erected should have four or five bedrooms, even though this may mean some under-occupation initially. Nor should we forget that the first immigrants will in thirty years' time also be the first middle-aged couples, whose children will have grown up and left home, and who may then need smaller dwellings. It would be a mistake to consign these people, including many of the then leaders of local society, to the geographical periphery of the community. This means that gaps should be left near the centre of any large new development for the later construction of small flats or houses.

Many immigrants to new towns will wish to own their homes. The number of owner-occupied dwellings in the established new towns is in fact rising rapidly. But certain difficulties must inhibit early sale of houses built by the developing authority; although coherent estate management can be preserved by the use of covenants, it remains vital to ensure that upon resale such dwellings are used to house people from the exporting city—and further, people whose housing need is greatest. It therefore seems essential to make it a condition of sale that resale within, say, twenty years shall always be to the developing authority, at a price calculated according to terms prescribed at the outset. There must be a further *caveat:* any private developer in a new town must be expected to make his contribution to the provision of non-statutory, and unprofitable, social amenities.

A standard complaint in the first new towns has often been a relative dearth of social amenities, whether commercial (cinemas, bowling-rinks, dance-halls) or provided at public expense (heated swimming-pools, playgrounds, playing fields, multi-purpose community centres). A development corporation is allowed to spend only £4 per head of incoming population on such amenities. This limit must certainly be raised to at least £10 per head, and perhaps to a higher level still in the early years when the reputation and attractiveness of a new town are being established, and when the pioneers inevitably endure privations unknown to those who come after them. Once again, the difficulties would be much eased if the developing authority were a regional council, subject to no such limit on its expenditure. This might also make it simpler to provide facilities which might be used by a school during the day and the wider community in the evening, or indeed to develop schools and other social facilities as part of the same integrated campus. But the crucial change required is to regard such amenities as an essential part of the development of the town, not as a bonus to be added or taken away according to the current availability of resources. Public and private enterprise can work together, where the developing authority leases land or buildings to a commercial undertaking, and uses the revenue to subsidize its own provision of non-profitable facilities. And where a private developer has a large stake in a new town or overspill development, he should contribute his fair share towards community amenities. In future there must be co-ordination of provision in this field, not just the haphazard efforts of a public authority whose resources rarely match up to the need.

Our towns of the future must be showplaces, not just of physical planning, but also because of the quality of the life lived in them. They must be balanced communities, with all the amenities essential to social vitality. 'New town blues' may always have been something of a myth, but myths die hard. Now is the time to kill this one.

If therefore the rapidly growing population of Britain is to be dispersed more evenly over the available land and we are to breathe new vitality into the remoter regions, we must improve upon the workings of the 'free market' more than ever before. Public policies must be co-ordinated and private investment guided, to a much greater extent than hitherto. We may need to recast the structure of both central government and local government. Social investment must certainly be increased: Crosland's 'decade of high spending' is over, but several decades of investment as high or higher are to come.

Some may argue that there are other ways of solving the problem. There are 'pure' regionalists, or local nationalists, who sometimes seem to think that all else will come right if only we have 'genuine' local democracy, in the shape of regional home rule in all save a few residual matters. But a change in the level of political control does not of itself produce new financial or physical resources. Nor does it help those congested regions which increasingly must export population. Nor finally does it reduce the attractions of the South of England to either the industrialist or the worker, let alone reverse the trend of migration. Home Rule for Wales would hardly bring all the emigrés flocking home from London, and heaven help the Welsh economy if it did.

There are also those who believe that we should interfere as little as possible, at any level, with the play of the 'free market', but wait patiently for the adverse economic effects of over-development together with the social discomfort and aesthetic unpleasantness of congestion to provide a 'natural' solution to the problem. Such laissez-faire idealists can have little notion of what really determines industrial location; all too rarely is such a decision the result of purely economic considerations — all too often it is based on motives of prestige or herd instinct or is the consequence of a failure to consider the alternatives. These theorists take account neither of the national economic loss resulting from permanent under-employment and low activity rates in the remoter regions, nor of the high social cost often entailed by this method of maximizing some private profits, while local and central government struggle to make life tolerable and movement possible for those in the expanding regions.

I have tried to set out a plan which combines the necessary central organization with the maximum possible local participation and control. Such a solution at least has the merit of giving us a map and compass to guide our march into the twenty-first century; blind faith in either the potentialities of the liberated regional democrat or the infallibility of laissez-faire economics is a poor substitute. But it also permits us to give due weight to social, as well as economic, values. Few Socialists will wish to bequeath to their heirs a country in which towns and cities sprawl and haphazardly coalesce; where more time each day is spent in commuting to work; where the Englishman's home has become his castle, because he must turn away from and shut out urban ugliness; where there are neither the facilities nor the time for him and his neighbours to lead a vigorous social life; and all this while the remoter regions continue to stagnate. Yet this could be the future which faces us, unless we take action now.

© 1967 BY GERRY FOWLER

A Socialist Policy for the Press

JOHN RYAN

The recent history and the future outlook of the British Press are gloomy. The merger of *The Times* and *Sunday Times* has been approved by the Monopolies Commission, but the visible difficulties of other major national papers are a reflection of the monopolistic trend in the commercial factors which shape our Press. Radicals are especially concerned, because it is the papers which are least inimical to them which appear to be in the weakest position. On the Left there is a growing demand for Government action to maintain the number of papers but often uncertainty about cohesive or practical ideas on which to formulate a new policy. The Government should urgently consider some of the measures which have been suggested to keep open the varied expression of news and opinions, while at the same time ensuring the Press's freedom from Government control.

The current difficulties facing the *Guardian* have highlighted the basic contradictions of the newspaper industry. Seriously high production costs, union intransigence regarding machine use and staffing policy, together with rising newsprint prices and the paper's dependence on a substantial advertisement subsidy, have conspired to threaten the future of the *Guardian* as a London-based national newspaper and to cast fresh doubts on the ability of at least six other national papers to continue.

The concentration of the Press into fewer groupings has now reached a point where most Socialists would demand positive action from the Government to frustrate the forces and pressures which cause this, but disagree when confronted with the problem of choosing a course of positive action. The Royal Commission on the Press in 1962 made a thorough investigation of the economics of newspapers. It was especially concerned with the problem of the socially valuable paper which was pleasing its large readership but which was failing as an economic proposition due to its inability to obtain advertising because of the lack of attraction of its readership for advertisers. Several proposals for diverting advertisement revenue to subsidize the weaker sections of the Press were suggested, but the Royal Commission was forced to the reluctant conclusion[1] 'that there is no acceptable or legislative way of regulating the competitive and economic forces so as to ensure a sufficient diversity of newspapers. The only hope of the weaker paper is to secure — as some have done in the past — managers and editors of such originality as will enable their publishers to overcome the economic factors affecting them.' This is an admirable sentiment, but does not admit the urgency of the situation.

Some people feel that the problem could be overcome by charging readers a more realistic price for their papers, thus diminishing the importance of the advertisement subsidy. This is an involved and usually marginal decision for any publisher to take and can rebound with a fall in circulation. The recent experience of the *Daily Mail* which gained circulation at 3d. when its main rival rose to 4d., but lost when it increased to 4d. also, is eloquent.

Other Socialists call, in Kaldorian vein, for a quota system on advertisements to 'spread them around' more evenly and so break the system of advertisers' 'short scheduling' the appropriations into relatively few successful papers. This idea merits serious examination, but in my opinion is impractical and might conceivably have an even worse effect on the situation. Such a policy could be applied in several different ways. It could be in the form of the fixing by legislation of a maximum ratio of advertisements to editorial matter in all papers, which would limit the paper's dependence on income from advertisements and so force up its retail price towards an economic level. If this formula were invoked it would not be unwelcome to some advertisers who are at present disturbed by the packing of some very successful papers with crowded advertisements which are competing for the reader's attention.

An enforced ratio of limitation could be used by the publisher to justify an increase in the advertisement rates charged because of the increased probability of readers' attention to the fewer advertisements. The factors controlling the amount of attention achieved vary greatly from paper to paper, depending on colour, page size and the advertisement's position, and are closely considered by the

[1] Cmnd. 1811 (H.M.S.O., 1962).

A SOCIALIST POLICY FOR THE PRESS

major advertiser who would be willing to pay an inflated price if it seemed worthwhile in real terms; but this inflationary price movement might draw the wrath of the Prices and Incomes Board. A quota system might also lead to attempts to evade it, by, for example, an increase in the number of P. R. supplements, stories and 'puffs'—a feature of advertising criticized by the Royal Commission. It would also bear most heavily on those who have a fixed page policy for production reasons which would limit the scope for increasing their revenue within the quota by creating better advertisement positions. No doubt this rationing policy might result in some redistribution and sharing of advertisements, but certainly would be no magical palliative and might have undesirable by-products.

A statutory limitation on the proportion of a paper's revenue to be derived from advertising has been suggested by the *New Statesman* as a method of forcing prices to an economic level and of helping the less fortunate in attracting advertisement revenue. This is more logical than a strict quota by ratios, but again it bristles with difficulties. The most important of these is that it would tax the 'heavies' more severely than the mass circulation papers—the *Sunday Times* derives about 80 per cent of its income from advertising and would be sharply penalized compared with, say, the *People*, or the *News of the World* which derive only about 50 per cent of their income from this source. It might result in the 'heavies' having to dilute their serious approach in order to build up a more popular readership. This may or may not be an undesirable effect: but it would be regrettable if the re-shaping were to take place under fiscal pressure rather than because of editorial intention and planning.

Any policy of quota restrictions could also lead to a diminution of the total advertisement subsidy to the Press as a whole. Advertisers are basically concerned with an absolute level of marketing achievement and judge each paper on its probable contribution to this end. If they are forced out of the best papers in each readership category by legislation, it is a far from automatic assumption that they would invest their advertising budgets in whatever other papers in each category had space inside the quota. They might invest if the next best papers were only marginally less effective for their strategy than their first preferences, but if the margin were considerable they might well decide to invest their money in other media, such as television, or posters, which might give them a better cost-effectiveness return. Furthermore if their objectives were unlikely to be attained by media expenditure because of restrictions, they might choose a totally different formula such as direct mail, better trade terms for consumer goods and increased P.R. for institutional advertising.

It is logical that if the margin between one paper's effectiveness and another's is quite small then any benefit which will result from the redistribution of advertisements will be equally small. To achieve the fundamental redistribution which the authors of this policy seek would involve the bridging of much wider commercial discrepancies.

A further method of re-orienting advertising revenue which has been suggested is a levy on all advertising revenue to be paid by each paper, on a similar basis to the present levy paid by the independent TV companies—but, in this case, with the levy fund being used to subsidize those who are less fortunate in achieving a high advertising income. Such a scheme would again be open to the objection of bearing hardest on the small circulation heavies and lightest on the mass circulation Press. When a levy was introduced on TV advertising it was passed on to the advertiser by the TV companies and if this happened in Press terms it might well lead to a contraction of expenditure in the Press as well as to an inflationary pressure. Allowing for these snags a levy would obviously raise funds: at 10 per cent it would raise about £11 million which could be used for a subsidy to the struggling papers.

But what criteria would the fund's trustees devise for defining 'struggling' and for calculating the level of payment to be made? If it was made to all papers whose income from advertising fell short of a defined proportion of their total income and was intended to balance the deficiency, then once again it would favour the mass circulation paper at the expense of the small sale 'heavy'. In either case it would be an excuse for inertia by their management and advertisement departments.

The criterion for receiving the subsidy which would be welcomed by most publishers would be to use the £11 million raised by the levy to make good the profit deficiencies for the struggling Press. At present most unprofitable papers are being carried as non-viable parts of quite prosperous groups. The *Guardian* is supported by the *Manchester Evening News*, the *Sun* by the vast resources of the I.P.C.,

A SOCIALIST POLICY FOR THE PRESS 183

and probably *The Times* will be supported initially by the rest of the Thomson empire. It would be a simple accountancy operation to show clearly what each paper was losing and even easier to write off a backlog of losses if a deficiency subsidy were proposed. The £11 million produced from a heavy 10 per cent levy would not go very far because the 10 per cent levy itself would push several papers below the viable margin into the queue. Of course, the Government could require that the losses of any individual paper in a group should first be absorbed by total group profits; but that would merely continue the existing situation which allows the publisher the option (and the incentive which many to their credit reject) of closing down the paper which is a drain on group profits.

Some Labour M.P.s have called for the Government to spread its own growing advertising into the papers which would not receive it if purely commercial criteria were applied.

AMOUNTS PAID BY GOVERNMENT DEPARTMENTS ON DISPLAY ADVERTISING SPACE IN CERTAIN NEWSPAPERS IN 1963-4 AND 1965-6

Newspaper	Expenditure 1963-4 (£)	1965-6 (£)
Daily Express	175,850	314,892
Daily Mail	119,878	125,602
Daily Mirror	200,116	381,485
Daily Sketch	18,045	20,933
Daily Telegraph	130,622	200,247
Financial Times	13,429	29,511
Guardian	15,194	36,605
Morning Star (Daily Worker)	nil	nil
Sun (Herald)	32,334	43,973
The Times	30,577	54,993
News of the World	117,221	142,007
Observer	50,664	104,798
People	115,875	182,231
Sunday Citizen	2,340	3,590
Sunday Express	135,357	199,322
Sunday Mirror	76,632	193,250
Sunday Telegraph	22,850	86,715

Newspaper	Expenditure	
	1963–4 (£)	1965–6 (£)
Sunday Times	106,979	198,589
Evening News	23,840	29,439
Evening Standard	17,064	29,791

Note: The amounts are those paid to the advertising agents. Advertising by the Post Office is excluded.

But I cannot agree with this suggestion for a solution. The *New Daily* would qualify as much as *Tribune*, the *Daily Sketch* as much as the *Guardian*. To preserve the essential freedom of the Press, it would not be permissible for the Government to discriminate. Yet the taxpayer might well object to the indiscriminate spreading of his largesse. If the Government feels it should give a subsidy, the best solution would be for it to reconsider some aspects of the S.E.T. which affect the Press. In any case it should not be ashamed of deciding openly to give a subsidy above-board as a policy decision, instead of attempting to disguise it.

Socialists believe that a varied and healthy Press is a precondition for a civilized and informed democracy. Papers should not be regarded as mere commodities whose size and existence should be governed by unchecked market forces, but should be cushioned by the Government from the effects of an inherited jumble of high production costs and large amorphous groups. It is not the role of a government to force people to read that which they find boring or heavy, or to prevent them reading that which is entertaining. It should be our aim to maintain *choice* as far as possible in the knowledge that as educational opportunities and standards rise there is likely to be an increasing movement away from the trivial to the more worthwhile. It should be recognized that this may not necessarily mean a switch from the popular papers to the 'heavies' but will probably result in an extension of 'heavier' coverage and features within the popular Press.

No one can argue that the present position in Britain in terms of the number, regional distribution, type and form of the Press is static, God-given and sacrosanct—or indeed should be. But we cannot ignore the fact that several papers which are satisfying large readerships are likely to go out of existence and that it is essential that the Government should act to maintain choice. It is a contradiction to introduce the open University of the Air in order to raise 'the quality of life', if worthwhile papers are meanwhile to be allowed to disappear.

I have tried to demonstrate that some of the remedies suggested so far are in fact naive double-edged weapons which would not give us what we want—indeed they express a very limited view of social policy. If you see a paper as being more like a theatre than a brand of beans—something which should be shielded from unfettered capitalist forces—then it is myopic to suggest squeezing the more successful theatres to subsidize the less successful. There is no justification for the Government shirking its responsibilities to provide a subsidy if it feels it necessary, rather than trying to redistribute income among papers. Some will point to the nucleus of extremely rich men who make fortunes out of the Press, but this is surely an argument for a more progressive tax system and a wealth tax not merely applicable to newspaper owners but to members of all occupations. There are more profitable business areas than publishing in terms of return to capital employed and it would be bizarre to concentrate one's policy only within the publishing field.

What I suggest as the best course of action is unashamedly ambitious and socialist. I believe the Government should consider the setting up of an independent National Press Corporation with power to purchase, if it so wished, the presses and assets of newspapers which were intending to merge or to close. This Corporation could then put out the business of producing a newspaper on the presses acquired to contracting companies on the same basis as the I.T.A. chooses the independent television companies. The contracting companies would be groups of journalists and newspaper executives who would lease the assets and publishing facilities. The selection of contractors could be done in a similar way to the I.T.A. selections on a basis of previous experience, resources, ability and qualifications. The contractor could be awarded the lease for an initial trial period and would have total absolute editorial and policy control over the paper published. It is obvious that a subsidy would be necessary in the amount charged to the contractor, for the return on the lease would normally be less than the real cost to the Corporation of the operational fabric and the newsprint; if it were an economic lease it would be prohibitive to the contractor to afford—or the previous owner would not have failed. The advertising revenue to supplement income could either be obtained directly by the contractor as is done by the TV companies, or it could be done centrally by the Press Corporation and offset against the contractor's lease payments.

This plan meets one basic social requirement in that its subsidy element is concentrated on those who really want to run a newspaper as salaried journalists and executives and are not influenced by the motive of distributed profits. This would not result in the monolithic state publishing concern which is a dismal feature of Communist countries, but could become a vibrant expression of what a civilized community's view of the Press's prime function is — the diverse advocacy of different views and opinions.

There would be many problems of detail unless safeguards were included, and there could be imbalances if, for instance, all the papers which disappeared were evening papers, and the contractors who were chosen to replace them were only interested in operating regional weeklies. Although no balance of papers is ever likely to be ideal, there might be a case initially for the Press Corporation giving priority in allocating contracts to those who had the best plan for a paper to replace in substance that which had failed.

If the advertisement selling operation were handled centrally by the Corporation, this would be a recognition of the Pilkington Committee's findings in the case of television:[1] that the contractors should basically be creative rather than geared to commercial advertising. In Press terms, it would mean the contractors could concentrate on the function they wanted to do and were best at — the production of newspapers; whereas the Press Corporation, as its base widened, could employ sophisticated and go-ahead advertising management on a scale which is extremely expensive for a single newspaper to afford.

A policy along these lines is worth considering as being more wide ranging and creative than some of the merely restrictionist ideas suggested. It would be a socialist scheme parallel to the concept of the Industrial Reorganization Corporation in that it would concentrate help to the right people in the right place — at the gap which would be caused to the community if a paper failed — and would give it in a way that ensured that it went straight to the newspapermen rather than to the proprietor seeking profits. It has

[1] Cmd. 1753 (H.M.S.O., 1962).

the advantage that it would not penalize the existing Press in the way any quota or levy scheme would. It would obviously be a difficult scheme to work in what is a complex field but the price is worthwhile if it halts the erosion of the Press.

Most important of all, it would be the recognition by a Labour Government of its responsibility to prevent any monopoly in the communication of the ideas which activate men's minds.

© 1967 BY JOHN RYAN

Modernizing the Labour Party

ALAN LEE WILLIAMS

Bill, a young scientist, thinks he will join the Labour Party. He has a vague feeling that ours is not the best of all possible worlds, that many things need improving, and that politics is the way in which things get changed. He has another ill-defined notion, perhaps one he grew up with, or acquired from his family, friends or from books: that the Labour Party wants equality, social justice and other intangible ideas which form part of his notion of a civilized society.

He asks friends, inquires in the local library, or perhaps sees a poster; somehow he contacts an official of the local party, and is told when and where their next meeting will be. To this he takes his vague feeling of dissatisfaction, and his general notion of the aims of the Labour Party. He feels a little strange sitting at the back of a draughty, gloomy hall, listening to long debates among a knowledgeable few about the arrangements for a social or a jumble sale, or the election of a representative to some obscure committee. He listens to fraternal greetings from a local trade unionist (which did not seem entirely fraternal), with perhaps some mutual back-slapping by worthy committee members. After a cup of tea and a biscuit he listens to an exhortatory speech urging him to do all sorts of things, from nationalizing all heavy industry to disestablishing the Church, with for good measure the speaker calling for the Government to be really socialist and sack all the bosses.

Will he be involved in any of these tasks? Would he canvass at the next election for this kind of organization? Will he be able to answer a question about his adopted party, if asked? Will he agree to pay a minimum subscription to help this still obscure cause? Will he even come to the next meeting? Or will he retire with his dissatisfaction to the TV or the pub?

It is Bill that the Labour Party is all about. He's an ordinary man who works for his living and pays taxes in the hope of a better society for not only his own children, but all children. It is for Bill that the Labour Party exists, it is to him that it looks for support, moral, financial and political. He may vote for the party occasionally, but the party needs more than this from him. It is my contention that the present organization of the party will not win that support; even if the example of the local Labour Party described is an example of the worst, the best still leave much to be desired.

Harold Wilson summarized the organization of the Labour Party in his 1955 Report: 'We are still at the penny-farthing stage in a jet-propelled era.' It might have been more accurate to say 'we are still at the horse-bus stage' for there have been few changes since the party structure was created in 1918. Since then we have had a world war, women's suffrage, the depression of the 'thirties, an increase in educational opportunity, several Labour Governments and their creation of a comprehensive welfare state; we have also had a wide increase in living standards, particularly in car ownership, and an expansion of systems of communication, especially radio and television. All these have had their effects on party organizations but—as Jim Northcott has shown in detail— little attempt has been made to change the organization to adapt to and absorb these changes.

This is not to say that we must tear down the structure and start again. In spite of the power of the media of mass communication, it is still individuals who matter; there will always be a need for local parties as rallying points for new members and as centres for political discussions, as foci of communications between the members and head office for the exchange of information and policy decisions, and finally as the headquarters of election battles, including the selection of candidates. What we need to do is to overhaul the structure, leaving the walls standing, but clothing them with fresh paint—having first made good the cracks which could in time widen and threaten the edifice.

If we begin our modernization with the foundations, in the local party, we find that there is too much overlapping of functions between the ward parties and the General Committees of each constituency. Too many ward meetings involve a dreary recital of what has already been, or will in due course be, discussed by the Executive Committee and General Committee—with the result that a new recruit like Bill may not come again.

We need to consider a division of the functions of the local party along the following lines (making changes in emphasis as appropriate for rural or urban constituencies, depending on size, transport facilities, car-owning membership, number of towns and so on). First, ward meetings could be reduced to the minimum necessary to elect delegates to the constituency General Committee. This would free a large number of members for participation in more interesting meetings, to be addressed by good speakers who are briefed to explain the Party's problems, priorities, proposed solutions, and policies. Bill would be more likely to come to meetings like this, especially if he received a newsheet every month to supplement the meetings which might themselves be bi-monthly.

For the real party activists the General Committee would provide the opportunity for debate on policies, the formulation of resolutions and the meeting ground of delegates from wards together with those from trade unions and co-operatives. It should concern itself as little as possible with the 'business' of running the organization, although continuing to adopt candidates and hear reports. The business should be left to the Executive Committee, which should be composed not of people who like just discussing problems, but of those who are prepared to decide action and carry it out. This would make the best use of the organizational talent in the Party, and free those members who want to debate politics or canvass support among the floating voters to do so. The Party often has a wealth of talent in its local organization, but at present too much of it tends to be concerned with the trivia of Party business, and not enough with the stuff of politics—debate, argument, education and persuasion.

The result would be to allow more active interest to be channelled into the broad issues of policy, while giving the organizers a better chance to take the decisions for which they were elected to a committee. Activities into which emancipated enthusiasm could be channelled might include the women's sections, which need to be freed from the drudgery of making tea for meetings, organizing bazaars and so forth, and given more opportunity for discussion at mid-week sessions (with the help of crèches provided for children), and for the study of one or two special topics each year which might then at Annual Conference be given a deeper examination than is possible at present when the whole range of policy receives only superficial debate.

Secondly, the youth movement should be helped to overcome its tendency to bitter and unproductive schisms. Its difficulties will not be helped by attempts to clip the movement's wings, and the attempt to abolish it has also failed. The Labour Party needs a strong youth movement, and young people have a great deal to contribute to the Labour Party. Local centres to provide the social and educational resources for young members could be set up by groups of constituencies. The incorporation of 25–30-year-olds as members of the youth movement, as is the case with the other political parties, could well lead to a maturer outlook and a more effective projection of Labour's policies to the younger generation as a whole.

Thirdly, local parties could employ energy released from the tedium of 'business' in exploring new avenues of recruitment—for example, discussions among groups of local teachers about the effects of Labour's policies on education or of doctors about improvement of the Health Service.

Finally, there is scope to make use of people who sympathize in general with Labour's aims but for one reason or another do not wish to join or take an active part. They might well, however, pay a small subscription for occasional literature, and might also be prepared to help at elections.

If the local parties are the foundations on which the Labour Movement rests, then the agency service can be regarded as the walls. In 1951 there were 300 full time agents; by 1965 this number had dwindled to around 200. Complaints about the rapid turnover in the agency service, and about the lack of experience (and, in some cases, low calibre) of its members, are widespread. Even those who are expert at their job are frustrated by their difficulty in communicating with Transport House and the party leadership. They are given no encouragement to submit proposals; they have been refused access to the N.E.C.; as employees they are without conciliation machinery for the settlement of disputes with their employer—a situation which the party would deplore in any other employment but tolerates for its own staff. It is true there is an adjustments board to deal with salary claims, but its failure to do justice to the agents' case is one of the reasons for the rapid drain of staff from the service.

Radical changes are required in this service, along the following lines. The Labour Government has rightly passed an Act to stimulate training in industry and the Labour Party should organize an effective training course for its agents. Over a period of, say, three years, recruits could assist full-time agents in constituencies selected as useful training grounds. This period should include attendance for some months on a special course at the Labour College (to be discussed later), and throughout this period the trainee should be encouraged and helped to study law, bookkeeping and the use of publicity media, as well as the more traditional subjects like party history and organization and the principles of Socialism. He might then qualify for some sort of diploma and proceed as a probationary organizer to work in constituencies for two or three years, after which he should be qualified to take over a constituency or take up specialist posts at head office or in the regional organization.

All this would require new and attractive pay scales to recognize length of service, ability and specialist qualifications. A grading and salary structure comparable to that of the executive class of the Civil Service might be suitable, and of course proper negotiating and consultation machinery should exist between the N.E.C. and the agency service. Such a new style agent would clearly be a skilled employee and as such should be relieved of the tasks of having to do his own typing and filing by the employment of adequate clerical assistance. He should also be able to call in the specialist knowledge which would be available on a regional basis, and to which he might contribute if he chose later in his career to do so.

As with recommendations for changes in the local parties, one result of such a reorganization would be to free time and energy for new techniques of political action—for experiments, for example, in the use of modern communications aids like telex and walkie-talkie at elections. Even a simple device like the telephone could be used more than it is at present for knocking up prospective voters. A study of the values of such experiments could be made at local and by-elections with a view to their more widespread use at general elections.

Before leaving the field to look at head office, it is necessary to make a few general remarks. None of these proposals should be seen as interfering with the democratic process of control of the local machine by the elected officials. All local parties deserve a first-class service, and today's safe seats if not properly attended are the marginals of tomorrow. The aim should be to separate the technical aspects of local party management and to put them in the hands of small executive committees who will execute them efficiently with the help of qualified professionals, properly recruited and trained for a worthwhile career. In this way, time, effort and enthusiasm will be released for fuller discussion of policy issues, for greater involvement in civic affairs, for the encouragement of new members and wider financial support. The net result would be that a new member would find our meetings more interesting, would know more about Labour's policies, and would be able to play a fuller and more effective part in the activities of the party which in turn would occupy a more important place in his life.

Much the same difficulties beset the central organization as are apparent in the agency service and in the constituencies. Generalized criticisms are subject always to amendment in the light of special cases, but I am concerned here with trends that can be identified as weaknesses that need to be removed if the party machine is to be able to compete in the age of the jet-liner. The malaise of Transport House has been widely publicized in recent years and nothing less than a radical rethinking of its organization and staffing will suffice. Most of the staff would agree that they are underpaid, and also bedevilled by committees and sub-committees which create volumes of paper work while making it difficult for them to concentrate on the organizational, planning and public relations work which are the shibboleths (but vital ones) of the modern world. This emphasis on servicing committees, together with the low pay and the restrictions on the scope of their work have combined to make the recruitment of experienced professional staff difficult and have led to a rapid turnover and the disgruntlement among those who remain which, when publicized, has embarrassed both them and the party.

The functions of the head office of a national political party organization are firstly, the initiation of long-term policy and its embodiment in the daily work of the party after consultation with the members; secondly, the publicizing of those agreed policies; and thirdly, the co-ordination of head office with local party organization and the preparation for elections.

At present these functions are carried out by the Research and International, Press and Publicity and the National Agents

Departments respectively; over all is the N.E.C. with its Home, Overseas, Publicity, Organization and Finance and General Purposes sub-committees. For three functions we have four departments, directed by five committees (six if the full N.E.C. is included). Simple arithmetic shows that there can be no clear chain of command, and a considerable overlapping of functions. When it is remembered that the General Secretary of the Party has his own important role to play, and that the people who sit on the sub-committees are extremely busy politicians and trade unionists whose lives include sitting on many other committees of one sort or another, one can see why the confused picture which Transport House gives to outsiders is a true one.

Any reconstruction of the machinery of Transport House must take account of the need for a high-powered research department. There are in essence four stages of long-term policy making. In the first place reliable and meaningful statistics must be collected about the wide range of governmental activities, taking a long view of what the state of the nation is likely to be in five or six years' time and what the nation's needs are then likely to be. This is followed by the reconciliation of conflicting opinions and the balancing of rival interest groups in order to achieve a policy which is an acceptable statement of aims and methods. The third stage is the testing of this policy, or hypothesis, in the light of the experience of other countries, where appropriate, and by comparing the need with the resources available to meet it. Finally comes the merging of inter-related policies into a cohesive whole, which may well involve elements of the second stage again, inasmuch as the need to alleviate the burden on financial and other resources will demand the preparation of an order of priorities, and this may in turn necessitate the conciliation and agreement of conflicting interests and pressure groups.

At present Transport House is ill equipped to handle policy research at this level. A salary scale with only three increments offers little incentive to staff to remain long, and the research department has therefore tended to include a large proportion of junior staff. Add to this the day to day demands of visiting journalists, party members, trades unionists, councillors, overseas guests, and the servicing of the policy sub-committees of the N.E.C. as well as the provision of material for the press, broadcasting authorities and the production of publications, and one can see why long-term policy has been neglected. It is not that ideas have been absent—on the contrary, during the Conservative administration, Transport House was full of bright ideas. But unfortunately there have not been the time and resources, especially of personnel, available to develop these ideas along the stages outlined above into the realm of practical policies. The result, as we have seen in three years of Labour Government, has been too many attractive slogans, like 'an integrated transport policy', coupled with too little appreciation of how to translate them into governmental action. As a consequence, Labour Ministers have been forced to rely extensively on the expertise of the Civil Service, with its built-in conservatism and its facility for finding reasons why a policy may not work and therefore should not be tried; or, and this is perhaps worse, demands have been made on the Civil Service to implement quickly policies only half worked out by Labour in opposition, with the result that many of the difficulties have been encountered but few of the advantages reaped.

A further deficiency in the present arrangements is the almost complete absence of what is best described as political education, by which is meant not propaganda but the availability of intelligent publications for the ordinary members of the local parties. Our chief rivals make a point of distributing good literature from their head office for discussion groups in the constituencies, and their comments on policies as a result of these discussions are invited by the Central Office. In the Labour Party by contrast the only way for members to express opinions is in terms of resolutions to Conference. The result too often has been that debates at Conference are relatively ill-informed, unsophisticated and over-emotional, apart from the semantic nonsenses which have sometimes been the result of compositing many resolutions into a few for debate.

What is needed is an entirely new department of research and information with more and more professional staff. The Director of Research should be a top-rank appointment with a status similar to that of a university professor or senior civil servant—and he would need to be paid accordingly. Under his control would be three sections—long-term policy (both home and foreign affairs), political education, and information. Between ten and fifteen youngish staff are needed for a research team, charged with the production of statistics and forward planning policy, producing and evaluating ideas and long-term policies with the available resources allocated on a basis of political priorities.

Alongside the long-term research section, a further eight staff should be employed in a careful programme of political education; in the preparation of good background literature, distilling the work of the researchers into documents for wider discussion, and examining the immediate implications. Better distribution of this literature would be encouraged by reviving the posts of constituency political education officers, who would thus be given a challenging and worthwhile job. Constituencies could discuss the local impact of national policies on welfare services, transport, etc.—and feed back the results of their discussions to head office for collation.

This is the point at which to propose the establishment of a Labour College, mentioned earlier when we looked at the training of agents. Some unions already have their own colleges: the Conservative Party has its Swinton College, and Norway with one-fifth of our population has three such institutions. The aim of the Labour College would be to act as a powerhouse for the party's political education services, to run full courses of training for agents and for elected officials of local parties to help them to give to and get the best from their own organizations, and also to brief and train the resuscitated political education officers in the constituencies. Such courses could call upon the services of the research and national agents' departments at head office, and would as well probably find many W.E.A. and other adult education practitioners willing to give their energy to a cause with which they are sympathetic.

Finally, the third section of the research department would be concerned with the provision of information—answering correspondence and telephone queries, seeing visitors, briefing M.P.s and preparing leaflets and other literature on Labour's policies for consumption by the general public.

Moving from research to publicity it is a relief to be able to record a greater improvement than elsewhere in recent years, certainly during the 1964 election. The need now is to consolidate these gains and remove the weaknesses which still remain. The campaign in 1964 was much more professionally run than previously, perhaps as a result of the widespread criticism of the party's machine during the campaign in 1959. In spite of Morgan Phillips's flair for publicity it is worth noting that this was achieved with one-third of the number of staff employed on this work by the Conservatives, who also had the services of a professional P. R. agency. If our success could be achieved with so few staff it is exciting to speculate what might be achieved with really adequate resources and better co-ordination of their effort.

In this age, whether we like it or not—and the puritan element in the party may well begrudge the resources needed—a full-scale public relations campaign requires the well-planned use of a wide range of media, each of which has a special function for which it is more suitable than the others. Press advertising, poster displays, radio and television coverage, opinion research, attractive literature for local campaigns—all these are tools suited to a particular job and all need to be skilfully deployed, and supported by good artwork and copy-writing. The volunteer services of professionals within the party is admirable, both from the point of view of those who give their services in this way, and that of the party which is sufficiently 'modern' to employ their services, but regretfully it is not enough in itself. (At present Transport House employs only one commercial artist, although a first-class one.)

This is just as important when Labour is in office as in opposition. Ministers are concerned with the work and relations of their own departments and the government Information Services serve a different purpose from political propaganda. The Labour Party still needs a first-rate public relations organization to project the themes of its policies and basic aims, in ways to which a more sophisticated public has become accustomed. Again, the accent must be on professionalism, under the direction of the elected representatives of membership who know what to ask of the professionals because they understand the machine at their command. For example, there is plenty of scope for greater use to be made of local media in marginal constituencies to publicize the achievements of Labour-controlled councils, and a team might be set up at head office to co-ordinate this work and deploy the available resources effectively.

Much the same criticism could be directed at the Party's use of broadcasting. We have too often insisted on making our own programmes for both radio and TV in spite of the authorities' offers to provide facilities in the form of studios and experienced producers, and committed the folly of not allowing a budget adequate for the purpose. Even worse, we do not even have videotape so as to be able to assess the suitability of people for the television programmes we have prepared, and as an aid to coaching the selected performers. We need to employ audience research, and to rely less on the 'TV personalities' in the party who have been criticized as interfering with the programming in order to impose their own views.

In all, a director of publicity is needed to deal with Fleet Street and with the leaders of the Party, a deputy director to shoulder the burden of administration, and a staff of about twenty who would include senior journalists and public relations experts—and once again who are adequately remunerated. In addition a peripatetic team to organize local campaigns is as desirable as the appointment of a permanent press officer. We need, too, the financial resources which will enable us to hire professional film-makers, advertising agencies and opinion pollsters. People who are primarily politicians cannot be expected to be experts in the sophisticated techniques which are necessary today. The professionals are available and their services are for sale; there is no reason why the Labour Party should not employ them, while at the same time using the talents of any experts within its own ranks.

Lastly in this critical analysis of the Transport House machine, let us consider the department of the national agent. Here the staff tend to be older and the turnover less rapid than in other departments; long-service medals are well earned if not freely given. The problem here is not one of retaining good staff, or constantly training new staff, but of persuading good, stable, experienced staff of the need to adapt their methods to rapidly changing conditions. There is too often an element of conservatism here which ill becomes a progressive party in the mid-twentieth century. To this may be attributed the tendency to neglect middle-class Labour supporters as if they were renegades in an old-fashioned class war, together with our perpetual failure (in comparison with our opponents) to take advantage of the increase in car ownership and of the telephone—particularly as regards the complex problems of getting voters to the poll and harvesting the postal vote.

The first area of activity in which changes are desirable is that of the regional organization. The twelve regional organizers are the representatives in their regions of the national leadership. As such, they need an improvement in status. At one time their pay was pegged to that of M.P.s, but now they are grossly underpaid. Only occasionally are large-scale meetings arranged for the party's organizing staff, and they rarely see the N.E.C. itself. The result, inevitably, is an absence of understanding of the problems and policies of the leadership. If the suggested improvements are made in pay, status and communications, it would also be as well to augment the numbers of specialist staff employed on a regional basis in youth work, women's organization, trade union liaison, political education, and as area organizers—in all of which categories there are too few at present.

Next, the agents themselves need a change of status. They have been seen in the past in the role of the party's civil service, and have not therefore been brought sufficiently into the party's counsels regarding the broad issues of policy. As a result the agents are ill equipped for political debate. Here again the proposed Labour College would be of great value, and agents could augment their six-month correspondence course with a wider training. The present system of appointment of agents by local parties has obvious advantages, but its great drawback is the absence of central direction. The best solution, if supported by a good communications system, would be the establishment of a national organization, centrally financed but preserving the local parties' right to choose their own agent.

One of the tasks that has been left in the past to the overworked agent has been the assessment of election results. Of course, the agent himself is an expert in so far as he knows his own constituency, but the party leadership's need for accurate assessments of election prospects at any given time suggests that the national agent's department should be able to call on the services of the specialist in this comparatively new field of expertise. Another advantage of a department with a greater degree of central direction would lie in the opportunity it would give for more careful planning of the organization for elections. We can no longer afford to leave the bulk of this to the local agent, relying on head office circulars to tell him not only what to do, but also, in many cases, how to do it. Nor can we rely any longer on the myriad part-time committees which exist in this field but which often serve only to confuse the agent and waste the time of professional committee-men whose real value lies elsewhere. What is needed is a unit at head office, consisting perhaps of an experienced regional organizer and two or three agents, preferably including some with organizational and methods and statistical experience. This team could experiment in modern techniques at local and by-elections, bringing their experience to bear on the assessment of the results, with a view to both improving techniques and sharing the knowledge of these improvements throughout the country.

The aim of all these proposals for a new Transport House is to make it a pace-setter, not a horse-bus. The relationship between the three main organs of the party—the N.E.C., the Parliamentary Party and Transport House—should be one of mutual respect, of a team working together for a common aim. These proposals therefore are intended to establish Transport House as the effective civil service for the other two organs. The policy will be, as it must always be in a democratic organization, decided by the N.E.C. and the P.L.P., but it should be based on high-powered research in Transport House entrusted to a Director General and a staff of experts.

The N.E.C. itself needs no more than two committees, one for policy and one for finance and general purposes. The former would be serviced by the Director of Research, who could present papers based on his department's work for decision as to priorities. Other departmental heads could report directly to the N.E.C. and should be empowered to set up study groups and expert committees, or call for advice from outside the party, instead of being, as now, restricted to part-time committees' advice.

The crux of effecting this transformation of Transport House is the recruitment of qualified people with expertise in a wide range of activities—from opinion-testing to film-making—and adequate payment of them. No one working for a cause expects to get rich, but he—and his family—have a right not to be exploited. The essential basis of all these suggestions is an increased budget, which would amount to between three and four times the present income at both national and local levels. The party has recently shown, by the emphasis given to fund raising at its 1966 conference, its awareness of the need to increase its income, as well as agreeing to the establishment of a Commission to make a rapid, searching inquiry into all aspects of party organization. Totes, lotteries and similar schemes will help, but it is vitally important that we also seek an increase in individual subscriptions (both by raising the subscription itself, and by increasing the number who pay it), and an increase in trade-union contributions. These new measures may not be popular, but we must convince our members, and future ones like Bill, that we are a progressive, modern party, in which the rank and file's role is in the political discussion of policies and priorities which experts will then help us to put into effect.

© 1967 BY ALAN LEE WILLIAMS

Socialist Law Reform

JOHN LEE

The term 'law reform' has at least three different meanings. Firstly, organization and methods, that is, improvement in the efficient running of the machinery of justice, a subject now being adequately dealt with by the Law Commissioners and one which does not call for comment in a general chapter for the layman. Secondly, the positive improvement or abolition of certain laws which, whatever may have been the position in the past, are no longer in accord with widely held views on the nature of justice. Thirdly, for a Socialist at any rate, the phrase connotes another meaning incomparably more important than the other two: the use of law as an instrument for achieving political and economic change. The second category includes many proposals of a more controversial character ranging from specifically political legislation, such as leasehold enfranchisement, to social legislation such as abortion and divorce law reform. With a Government in being largely favourable to most of them there seems every likelihood that these will be enacted in the near future. It is, therefore, with the last category, law reform as an instrument of socialist advancement, that this chapter is concerned. Remarkably little attention has been given to this. Quite a few lay people, and even some lawyers, seem to regard legislation as little more than a regulative and somewhat minor factor in our affairs. Yet nearly all the great milestones of social advance—free education, free health services, municipal housing and so forth—have all depended on the passage of legislation for their very existence. This is because legislation, and legislation alone, can authorize and define them. It is true that in the period immediately following the end of the post-war Labour Government there was some reaction against legislation in favour of greater reliance on fiscal measures and on budgetary policy; possibly this came about as a reaction against statutory corporation nationalization caused by disappointment when some of the new nationalized industries did not immediately fulfil the high hopes that had been held of them. It was a mood that soon passed and even those Socialists who are unenthusiastic about orthodox measures of nationalization now accept that a socialist society cannot be achieved without an ambitious programme of legislation. What they and many others do not realize is that an immense amount can also be achieved by a few simple changes in certain *existing* laws of major importance: laws which for the most part are of long standing and outside the usual recognized field of political controversy. The thesis of this chapter is that some twenty quite small changes in only seven Acts of Parliament could well-nigh transform our political system.

If the Labour Party is to bring about a society that is both democratic and socialist within the foreseeable future it has to solve three great problems of political science: the attainment of economic equality; the settlement of the political changes necessary for this equality, and the enlargement and preservation of civil liberty in the widest possible application. These are the tasks for which some solutions are attempted below.

In order to become a socialist society in this century, there will have to be in this country a massive redistribution of wealth. It is a curious fact, often unnoticed, that in spite of two world wars, very high nominal death duty rates, increasingly high rates of interest, and a quarter of a century of a high standard rate of income tax, the distribution of wealth remains substantially unaltered. The percentage of the population owning half the totally owned private wealth has changed little in the last fifty years and two per cent of the population still owns about half of all private wealth. Moreover, although there has been considerable improvement in the middle range of incomes (but not of capital assets) since the beginning of the second world war, this is not so in the case of those at the bottom end, while the number of very large incomes remains strikingly unchanged. Even the number of millionaires has not altered, though perhaps their social composition has altered somewhat. The same number of people had assessed incomes of £100,000 a year or more in 1963–4 as had them in 1937–8. The number fell immediately after the war but rose again later. It is clear, therefore, that as a means of bringing about greater equality high taxation has been unsuccessful. Nationalization, on the other hand, whilst it undoubtedly puts an end to subsequent accumulation of private capital wealth in specific sections of the economy, only applies to between ten and fifteen per cent of the capital of the nation. Even if one assumes a long run of election successes for the Labour Party, a dangerous assumption to make (as those who in 1945 rashly prophesied twenty years of continuous Labour rule will have cause to remember) it would take a very long time before present methods of nationalization could completely bring to an end all possible sources of private capital. It is obvious that some very different policy is necessary, if this is to be achieved in the foreseeable future. As I hope to show, here is a problem where some simple law reforms could come dramatically to the rescue, and the first of these involves striking at the roots of what is the most important form of capital wealth of all, namely the land.

In spite of town planning prohibitions, extensive local authority and central government purchases, heavy death duties, and extensive bequests to the National Trust, the fact remains that private land ownerhsip still exists on a massive scale and—this is the really significant point—the *definition* of the meaning of the word 'ownership' itself has remained unchanged over many years. The latter is defined in the first section of the Law of Property Act 1925 and means in practice that anyone who owns land or buildings freehold owns it absolutely to any depth beneath the soil and (in theory at least) to any height above the surface. He can sell it or give it to whom he likes, or it will pass on death by will or intestacy and will remain with his successors in title endlessly. Compared with the total of privately owned cash or other movable or liquid assets, land is much more important in relation to the problem of inequality because it appreciates in value more quickly and because of its endless durability (even if you scoop out a quarry you still own the area underneath) and because of its increasing scarcity due to population density. A revision of the Law of Property Act which, among other things, redefined ownership by reducing the highest form permitted to an individual from freehold to something very much more limited in character, would do far more than all the compulsory purchase orders, with or without the aid of a Land Commission (admirable though this may be), to reduce the scope of enduring private wealth.

One can reduce the degree of ownership by limiting title either as to its duration or as to its usufruct. There are many examples of both under our present law: leaseholds for a term of years, yearly tenancies, tenancies at will, and life tenancies under a trust, and for examples of the latter one has only to look at the great variety of covenant restrictions that exist. Modern town-planning legislation has created even more varieties of title. Now the Land Commission Act will bring into existence on a large scale many examples of another kind, Crownhold. This gives unlimited title as to time, but the owner is limited as to the purpose for which the land can be used. This restriction kills speculative development and speculative buying and selling, the basic causes of our inflated land values. Both methods of title limitation have their merits. Limitation as to time has, however, the very decided disadvantage that many of the problems that arise now out of leasehold tenure, fagend speculation, the 'running down' of property and so forth, might manifest themselves on a vast scale, and the task of estate management presented when so much land passed by remainder to the Crown could be really formidable. Moreover, if such a change was made to take effect over a very short period of time the administrative problems would be overwhelming. The great advantage of redefining all privately owned freehold as Crownhold on a given date is that there would not then be any special problem of estate management since the land would continue to be owned by the existing owners — and no one owner would be worse off relative to any other owner. Sections 1-4 of the Law of Property Act 1925 should therefore be amended to deprive private persons of the legal capacity to own freehold. One can perhaps compare the situation that would arise with the position under the present law whereby an infant lacks the legal capacity to own land though he may possess an equitable interest. Thus the 'free market' in land would be radically deflated, because no private owner could sell it for development, at any rate to other private persons; there is every reason why statutory corporations should continue to be able to own freehold for their own purposes. The very universality of the change would reduce the sense of injustice that arises from selective compulsory purchases. The new Crown Land Commission would still be necessary in order to make outright acquisitions for public purposes, but the title to land acquired from private individuals should become a freehold title on the completion of conveyance. In this way land would become available for development far more easily and so benefit new town development, town planning, the building of cheap housing, agricultural husbandry and land reclamation alike. The inflation in land capital values would be drastically reversed and a genuine and universal disinflation effected.

Revolutionary though this seems, it is certainly not without precedents, some of them far more drastic in character. When I was in Ghana I was at one time the Government Agent (or District Commissioner) of a part of the country called the Akwapim New Juaben district. All the land in that portion of the district which comprised New Juaben was owned by the State and all occupants living there were mere tenants at will. Elsewhere in Ghana, in the Northern Region (about half of the total area of the country), there existed a similar situation where some forty-five years ago, by virtue of the so-called Land and Native Rights Ordinance, the title in law passed to the community. It may be argued that any proposal to end private freehold is so revolutionary that it would provoke enormous opposition because it would be regarded as confiscatory, but if a very traditional colonial administration could be imaginative enough to effect even more radical innovations so many years ago, is it really too much to hope for the introduction of this proposal here? Absolute private ownership of land is not a sacrosanct principle. It is still unknown in many parts of the world and resented where it has been imposed in others. For hundreds of years, whilst land passed through enfeoffment, it was unknown to English law. A change which ended private ownership of freeholds would certainly be no more revolutionary than the Act of the reign of Edward I which prohibited subinfeudation and it could be as beneficial to our society as that law was to his.

Company law is, next to property law, probably the most important sector in which reform could accelerate our belated advance to a socialist society, since this regulates the conduct of by far the greater part of all business activity. Reform of the Companies Act 1948 has been in the air for some considerable time; but most of the reforms that are now proposed are concerned with such matters as the safeguarding of the interests of shareholders, the disclosure of more information at company meetings, and the prevention of new forms of fraud by directors and others abusing their powers. Little attention has been paid by the proponents of reform to the question of using changes in the law to place more of the nation's resources at the disposal of the community and to protect its interests against the predatory conduct of directors and shareholders alike. It is important that this should be done, not only in order to promote equality, but also to ensure a greater measure of efficiency. A few carefully selected amendments to the law could provide a short cut to large scale nationalization in a way incomparably simpler, less costly, and less time consuming than the cumbersome process of statutory nationalization industry by industry.

It ought to be said at the outset that the so-called public company is not sacrosanct (neither is it public any more than the public school or the public house—none of them belongs to the public). There was plenty of commercial enterprises long before 1862 and the Limited Liability Act and even in the period between 1862 and 1914, the period of capitalism's greatest success, much commercial activity existed outside the scope of the Act. I have in mind five major changes: the ending of the principle of limited liability for the public company shareholder; the abolition of the so-called exempt private company; a very great increase in the powers of auditors who would be made responsible not to the company but to the Board of Trade; the vesting in the Board of Trade of the right by Order in Council to acquire the shares of any new public company created after the passing of the amending law at par valuation; and finally, the vesting in the Board of Trade of power to determine by Order that at some future date the further creation of companies within the meaning of the Act should cease altogether. The objective behind these changes is to bring to an end, with the minimum dislocation of the economy, of the system of large-scale private commercial enterprise which has existed for more than a century.

The principle of limited liability whereby the shareholder's risk was limited, in the event of insolvency, to (at worst) the value of the share he purchased, was introduced in the pioneering days of large-scale enterprise to protect investors from the then very real dangers of heavy loss from company failures. This is totally unnecessary nowadays. Shareholders have at their disposal a whole gamut of aids, ranging from their own bank managers, stockbrokers and solicitors and the City editors, to the vigilance of the Stock

Exchange Council—to say nothing of the unit trust system. They may still need protection, but of a different kind. In any case, with the growth of very large scale commercial organization more and more investment is effected by self-financing, or alternatively by borrowing, so that the share grows less and less necessary. It survives merely as a means of disbursing unearned incomes. Many companies themselves, in practice, have recognized this; hence the creation of 'capital aim' A Class or non-voting shares. Nevertheless, year by year dividends are paid out, often rising at a rate which greatly exceeds the increases in prices, wages and salaries. Yet the sole justification in law of dividend payment is the risk which a shareholder is alleged to take when investing. If practice were to conform with theory, the bigger and more secure the company, the smaller the dividend declared should be, and the smaller the company, the greater the dividend: whereas the reality is often the opposite. A share is paid out of the profits and since on balance larger companies tend to be more profitable than smaller ones, the least-deserving shareholders receive the richest rewards. By Section 26 of the Companies Act 1948, a shareholder is a member of the company in which he holds shares, and yet if the company is a limited one (and most are), by virtue of Section 2 he cannot be sued for torts or breaches of contract of his company. If this were altered, not only would there be fewer fraudulent and incompetent directors (because shareholders would then be obliged, if only for reasons of self-defence, to take more interest in the affairs of their companies than they do now), but the shareholders would at least be doing something for their money for so long as the present system of private enterprise exists. The logical alternative would be to limit dividends to a sum based on an actuarial assessment of the risk of company insolvency: most would be minimal, probably less than 0·5 per cent in many cases. To force all companies simultaneously to reduce their dividend disbursements to such levels would be politically quite unrealistic, and so long as sterling remains vulnerable to overseas pressure would provoke a massive exchange crisis. On the other hand, this quite simple change would end the present unsatisfactory state of affairs without the risk of such a furore, and make shareholding for so long as it continues to exist a serious business rather than a device for syphoning off large portions of the national product in the form of unearned income.

The exempt private company was a device created by the Companies Act 1947 to afford the small and medium-size family business some of the advantages of company incorporation, such as survival on the death of members and limitations as to common law liability, not enjoyed by business partnerships. Unfortunately, the system has served to exclude a very considerable portion of commercial activity from proper supervision by the Board of Trade. It has also served for various reasons as an instrument of tax avoidance, largely because of the lack of proper audit control (auditors need not be qualified, and can be members of the company), and because the actual returns that have to be submitted to the Board of Trade are sketchy in the extreme. Amendments to Section 129 of the Companies Act could end this, either by requiring the company to furnish the Board of Trade with as much information as will be required of public companies under the new law, or by abolishing the exempt private company altogether, so that all businesses so constituted will have to revert to the status of partnerships, or themselves become public companies and thus subject to a correspondingly greater discipline. The advantage of the latter is that private businesses would henceforth be confined to small-scale activity and the Board of Trade would not be over-burdened by the task of scrutinizing the activities of a vastly greater number of organizations, as at present.

As the law stand, auditors—even of the largest public company—are appointed by it and are the servants of the company. They must ascertain the true financial position of the company but they are not expected to track down ingenious or carefully prepared schemes of fraud, unless their suspicion has or ought to have been aroused. Incredible as it may seem, they are not concerned with the policy of the company or whether it is well or ill managed. They can report and criticize, but they have no power to disallow improper expenditure or order restitution. It would be easy to give them real powers if the appointment of auditors was made by or had to be sanctioned by the Board of Trade and they were required to examine accounts from the point of view of the interests of the public at large and not just of the company.

As the remainder of the private sector of the economy becomes concentrated in a rapidly diminishing number of the very big companies, it will be necessary to nationalize it more quickly in order to prevent the existence of uncontrollable private monopolies. This could be done with the minimum of difficulty if the Board of

Trade were empowered to acquire, by compulsion if necessary, at no more than current market valuation, all the shares of any given public company. The least-memorable act of nationalization of the post-war Labour Government of 1945–51 was also the one which caused least difficulty—that of Cable and Wireless. It is an example that could well be followed in many other cases. This is especially so as it becomes necessary to take over those concerns which are comparatively efficient so that the change of ownership does not need to be accompanied by any restructuring of the organization. Such a power hanging over the head of the private sector could give the Board of Trade immense power for directing the economy, not least because of its deterrent value.

The House of Lords is often criticized, among other reasons, for the persistent non-attendance of a very large portion of its membership, but it is a veritable hive of activity when compared with the normal company meeting. This is true even though the House of Lords meets almost as frequently as the Commons and its membership, although considerable, is far smaller than that of any of the big commercial concerns. Only a minute proportion of members attend the Annual General Meeting, or even bother to appoint a proxy, unless there is a take-over bid in the offing or a more than usually spectacular dispute in progress between the directors and the shareholders or amongst the directors themselves. No doubt this would alter if the protection afforded by limited liability were to be ended, but it is still unlikely that very many members would wish to attend. Poor attendance is unsatisfactory for many reasons, amongst them the fact that by not attending meetings of their company shareholders are failing to do one of the very few duties that the law provides for them—and neither they nor the community as a whole can complain about absenteeism by the company's employees. At present, to form a quorum for a meeting of a public company, only seven members are required to attend, irrespective of the size of the company. If this were altered so that no meeting would be valid without the attendance by person or proxy of 20 per cent, say, of all members in the case of a public company, and perhaps as much as 30 per cent in the case of a private company, this would oblige many more shareholders to take a proper interest in their company, as well as let the directors feel that there was someone taking an interest in their conduct of the business besides the institutional investors; it might also make those employed by the company a little less cynical about it, and there might be fewer scandals in the insurance world.

As an instrument of money-raising for investment, the shareholder has already outlived his usefulness in large-scale enterprises. The relentless process of concentration and the measures of government intervention which even Conservatives accept as being unavoidable, make it hard to believe that the shareholder will be necessary for the promotion of any kind of economic endeavour for more than a few years longer. Like the piston-engine aircraft and the steam locomotive, the system of equity shareholding is coming to the end of a long and, on the whole, honourable history. It would be convenient, therefore, if our revised company law provided the Board of Trade with the power at some future date to prevent the creation of any further companies. This would not extinguish those already in existence, some of which might well continue for many years; but the time is approaching when it will be no more appropriate to incorporate a company with shares than it is nowadays to have a commercial enterprise founded by Royal Charter.

Next to an onslaught on the maldistribution and misuse of wealth, the most difficult problem for which reform of the law could be called in aid is that of how to protect the political advances that have already been achieved, not just from being run down through neglect (as has happened to the Health Service) but from subsequent assault by means of antagonistic legislation. One of the most novel and disturbing, but surprisingly little-noticed, constitutional changes of the 1950s was the phenomenon of denationalization. Here I am not concerned so much with the political merits or demerits of nationalization, but with the implications of denationalization with regard to continuity in government. Since the beginning of the nineteenth century there have been at least four periods of major political turmoil in British history during which the main political parties of the day disputed with especial bitterness. In the 1830s and again in the 1860s, they were concerned with parliamentary reform, and in particular the extension of the franchise. In between there was the dispute over free trade. From the 1880s onwards, the Irish Home Rule controversy became the most serious domestic political issue in Britain, and it remained so until 1922 and the founding of the Irish Republic, overlapping the constitutional and fiscal enactments of the last Liberal Government. All the changes in the law proposed by the party of change (generally the Liberals) were strenuously opposed by their opponents. Yet all of them became law, and all of them (with only one exception—free trade—and that was a fiscal and not a legislative change) have either remained law to this day or have been altered in an even more radical direction, long after the politicians and governments that enacted them have passed from the scene. For until 1951 it was tacitly accepted that successive governments would not repeal the positive legislation of their predecessors, however distasteful such legislation might have been. Indeed, as a general rule, successor governments did not even reverse the fiscal changes, and certainly not the fiscal trends, of their predecessors. Trends in income tax, though rates have fluctuated from time to time, have been unmistakably in the direction of higher rates and higher allowances, but the death duties and surtax introduced respectively by Sir William Harcourt and by Lloyd George for the first time amidst tremendous opposition, have increased, having long survived their originators. Since 1951, however, the principle of the permanency of change has been thrown aside. The denationalization of steel, of much of road haulage and civil aviation, of development values, and of raw-cotton purchasing are examples of this. It is not just that these Acts of Repeal were retrograde measures in themselves; it is that they challenge the very basis of two-party democracy. If a political party cannot introduce a reform in the confident expectation that once passed by Parliament that reform would become a permanent part of the political system, then that party must sooner or later become reluctant to share the privilege of government with its opponents. Democracy necessarily involves sharing power, or the prospect of power, with opponents, because those countries which have a free and universal franchise sooner or later get tired of government by one party and seek to change to another. Moreover, if provoked too far the party of change may itself be tempted to copy its opponents by way of retaliatory action. So far, the present Labour Government has shown no signs of doing this: for example, it has not repealed the Government of London Act 1963, or the Television Act of 1954.

Has the present Labour Government any idea how to deal with this impasse? If not, the constitutional lawyer will have to come to the rescue. It is a well-known but curious fact that Britain, which has given more than twenty countries in the Commonwealth written constitutions, many of them containing provisions quite severely restrictive of their government's freedom of action, has no written constitution of its own. In Britain, Parliament is omnicompetent: it can do anything, it is said, except make a man a woman, and a woman a man. The trouble is that it can also undo anything. There are great advantages in the present situation. No legislation once passed, however controversial it may be, is ever harassed with doubts about its basic validity; nor does any legislation have to be subjected to the protracted agonies of constitutional amendment procedure, as in the United States. One does not lightly abandon a system that has worked remarkably well for nearly three centuries. On the other hand, the present difficulties are serious and would be infinitely more so if the Labour Government were to embark on more measures of nationalization. Even on the assumption that the present Government's moderate policies are to continue, it is very hard to believe that there will not be quite a number of measures, in addition to steel nationalization, that will be so abhorrent to the Conservatives that they will be tempted to repeal them in the future, if their previous violations of the constitutional convention are left unremedied. It may be argued that a firm undertaking on the part of the government introducing any legislation threatened with subsequent repeal not to pay a second round of compensation in the case of nationalization, or otherwise to renounce commitments and undertakings given by the repealing government, would be an effective deterrent. If legislation can be repealed, so the argument runs, so also can it be reintroduced. I fear this is not enough. Although governments do change sooner or later and change back again, they tend nowadays to last a long time, so that the period of uncertainty while the battle continues to rage can be crippling to the economy. The battle over the steel industry was joined in 1947 and now, nearly twenty years later, it is still not over.

There would seem to be several ways of dealing with this situation: none of them very easy, and most of them somewhat complicated. One way would be to incorporate words in the preamble to the Bill concerned declaring it to be unrepealable. There is a distant precedent for this: the Act of Union of England and Scotland, 1706, contains a proviso to the fact that it can never lawfully be repealed. One has doubts about the effectiveness of this.

The courts have never been called upon to test the validity of the Act of Union, and if they were it might be that they would hold that Parliament had no power in the first place to pass irrevocable legislation, on the ground that each individual parliament is sovereign. Moreover, the climate of opinion in both England and Scotland has hitherto been such that this particular legislation has never been subjected to severe political strain. In any case, for Parliament to pass legislation that could *never* be repealed might create tiresome and unnecessary difficulties for future governments centuries hence. In theory it ought to be possible to make constitutional changes in parliamentary practice so as to distinguish between ordinary legislation requiring a simple majority in the House of Commons, and fundamental legislation requiring, say, two-thirds majorities. In this way a government of change, successfully carrying its programme into law but facing the prospect of its repeal by a vengeful successor, would have the reassurance of knowing that unless the pendulum swung really violently against it at a successive election (in which case it would hardly be in a position to complain), its work would be safe from undoing; and since 1935 no British government, except for the wartime coalition, has controlled two-thirds or more of the members of the House of Commons.

Unfortunately, there are serious objections to this safeguard. The first lies in the omnicompetent character of Parliament. Since the passing of all legislation specially protected in this manner would, it seems, have to be preceded by an enabling Parliamentary Bill embodying the procedural changes, the question arises how far such an enabling Bill *itself* would have to be passed by the special majority in order to offset the possibility that it could be lawfully repealed by a simple majority — thus destroying the protective procedure before it could become operative. Although there seems to have been no serious judicial challenge to the validity of legislation since the early seventeenth century, as recently as 1961, in the course of debates on the Strauss parliamentary privilege case, the then Attorney-General talked of the possibility that there could indeed be matters *ultra vires* Parliament. Therefore such a procedure would not only be complicated but might also be vitiated by uncertainty. Such a problem has never confronted the courts of England before, but the concepts that a majority of one is a majority, and that one does not look behind an Act of Parliament into the proceedings of Parliament, are very deep-rooted. A better and simpler alternative would be to make any important legislation only repealable after a national referendum on the subject had been held and an overall majority found in favour of such action. This would have the very considerable advantage of being more flexible and much more democratic in character. There is nothing intrinsically wrong in governments repealing positive legislation, always provided that there is clear, unambiguous, popular support for their doing so, and provided that such popular support has been obtained from an electorate fully seized of the implications of what was being done. This could never be said of the Iron and Steel Act 1953. The Conservatives had been elected on a minority vote in 1951 and that election was concerned with many issues besides steel. We have never conducted official referenda in this country, but in recent years they have sometimes been suggested as a means of dealing with contentious issues—such as the Common Market and capital punishment—that cut right across the normal lines of political cleavage. Because a general election is always fought about a number of different issues and increasingly as well about the choice of Prime Minister, it is rarely possible to be certain whether the electorate is in favour or against a particular issue, and governments are tempted to interpret the successful outcome of an election campaign as a vote in favour of anything they choose to do or not to do. Referenda would put a stop to that; and the day will surely come when a more educated electorate will want to do more than put a cross on a ballot paper every five years.

This book is being written at a time when British politicians are in the throes of debate over the prices and incomes policy and are acutely divided about the desirability and practicability of a comprehensive system of control over the prices of goods and services and the remuneration of the worker. The least that can be said in criticism of the 1966 Prices and Incomes Act is that it was drafted in a hasty and slovenly manner. Many would criticize it on the much more serious grounds that it does not take effective control over some forms of remuneration, especially dividends, the profits of unincorporated businesses and professional fees. There is a further criticism to be made that, assuming the policy itself is a sound and just one, legislation so hurriedly prepared and passed is really unnecessary. The powers that government can acquire under the provisions of the Emergency Powers Act 1920 are immense. This Act was introduced to assist the discreditable post-first-world-war Lloyd George coalition to defeat industrial militancy, and operates when a state of emergency is proclaimed. Because of their extensive character it is rare for all of the emergency powers to be activated for any one emergency. The only important restriction on these powers is that a state of emergency has to be renewed every few weeks.

It is possible for a government, by using the Act, to acquire a far wider measure of control over the economy than it can through the medium of the Prices and Incomes Act 1966; powers possibly wider than those contained in the wartime legislation. Looking back on the events of October and November 1964, it seems strange that it was not used to prohibit the speculative movement against sterling that precipitated the first of the financial crises with which the present Labour Government has been confronted. Labour Governments have never felt inhibited from operating the Act and movements of sterling are as important to the well-being of the nation as movements of shipping and by rail. Perhaps the thought of putting emergency powers to such a startling and novel use led to doubts as to whether they really were applicable. Perhaps, too, bold and drastic measures were a little too much to expect of a new government taking office for the first time for thirteen years. Certainly in the mind of the public and not least of trade unionists, these powers are now almost exclusively associated with industrial emergencies.

Of course, the power to deal with sudden emergencies must be there. Political situations apart, the possibility of some widespread natural catastrophe renders this necessary. The real problem is how to preserve this without endangering civil liberties through its misuse by a disreputable government. At present, provided they are renewed every twenty-eight days, emergency powers can be continued indefinitely; and this despite the fact that any emergency in the sense ordinarily understood by what word is normally of limited duration (and when it is not, then there is time for the enactment of measures designed specifically to meet it). The Emergency Powers Act ought to be changed so that it should not be possible for a government to keep the powers in being for longer than twelve months at a time.

The creation of the new post of Parliamentary Commissioner is an extremely welcome innovation. Amongst other things it has for the first time enshrined in the constitution the place of the Member of Parliament *qua* representative of his constituents' interests, as well as *qua* legislator. The fact that it has been fathered by a Labour Government gives the lie to the allegation so often made that Socialists are less concerned with civil liberties than they are with economic equality. If the Conservatives had really cared for the liberty of the subject they would themselves have created such a post after the Crichel Down affair. Welcome though it is, however, there are weaknesses in the new Act. It does not extend to a large number of departments such as hospital boards, the police and the armed forces, nor to statutory corporations like the National Coal Board, nor to semi-public organizations in which the Government has the controlling or major shareholding interest. The Parliamentary Commissioner cannot initiate inquiries; he can only act on the complaints referred to him by Members of Parliament. He has no power of sanction, only of inquiry and report. There is no reason why after a short while most of those limitations should not be removed, particularly on the right of the Commissioner to initiate inquiries of his own and extend existing inquiries. There cannot be too much vigilance where human liberty and justice are involved.

Important though the creation of the Parliamentary Commissioner may be as providing a means of scrutinizing injustice of a kind that does not readily lend itself to orthodox legal remedies, it must be remembered that government bureaucracy is much more inclined to be wasteful than to be unjust. With the vast growth of technical and scientific industries either directly under its control or in contractual relationship with it, the government machine often fails to measure up to the task of scrutinizing and controlling the cost of government projects. The sorry truth of this has been spectacularly shown up by episodes such as the Skybolt, Blue Streak and the Bloodhound Missile weapons projects, and by the escalation of the Concord and various motorway contracts. Not only this, but to a very large extent there is a failure to show the liveliness and flexibility which modern government requires if it is to be well served. This is a matter which lies largely outside the scope of this chapter, but change in the law impinges upon it in one important respect. Just as the present company law is very weak in the matter of the auditing of private and public companies, so the control of public expenditure suffers for somewhat the same reasons. The function of the Comptroller and Auditor-General is to scrutinize, advise and make reports. He, too, has no power of sanction or discipline; nor any power specifically to disallow improper or wasteful expenditure. This, in practice, means that a very long time will normally elapse between investigation and the taking of any remedial action. For the law depends upon Parliament taking notice of the report, and very frequently the competition of other more pressing matters distracts attention from adverse reports; sometimes neither remedial nor disciplinary action ever follows. One cannot help contrasting the essentially advisory character of the Comptroller and Auditor-General in the United Kingdom with the power of the Auditor-General in a Colonial territory, and indeed with the power of a district auditor in relation to a local authority. Both these officials can disallow expenditure and also surcharge the offenders. Colonial Auditors-General are no respecters of persons and have been known to order contributions from quite senior members of the Service who offended against the rules. An amendment to the Exchequer and Audit Departments Act 1866 could change this. It is not suggested that there should be any diminution in the powers of Parliament and the Public Accounts Committee, but if the Comptroller and Auditor-General were provided with the same powers as his colonial counterpart one can imagine the salutory effect this could have. Many a local councillor has at some time or other suffered for supporting some improper expenditure: it is strange that we demand a higher standard of discipline and of personal probity from our local councillors than we do from Members of Parliament. No doubt the recruitment of more professionally qualified accountants capable of standing up to private manufacturers (particularly in the civil and electrical engineering worlds) could also produce the desired effect. But there is a dearth of these which does not look like being rectified for a long time to come, and this change could be effected easily and with the very minimum of administrative complications.

The battle for freedom of expression was won quite a long time ago. The battles for the rights of the individual in matters of private conduct, and for the legal emancipation of women, whilst not quite over, are as good as won. Indeed, the legal emancipation of the individual is almost complete: only the atheist, the republican, and the legal infant of mature years (18–21) may still be said to be at some disadvantage—and the first two suffer more from social disapproval than legal disabilities. The real difficulty that stands in the way of the enlargement and preservation of civil liberty is the problem of the concentration of power. For the most part, this is seen as the concentration of power in the hands of the State, or, on a world basis, concentration of power in the hands of two or three giant nations: while the process has its parallels in every field of activity, particularly in economic affairs within each nation. Economic power has been rapidly concentrated in fewer and fewer hands, despite lamentations (real or bogus) of those who call for continued competition, and despite anti-monopoly legislation. To take a simple and obvious example: thirty years ago the Unilever organization and I.C.I. were exceptional, both in their size and the scope and diversity of their operations. Today not only are these generally accepted as being normal for most kinds of business activity by both Left and Right in politics, but there is great concern that we are not hurrying on the process fast enough to promote industrial efficiency, and the chief political argument between Left and Right in relation to such matters is about whether such organizations should be publicly or privately owned. The problem of the undesirable concentration of power in private hands can always be dealt with by simply removing it from private hands, by nationalizing it; but the problem of state power concentration presents a much greater difficulty.

Both socialists and non-socialists frequently assume that judicial independence is no problem nowadays and are a little surprised if the contrary is suggested. Unfortunately, such are the stresses of our modern State with its great concentration of power, we cannot take this for granted; and we still have to ensure that, whilst nothing is put in the way of government extending its functions, especially in the economic field, the judiciary remains completely independent and there is no suspicion of partiality towards the State. Efficient governments are not always the most sensitive ones. The possibility of conflict between the judiciary and the executive is not theoretical. Governmental enthusiasms and the pressure of a modern legislative programme do not make for undue scrupulousness where constitutional proprieties are concerned. There have been disturbing instances in recent times of both Labour and Conservative governments cutting the corners when legislating. In 1961, the Conservatives very rightly introduced a provision in the Budget of that year to end dividend-stripping; unfortunately they attempted to make it retrospective and were stopped only by the pressure of their back-benchers. The present Government tried to 'anticipate' recent building controls before they had been made law, and even went so far as to suggest that contracts contrary to the prices and wages freeze *policy* were invalid even before Part IV of the Prices and Incomes Act had been made operative by Order in Council. Both parties, moreover, supported legislation to reverse retrospectively the judgment in the Burmah Oil Company case. There may be more occasions when comparable stresses and strains will occur in the course of which governments will be tempted to treat the law in this fashion. This is particularly likely if, as I hope, there is a massive extension during the next few years of the public ownership of the means of production, distribution and exchange. The judiciary has not always been robustly independent of governments. In the first place, judges are in fact appointed by the government of the day. In the second place, until quite recently the difficulties facing an individual seeking redress against a government department by litigation were formidable; and although the position has been improved by the Crown Proceedings Act of 1947, it can still be very difficult when questions of Crown privilege are raised with relation to confidential matters of State. In addition, the judiciary, especially in times of great political controversy, have not always conceived it to be their duty to be indifferent to the plea of 'reasons of State' (perhaps understandably so in wartime). For example, one cannot be entirely happy about the approach to certain post-war treason trials, nor about the handling of the various scandals of 1963. The fact is, of course, that the judiciary is *not* independent of the State. Its head is the Lord Chancellor who is a member of the Cabinet of the day, changing with each change of government, sometimes for reasons totally unconnected with the administration of justice—as in 1962. The Law Officers of every government are also party politicians. Nothing is more extraordinary than the contrast between the posts of Lord Chief Justice and Master of the Rolls and that of the Lord Chancellor, an active politician and spokesman for his party in the House of Lords. It is not seriously suggested that any Lord Chancellor of any political party would behave improperly, but his position must from time to time surely present him with perplexing dilemmas and cannot be regarded as satisfactory. It is not long since the Attorney-General was relieved of the painful embarrassment of having to decide in a judicial capacity who should be allowed to proceed to the House of Lords (Criminal Justice Act 1961), even in respect of cases in which he himself was the prosecutor. The situation placed him in an invidious position and had to be changed. Now it is even proposed that the Attorney-General should not appear at tribunals of inquiry. If the judiciary is to be in an unassailable position so that it can stand up to even the strongest governments when they show a tendency to assume arbitrary power, the judicial and political functions of the post of Lord Chancellor must be separated. If it is necessary for a member of the government to be charged with the supervision of judicial affairs, then a Minister of Justice should be created who should be an ordinary political member of the government.

This still leaves the question of the appointment of judges. Here I advocate what has been done in a number of overseas territories on the eve of their independence to safeguard their judges from political interference (alas, not always successfully). A Judicial Service Commission should be appointed which might be composed of five or seven senior judicial office-holders, including the Lord Chancellor and the Lord Chief Justice. It might be desirable, in order to guard against the possibility of judges becoming too remote from the community, to include some prominent lay persons. Unlike the Lord Chancellor, the incumbents would hold office indefinitely until a specified retiring age and would not change with governments. In this body would be vested the power of appointment, promotion and dismissal of judges and magistrates. Of course, this would not entirely solve the problem, because clearly the government of the day would have to appoint to vacancies in the Judicial Service Commission itself, but by vesting the supervision of the judiciary in a non-political body it would place the judiciary that much further away from executive control. Parliament has always had the power to remove a judge from office, by resolution of both Houses, though this power has never been exercised. Possibly in the past the fact that the exercise of such a power would have seemed so objectionable politically may have had the paradoxical effect of actually protecting unsatisfactory judges who ought to have been removed. There is no reason why judicial office-holders should not be subjected to the same kind of discipline as other members of the community, always provided that the supervision does not inhibit their judicial independence.

Clearly Parliament should renounce this power in favour of a system which at one and the same time is not open to the objection of political influence, but does subject the judiciary to a more modern kind of administration than exists at the moment, akin to that which regulates the Civil Service.

The sternest test of a government's integrity is whether or not it is willing to forego some at least of the many electoral advantages that stem directly from its holding the reins of power. No government, however pure-minded, will ever forego all of them; indeed this may not be possible. However, the long years of Conservative rule between 1951 and 1964 witnessed an alarming slide in standards. Budgetary manipulation in order to create pre-election booms, the misuse of the Honours System, and the telling of blatant lies in election campaigns together helped to keep in being a government that very probably would otherwise have ended its life some years before it finally went out of office. These are not new devices, but they have been supplemented by one that is new and is already more important than any of them: namely, the choice of election dates based upon opinion poll intelligence. The General Election dates of 1955, 1959 and 1966 were largely influenced by the fair weather discernible from the opinion polls; and it is at least arguable that if the Conservatives had been less divided over their leadership and other matters they would have chosen a little more skilfully the date of the 1964 election.

In the United States, where the science of opinion polling is even more highly developed, the government of the day has no power over the choice of the election date either for President or for Congress. Those elections have to be faced on a fixed known date, fair weather or foul. United States' politics suffers in its way from tactics of doubtful morality; but at least they are spared the degrading situation that existed here in 1964 when a government continued Parliament to the last possible moment that it legally could, postponing urgently needed decisions and thereby creating additional difficulties for its successor. The right of the Prime Minister of the government in being to advise the Sovereign on the date for the dissolution of Parliament has long existed. With rare exceptions, such as Baldwin's dissolution in 1923 and Attlee's in 1950, few Prime Ministers have ever been able to resist taking advantage of the right to choose a date they consider most favourable to themselves, regardless of objective considerations. It is said in defence of the status quo that once having struggled into office a party leader's job is to stay there and govern; and so it is, but he also has a duty to the electorate to ensure that the country has a fair and genuine opportunity of choosing which party and party leader it really wants. It is also said in defence of the system that a Prime Minister may lose control of Parliament by losing control of rebellious members of his own party unless he has the power of summary dissolution in this way; and it is said that if he cannot dispense with an unruly Parliament, government might lapse into weak ineffectiveness, as French governments did during the Third and Fourth Republics. This argument, though plausible, is neither edifying nor even sensible. A democracy depends in the last analysis both on the right of a free people freely to choose and upon the right and duty of Members of Parliament freely to exercise their conscience, and on governments to stick to their election mandates. The best and the hardest thing that the Labour Government can do is to face this, to resist the temptation of following the contemptible example of its opponents, and to make the length of parliaments a fixture.

© 1967 BY JOHN LEE